Learning Commons

Evolution and Collaborative Essentials

EDITED BY
BARBARA SCHADER

Chandos Publishing
Oxford · England

Chandos Publishing (Oxford) Limited
TBAC Business Centre
Avenue 4
Station Lane
Witney
Oxford OX28 4BN
UK
Tel: +44 (0) 1993 848726 Fax: +44 (0) 1865 884448
Email: info@chandospublishing.com
www.chandospublishing.com

First published in Great Britain in 2008

ISBN:
978 1 84334 312 7 (paperback)
978 1 84334 313 4 (hardback)
1 84334 312 6 (paperback)
1 84334 313 4 (hardback)

© The contributors, 2008

Typeset by Domex e-Data Pvt. Ltd.
Printed in the UK and USA.

Contents

Jan Howden

List of figures, tables and box

Figures

Tables

Box

Preface

In 2005, I was hearing a great deal of discussion about 'Learning Commons', 'Information Commons' and 'learning spaces'. I wondered, what were these entities and were they effective? How did one develop a Commons? Was it expensive? Was it difficult? Where should we locate it? Because I had so many questions, I decided that others probably did too, and so with two intrepid colleagues, Mary M. Somerville and Sallie Harlan, I decided to do a survey of California academic institutions of higher learning. We surveyed 88 institutions and discovered that only 30 per cent of these institutions had a designated Learning or Information Commons. However, 43 per cent of these institutions were considering developing a Commons and were very interested in learning how to proceed. The results of this survey led us to develop a full day pre-conference at the 11th California Academic and Research Libraries (CARL) Conference in April 2006. We invited several West Coast USA librarians to discuss their experiences with planning an Information or Learning Commons. Our speakers included Jill McKinstry, Director of Odegaard Undergraduate Library and Learning Commons from the University of Washington; Shahla Bahavar, Information Services Coordinator for the Leavy Library at the University of Southern California – the oldest US Information Commons; Patricia Davitt Maughan, Facilitator for the Mellon Fellows Program at University of California, Berkeley and currently heading up a task force on learning spaces at University of California, Berkeley; Jennifer Ramsdell Stringer, Associate Director for Education Technology at the Stanford University School of Medicine; and Mary M. Somerville, then Assistant Dean for Information and Instructional Services at California Polytechnic State University at San Luis Obispo. The full day session was well attended and well received. Valuable information was provided and shared at this preconference. The pre-conference was so informative that I thought it was a pity that only 40 people heard the presentations. A conference reaches only a small percentage of interested individuals, but an entire book of 'learning stories' might inform interested persons around the globe. With an expanded international framework, I then set about discovering what academic librarians around the world were doing to reach their millennium generation students.

Somerville and Harland provide an intensive and informative survey of the literature on the evolution of Information and Learning Commons. Their research informed my contacting librarians from around the world over the next several months. Fifteen individuals were selected to impart their stories of planning, developing, collaborating, implementing and then managing and assessing/evaluating their Learning Commons over 11 chapters, wonderfully told. You can feel the excitement that each of these authors has for his or her learning spaces.

In reading these chapters, I have discovered that there are many common elements in these learning spaces. Most Commons, for example, offer flexible space and require campus collaborators. In addition, most need many small group study rooms, special computer tables that accommodate two or three students working at the same workstation, quiet and noisy areas in the same library, and sustenance via cafes on premises. In addition, most offer a wide range of production software on all or most of the computers. These commonalities are important and can serve as a guide to planning one's own learning spaces.

There are also many unique approaches to learning spaces discussed in these chapters and this is where the fascinating adventures begin. These Learning Commons were chosen because they are examples of tremendously successful learning spaces. Each institution has successfully melded the basic necessities for learning spaces with their unique imprints. Sometimes it is an unexpected department added to their list of collaborators, sometimes it is the libraries working with furniture manufacturers to develop furniture or lighting to their specifications. Some learning spaces have been so successful that at least three of our authors are now developing faculty Commons. And each of these faculty Commons is developing to fit local culture.

I hope you enjoy this reading journey as much as I have. I anticipate that you will be rewarded with many wonderful ideas that will fit into your local situation. The libraries chosen represent a wide variety of sizes, private and state supported, well funded and struggling. There is something here for everyone.

Enjoy.
Barbara Schader

About the authors

Susan Beatty is the Head of Information Commons at the University of Calgary, Canada. Her main responsibility is coordinating the delivery of reference service and technical support in the Information Commons and working with her collaborators to ensure delivery of a service that meets the needs of the Commons users.

Barbara I. Dewey has been Dean of Libraries at the University of Tennessee, Knoxville, TN, USA, since 2000. She has also held positions at the University of Iowa, Indiana University and Northwestern University. She has published and presented on a wide variety of topics related to research libraries, including collaborative learning spaces. She is on the Digital Library Federation Board, the Association for Research Libraries (ARL) Board, and serves as Chair for the ARL Research, Teaching, and Learning Committee.

Sallie Harlan is formerly the College of Liberal Arts subject librarian for the Robert E. Kennedy Library at California Polytechnic State University in San Luis Obispo, CA, USA. She also coordinates the AskNow 24/7 chat service for the campus. Sallie has published and presented on web-based information literacy tutorials and ICT (information and communications technology) assessment. She co-coordinated a pre-conference session on Learning Commons planning, implementation and assessment at the 2006 California Academic & Research Libraries (CARL) Conference.

Jan Howden is Associate Director in Learner Support at Glasgow Caledonian University, Glasgow, Scotland (j.howden@gcal.ac.uk). Jan has worked in health libraries and academic libraries, is Chair of the SCONUL (Society of College, National and University Libraries) Working Group for Information Literacy and Treasurer of the Scottish Council of University and Research Libraries. Her interest in taking a wider look at the student and researcher experience was sparked by a 3-year secondment to a JISC (Joint Information Systems Committee) project looking at improving and providing certification for the learning and teaching skills of library and IT people. At the moment Jan writes for many publications on learning environments and on information skills.

Dr Gary A. Hunt (ghunt1@ohio.edu) has recently retired as Associate Dean of Libraries at Ohio University, where he led the planning process for the Learning Commons and Faculty Commons projects described in his chapter. His experience includes strategic planning, budgeting, human resources management, facilities planning, and private fundraising. In addition to a Masters in Library Science from Simmons College, he holds a BA in English from the University of California at Berkeley and a PhD in English & American Literature from Brandeis University. As a private consultant, Dr Hunt specializes in the design of learning spaces for academic libraries.

Shay Keating M Ed Dip Voc Ed and Training Cert IV Assessment and Workplace BA (Hons). Shay has 6 years experience as Research Officer at the Victoria University (Australia) Postcompulsory Education Centre (PEC), which conducts research on student transition and attrition, learning in the workplace and learner-centred teaching practice. Shay co-authored a literature review (Keating and

Gabb, 2005; internal VU publication), which recommended a series of principles to underpin Learning Commons design at VU. A subsequent paper (McLennan & Keating, 2005; internal VU publication) explored learner-centred teaching further. Shay recently collated 4 years of evaluation data from a subject based peer-mentoring program at VU.

Philip Kent BA Grad Dip Lib Sc AALIA MBA. Philip joined Victoria University, Australia in April 2006. He came to the university with 25 years of library and information management experience in higher education and research organisations including CSIRO, Australia's national science agency. A career highlight was the building of a large, onsite digital library of full text science literature. He has presented papers at national and international forums, been an active member of many professional associations and published widely in a variety of disciplines. In seeking to optimise VU's learning environment, the Library is a lead player in implementing integrated Learning Commons facilities at multiple campuses. This initiative will provide a major challenge for Philip and the University Library over the next few years.

Jill McKinstry is the Director of the Odegaard Undergraduate Library and Learning Commons and Special Assistant to the Dean of University Libraries for Undergraduate Education and Programs at the University of Washington, Seattle, WA, USA. As a librarian at the UW for over 20 years, Jill is a passionate advocate for libraries and partnerships within the campus and community. Working closely with the Office of Undergraduate Academic Affairs, Jill co-founded the lecture series, "Research Exposed" to introduce students to the varied research efforts of faculty on campus in a variety of disciplines. In 2003, Jill created a program to celebrate and reward students' research and creative activities, called the UW Library Research Award for Undergraduates. (In its fourth year, $10,000 was awarded to outstanding research projects of UW students.) Jill has also participated in several video tours and discussions in the last couple of years: *Equal Access: Campus Libraries*, interviews about equal access for students with disabilities produced by DO-IT, University of Washington, 2005. *Libraries tour, with Jill McKinstry* (UWTV Production) won a Bronze Award at the 21st Annual Telly Awards, and the video *Jill and Linda* was chosen as "Spot of the Day" by Ad Critic, October 16, 2003 as a television spot to promote support for the homeless through the newspaper, *Real Change*.

Jill is also co-chair of the selection committee for the UW Common book Program for incoming freshman, creating a community of inquiry around an important theme or question.

Belinda McLennan has a background of over 25 years in vocational, further and higher education institutions, in teaching and administrative roles. Belinda is currently the Pro Vice-Chancellor (Teaching and Learning) at Victoria University, Australia. She has overall responsibility for all aspects of teaching and learning including the building and improving of learning, teaching, career development and work experiences for students, as well as professional and career development for all staff of Victoria University.

Belinda is the sponsor of a number of strategic initiatives in teaching and learning at Victoria University, including the development and implementation of a Learning Commons approach across the University's campuses founded on a student-centred learning and teaching philosophy. Belinda has teaching qualifications, an M Ed (Leadership and Management) and is currently completing a Doctorate in Professional Studies in work-based learning.

Hester Mountifield is Assistant University Librarian (Information Commons & Learning Services) at The University of Auckland Library in New Zealand. She has been with the University Library in various roles since 1996 and prior to that worked in the university and secondary school sector in South Africa. Her current role includes the management of the University Library's Information Commons Group and the development and coordination of information literacy and integrated learning support initiatives in collaboration with institutional partners. She is interested in the pedagogical and learning support issues raised by the blending of e-learning technologies with digital libraries, resources and services, the educational design role of librarians and the learning support and e-Literacy needs of the Net Generation. She holds a Masters degree in Library and Information Science and a Postgraduate Diploma in Higher Education. Her publications include conference papers and articles on the Information Commons and e-Literacy. She has also contributed chapters to various books on these topics.

Barbara Schader, Assistant University Librarian for Collections and Scholarly Communication, University of California, Riverside, Riverside, CA, USA, has spent her career working in academic and medical libraries. She co-planned a 1-day pre-conference on Learning Commons Planning, Implementation and Outcomes at the 2006 California Academic & Research Libraries (CARL) annual meeting. She has authored a number of articles and presented at conferences as wide ranging as the Medical Library Association and the Charleston Conference.

Dr Mary M. Somerville serves as Associate Dean for the Dr Martin Luther King, Jr. Library (San Jose, CA, USA), a future-oriented collaboration between the San José State

University Library and the San José Public Library. Her responsibilities are to oversee advancement of knowledge management, scholarly resources, organizational development, and user services. She has published and presented on the subjects of Learning Commons' and learning spaces in Europe, Australia, and the United States. In addition, she led the planning process for the Learning Commons at California Polytechnic State University in San Luis Obispo, Ca, USA. Presently, she leads planning for Learning Commons and learning spaces in the King Library, the largest joint library facility in the United States.

Gabriela Sonntag Coordinator, Information Literacy Program and Reference Service at the California State University in San Marcos (CSUSM), CA, USA. As Coordinator she provides leadership for a team of nine staff implementing an innovative program of information literacy instruction delivered through the lower-division General Education program, currently viewed as a model for other universities. Extensive instruction in support for degree programs, as well as pioneering reference services, are also her responsibility. Gabriela was the team leader of CSUSM librarians serving as Consultants for Information Literacy for the Association of College and Research Libraries. Additionally, she was the project manager for a 2-year grant from the Institute for Museum and Library Services to train academic librarians in assessing student information literacy learning outcomes. She is the library representative on the Academic Senate Curriculum Committee, and has been chair of the University Program Assessment Committee since 2004. She is a member of the campus Western Association of Schools and Colleges (WASC) Steering Committee and sits on the Academic Senate Executive Committee. Gabriela has several publications on information literacy, assessment of student learning, reference services, and first year students. She has also presented at numerous conferences and conducted professional development workshops in the United States, Spain, Mexico, Chile and Argentina for teams of instructors and librarians on teaching information literacy competency.

Jenn Stringer, Director, Educational Technology, Information Resources and Technology (IRT) Stanford University Medical Center, Stanford, CA, USA. Jenn is responsible for setting strategic direction for educational technology support for the Medical School, budget prioritization and management, and planning for new technology enhanced educational spaces. She manages programs and projects in knowledge-based learning, instructional content development, learning facilities and integrative services. She directs the support for over 40 technology enhanced spaces, manages the learning management system (LMS; WebCT), supports faculty technology training, provides video capture and streaming, offers videoconferencing services, and develops online teaching modules and multimedia content. She works collaboratively with other groups within the School and the University to facilitate the use of technology in teaching and in support of the School's educational mission.

Crit Stuart is Program Director for Research, Teaching, and Learning for the Association of Research Libraries (ARL), USA. Prior to taking the ARL position in May 2007, Crit was associate director for public services at the Library and Information Center, Georgia Institute of Technology, Atlanta, GA, USA. There, he coordinated the evolution of "library as place," emphasizing enhancements to spaces, technologies, and services to support student productivity and success in a 24-hour environment, and expanding practical partnerships between the Library and students, faculty and student support services. The library received the ACRL Award for Excellence in Academic Libraries, University Library section, for 2007.

Susan M. Thompson holds an MLIS from the University of Denver and has over 20 years of experience with libraries and technology. As the Library Systems Coordinator at California State University San Marcos, CA, USA for the past 9 years, she is responsible for all aspects of library technology. She was heavily involved in the library's recent building project, planning the technology and working closely with library faculty and staff as well as campus IT. She has presented at a number of national and regional forums on topics ranging from re-imagining technologies role in the library building to technological solutions to plagiarism. She has also published several articles in periodicals such as Information Technology and Libraries and Computers in Libraries and is editing an upcoming book on core technology competencies for libraries.

From Information Commons to Learning Commons and learning spaces: an evolutionary context

*Mary M. Somerville
and Sallie Harlan*

Since 1994, when the University of Southern California opened an Information Commons (Holmes-Wong et al., 1997), college and university libraries across the globe have adapted the generic 'Commons' concept to their particular circumstances. Often, this has involved 'replacing books with bytes' (Swarz, 2006) in a computer lab that provides access to electronic resources and productivity software. The enhanced Information Commons model offers integrated services (Crockett et al., 2002). Some Information Commons even provide a 'continuum of service from resource identification and retrieval on through data processing and format conversion to the desired end state of preservation, packaging, or publication' (Beagle, 2004). The University of Michigan's Media Union, for instance, brings together information resources, information technology, and media production (Miller, 1988).

These innovations have inspired some campuses to evolve the Commons concept still further. Driven by deep appreciation for the potential synergy of 'student success' partnerships, the resulting 'Learning Commons' can provide resources and services similar to those in an Information Commons. However, it does so in collaboration with other campus units, such as campus information technologists, instructional designers, pedagogy experts, peer mentors, and writing specialists. In addition, Learning Commons aim to align with and contribute to other campus priorities such as course management systems and e-portfolio initiatives. The Learning Commons merges 'functions formerly carried out *within* the library with others formerly carried out *beyond* the library's purview' (Beagle, 2004). Well aligned with the shift in higher education from a focus on teaching to an emphasis on learning, Learning Commons demonstrate how libraries can migrate to new 'service paradigms' (Moyo, 2004) that heighten the organisation's visibility on campus. Characterised by one author as 'Campus Library 2.0' (Albanese, 2004), new integrated service and delivery models meet 'the needs of faculty as course authors, knowledge creators, learning coaches, and scholarly communicators' (Beagle, 2004).

> The 'Commons' concept and Information Commons and Learning Commons implementations offer learners, researchers, and information professionals a physical, technological, social, and intellectual location to pursue various educational and research curricula and activities. The learner and researcher find opportunities for independent, self-sufficient contemplation, research, productivity and creativity facilitated by the seamlessly integrated continuum of resources and services in the Commons. While the various iterations of the Commons concept in academic libraries are less than two decades old, it is clear that they hold promise for an

enlightening era of vibrancy and intelligence in libraries and great hope for those of us who strive to collaboratively produce and share the vision of the dynamic library Commons. (Bailey, 2005)

Recently, recognition of the far-reaching implications produced by redesigning and repurposing space in academic libraries has prompted widespread interest in creating 'learning spaces' throughout the campus environment. In acknowledging the essential social dimension of knowledge and learning (Latour and Woolgar, 1979; Brown and Duguid, 2000), this third iteration of the Commons concept encourages the facilitation of formal and informal social exchanges in campus spaces such as dining halls, residence halls, reading rooms, scientific laboratories, and university bookstores. Grounded in the recognition that learning occurs when information is transformed into knowledge by some person or group of persons (Bruce, 1998), even classroom design concepts are now changing, as professors increasingly adopt pedagogies enabling of discovery (Marcus, 2001) that provide students with 'knowledge making' experiences transferable to lifelong learning (Bundy, 2004). Clearly, the evolving Commons concept in higher education holds significant promise for fundamentally transforming both higher education and academic librarianship.

The evolution of the Commons conception

In his provocative essay, *Libraries Designed for Learning*, Yale University Librarian Emeritus Scott Bennett (Bennett, 2003) recalls the long heritage of common rooms in higher education, where all members of the academic community meet informally around shared interests, especially after meals. Despite shared origins, Bennett sees quintessential differences between the Commons concept that became popular in libraries in the 1990s, and the twenty-first century Commons concept that anticipates the current evolution of campus learning spaces. The early Information Commons construct, Bennett says, only enables knowledge seeking. In contrast, Bennett proposes that a Learning Commons has knowledge creation goals:

> It would bring people together not around informally shared interests, as happens in traditional common rooms, but around shared learning tasks, sometimes formalised in class assignments. The core activity of a Learning Commons would not be the manipulation and mastery of information, as in an Information Commons, but the collaborative learning by which students turn information into knowledge and sometimes into wisdom. A Learning Commons would be built around the social dimensions of learning and knowledge and would be managed by students themselves for learning purposes that vary greatly and change frequently. (Bennet, 2003; p. 38)

Furthermore, according to Bennett, a Learning Commons must be 'owned' by learners, not by teachers, whether faculty or librarians. A Learning Commons must be capable of accommodating frequently changing learning tasks that students define for themselves – 'like an academic playground of sorts' (Bennet, 2003; 38), not information management tasks defined and taught by library or academic computing staff. A Learning Commons would most likely also provide food service, maintaining the strong customary association of food with sociability and dialogue.

A second body of literature offers a complementary framework for appreciating the evolution and elaboration of the Commons concept in terms of institutional alignment, strategic fit, and functional integration (Beagle, 1999, 2002, 2004; Bailey and Tierney, 2002). These characteristics are useful in describing the change dynamics and service priorities that continue to push the evolution of Information Commons, Learning Commons, and learning spaces through strategic collaborations (Dewey, 2004; Davis and Somerville, 2006), professional retooling (Somerville et al., 2005b), planning processes (Bailey and Tierney, 2002), resource reallocation (Miller, 1998; Halbert, 1999), delivery models (Spencer, 2006; Whitchurch et al., 2006; Dallis and Walters, 2006; Jager, 2004), evaluation strategies (Malenfant, 2006; Gardner and Eng, 2005; Garriock, 2004), building design (Misencik et al., 2005), and staff development (Cowgill et al., 2001; Somerville et al., 2005a, 2005b). Drawing from the American Council of Education matrix for change (Eckel, 2000), the evolution from Information Commons to Learning Commons can be understood in terms of a continuum: adjustment, isolated change, far reaching change, and transformation.

In a paper titled 'From Information Commons to Learning Commons' distributed at the Information Commons conference sponsored by the University of Southern California on the occasion of their tenth anniversary, Beagle (2004) offers a typology for distinguishing between Information and Learning Commons. Of Information Commons (IC), he writes:

> **IC as adjustment:** described as a computer lab on the first floor of the library with a suite of productivity software (Microsoft Office) combined with access to electronic resources. Focus broadens from print to integration and coordination of information technology resources for students.

IC as isolated change: described as the same lab but with media authoring tools also included, and with coordinated in-library staff support designed to carry the user through a continuum of service from resource identification and retrieval through data processing and format conversion to the desired end of presentation, packing, and publication. Here, the library has altered its pattern of service delivery to better align itself with changing campus-wide priorities, and has done so by integrating functions formerly carried out by separate units within the library to project a new service profile. This level portrays an IC model that is still library-centric, however. While it better aligns the library with other campus priorities, it is still not intrinsically collaborative with other campus initiatives.

At this point, Beagle marks the threshold that he is proposing between Information Commons and Learning Commons. In continuing, he says of Learning Commons (LC):

LC as far-reaching change: described as the above plus coordination with other unit(s) such as a faculty development centre or centre for teaching and learning, as well as the frequent inclusion of a campus-wide course management system meaningfully linked to and integrated with library electronic resources and virtual reference services. Here, the library has further altered its pattern of service delivery to better align itself with changing campus-wide priorities, and has done so by integrating those functions formerly carried out within the library with others carried out beyond the library's purview. The service profile is no longer library-centric, and becomes essentially collaborative.

LC as transformative change: the above carried out with reference to (or within a framework of) campus-wide schema and/or faculty innovation such as core curriculum revision, writing/authoring across the curriculum, cognitive immersion learning paradigms such as the 'classroom flip' and 'learning object'/IMS implementation, such as D-Space. At this level, we continue to see functional integration across a horizontal plane, but we begin to see vertical differentiation as the former service delivery profile projected toward students becomes enhanced with another (or multiple) service delivery profile(s) projected at the needs of faculty as course authors, knowledge creators, learning coaches, and scholarly communicators. This also involves an enriched suite of services and toolsets.

In its maturity, then, the Commons concept illustrates that 'what begins as the reconfiguration of an academic library becomes a reconfiguration of the learning environment' (Beagle, 2002; 289).

Campus advancement of library centrality

It is fitting that Information and Learning Commons developed in the library because 'The academic library as place holds a unique position on campus. No other building can so symbolically and physically represent the academic heart of an institution' (Freeman, 2005; p. 9). In keeping with its historic role as an institution of learning, culture, and intellectual community, a library location offers 'a rich, comprehensive environment of print, electronic and human information resources' (Bennett, 2003; 39). Predictive of its future potentialities in the dynamic higher education environment, 'In recent years we have reawakened to the fact that libraries are fundamentally about people – how they learn, how they use information, and how they participate in the life of a learning community' (Demas, 2005; 25). So, while Information Commons assist users in knowledge seeking, Learning Commons are designed to enable knowledge creation through cross-disciplinary, cross-campus, and cross-functional collaboration.

Symbiotic relationships nurtured through cooperative endeavours can produce extra-ordinary outcomes, as demonstrated in the Dalhousie Learning Commons' collaboration with statistical computing consultants and geographic information system specialists. Of this, Nikkel (2003; 214) writes: 'The project sparked an unprecedented level of cooperation among university departments – facilities management, networks and systems, hardware services, and of course the libraries – because all understood the value of the new centre, not only to our students as a computing resource, but also to the university itself'. In this spirit, at the University of Auckland's Kate Edger Information Commons, the campus 'student centred university' approach has been successfully leveraged both strategically and tactically through establishment of a library-located Information Commons to advance campus-wide life long learning e-literacy priorities (Mountifield, 2004, 2005).

Both of the aforementioned initiatives demonstrate local customisation of the universal Commons concept, appropriate to a particular campus environment. This is true as well at the University of Nevada, Las Vegas (UNLV) Library, a state of the art building located in the literal centre of campus and identified regularly by campus leaders as its figurative 'heart'. Within the UNLV library mission to 'bring people and information together in innovative ways' (Starkweather and Marks, 2005; 22), the notion of an Information Commons set apart from the library has been substantively transformed. Originally, the Information Commons was a focal point of the building (Church et al., 2002). Physically located on the first floor, the spacious area included 12 built-in furniture pods of workstations totalling 92 desktop computers, plus three scanners, and two large-scale study rooms. However, 'technology and productivity software within the library were far from constrained by these physical limits' (Church, 2005; 75) because 'the principles and technology of the Information Commons were interwoven with the library on every floor' (Church 2005; 76).

So, while in the beginning, the Information Commons was a distinct location with a set number of workstations, the conception guided many of the initial operating assumptions for the setup of both workstations and service points throughout the new library. Users' perceptions – which did not recognise if questions were information-, technical-, or research-related (McKinstry and McCracken, 2002) – prompted merging departments and service points to expand the original vision for the Information Commons. 'This dynamic interweaving of tools and services requires a constant rethinking and reorganisation of ideas, methods, and space' (Church, 2005; 80), including cross-campus collaboration activities, as the Commons continues 'to evolve and assist in the process of turning information to knowledge to final product' (Church, 2005; 81).

The Association of Research Libraries (ARL) SPEC Kit 281, *The Information Commons* (Haas and Robertson, 2004), offers still further examples of the range of definitions and outcomes in Information and Learning Commons throughout the United States. Illustrative of this diversity are the variety of names assigned to these initiatives – i.e., media union

(University of Michigan), electronic information centre (Colorado State University and University of Texas, Austin), information arcade (University of Iowa), digital learning collaboratory (Purdue University), UWired: Center for Teaching, Learning, and Technology (University of Washington), information gallery (Winona State), Information Commons and information café (McGill University), research Commons (Indiana University), knowledge navigation centre (University of Michigan), information hub (University of Calgary), InfoCommons (Kansas State University), and cybrary (University of Buffalo, SUNY). In proposing a working definition of Information Commons, authors write that the model typically brings together resources and services typically found in an academic library's reference department and the campus computer lab – i.e., 'an evolving way of offering resources and assistance not found in one area, but being sought by users in both areas' (Haas and Robertson, 2004; p. 11).

This movement toward co-location, cooperation, and collaboration (Lippincott, 2004) in support of cooperative learning and group study in Information and Learning Commons – enabled by multimedia tools and staff assistance – recognises changes in the way students use academic libraries and library resources (MacWhinnie, 2003). This paves the way for campus-wide exploration of new ways to combine information resources, technology, and research assistance.

Within the rich context of 'universal' Commons possibilities, campus discussions have informed decisions about local 'particulars'. This is grounded in the recognition that 'learning is fundamentally a social construct that allows access to instruction, collaboration, informed research, relevant resources, critical analysis, and integrated results' resulting in 'knowledge and often in wisdom' (Wedge and Kearns, 2005; 1). The social/communal aspect of knowledge acquisition predicts the fundamental importance of learning ecosystems, where 'knowledge arises out of a process [that is] personal, social, situated and active' (EDUCAUSE Learning Initiative, 2006). This suggests that in today's technology rich world, educational institutions have a responsibility to explore and implement technology-enabled solutions that advance learners' opportunities to collaborate, create knowledge and engage in both physical and virtual communities of practice. This 'cyberinfrastructure' can enable learner interaction and knowledge creation by transcending formal educational boundaries and blending formal and informal modes of learning interaction (Computing Research Association, 2005).

The social dimension of learning and knowledge is a recurrent theme in writings about the relation between information, information technology and education. In *The Social Life of Information*, Brown and Duguid argue that social context 'helps people understand what....information might mean and why it matters' (Brown and Duguid, 2000; p. 5) so social networks, 'communities of practice', provide for peer-to-peer enculturation and the creation and sharing of knowledge. In a later article, Duguid elaborates on communities of practice as places where knowledge, identity and learning are situated (Duguid, 2005). In particular, he reflects on the tacit dimension of knowledge ('knowing *how* as opposed to knowing *that*') that is acquired through action, interaction and sharing with others. Lippincott concurs and urges educational planners to design spaces that encourage student teamwork and collaboration, support student multitasking and nurture creativity and communication – i.e., the learning environment must be 'both academic and social' (Lippincott, 2006; section 7.15). Widespread convergence of new understanding promises to change learning approaches still further in the twenty-first century.

Learning space design elements

There is now abundant literature codifying learning space design theory and practice (Brown, 2005) and technology integration in learning and teaching practice (Brown and Lippincott, 2003). This convergence of technology, pedagogy, and space considerations is driving the transition of both classrooms and libraries into learning spaces, as exciting new campus collaboration models (Oblinger, 2005) re-energise teaching and learning. This transformation is at least due in part to the evolution of the Commons that demonstrated the efficacy of a learning focus. In addition, technologies used in learning, such as interactive whiteboards, personal learning environments, wireless networks, and mobile devices, plus Internet-enabled high quality digital learning resources – and the ability to access many of these from home and the workplace – are altering users' experiences in twenty-first century learning environments.

Commons' planners now aspire to do more than simply reconfigure and/or update facilities with technology (Beagle, 2006). Their efforts increasingly highlight the larger academic institution's educational mission and purpose. Kuh and Gonyea reflect this transformation in thinking in their study of student experiences within the academic library. They call attention to the importance of asking the question 'just what does the library contribute to student learning?' and of determining how library experiences affect 'desirable outcomes of college' (Kuh and Gonyea, 2003; 256). Bennett reiterates the centrality of the educational function of libraries in his review of new and renovated libraries during the 1990s (Bennett, 2003). Building design, he emphasises, must be informed not by the traditional service operations of libraries, but rather by an analysis of how students learn and faculty teach. Continuing the theme of planning space based on learning, Oblinger highlights design principles that encourage intellectual interaction. Arguing that changes in pedagogy and technology demand a transformation in space planning, she urges planners of Commons and other educational spaces to observe, study and seek input from the learners themselves.

In their literature review of the Learning Commons, Keating and Gabb apply Beagle's concept of an information to Learning Commons continuum to evaluate the design, development and operation of initiatives to date. Although they conclude that many Commons fall short on learning – i.e., 'Learning Commons is being oversold' (Keating and Gabb, 2005; 4) – they affirm planning principles that are fundamentally learning-oriented, learner-centred and responsive to the changing needs of learners. In response, academic and library faculty at California Polytechnic State University (Cal Poly), San Luis Obispo, have evolved a 'collaborative co-design' approach that aims to close the gap between Commons planners and Commons beneficiaries through using user-generated research results to plan, implement, evaluate, and improve the Learning Commons (Somerville and Brar, 2006; Somerville et al., 2007; Mirijamdotter et al., 2007). By embedding action research into the Commons' development process, the Cal Poly SLO approach demonstrates that, although libraries have always been places of learning, if they are to remain viable they must host 'new forms of learning' – i.e., enabled by technology, libraries must reinvent learning communities and 'place-based social forums of learning in cyberspace' (Lynch et al., 2004; p. 13).

Ideas about the social dimension of technology-enhanced learning have impacted theories of educational space design. Writing on the nature of study/learning environments, Bennett argues in particular that plans for educational spaces must recognise the 'communal character of knowledge'

(Bennett, 2005). With regard to library space, Bennett emphasises the need for places 'congenial to conversations that share knowledge gained from class', spaces where 'classroom inequalities of authority are neutralised', areas promoting the notion of study as having a strong social context.

A number of case studies exemplify ways in which ideas on the social dimension of learning have been applied in Commons and other educational environments. Detailing the results of an experiential learning project based on the idea that individual cognition occurs in a social setting, Selzer and Woodbridge (2004) report on the dynamics and results of the project's group problem solving and interaction. They conclude that the social dimensions of the endeavour – teamwork, interpersonal communication, the sharing of information and the negotiating of meaning – create a transformational environment that helps students make sense of tasks and contexts and results in the co-construction of knowledge. At California Polytechnic State University, for instance, the concept of social-cultural learning informed creation of a 'zone of innovation' in the Learning Commons where faculty and students collaborated on 'knowledge making' projects (Gillette and Somerville, 2006; Somerville and Gillette, in press).

As Commons advocates refocus on the primary mission of academia – learning – and its social context, they also reconsider a new cohort of learners. The generation that has grown up with the Internet – referred to interchangeably as Millennials, the Net Generation, Generation Y, and the Digital Generation – differs greatly from previous learner generations in terms of needs, expectations, behaviours, and learning styles (Howe and Strauss, 2000; Lenhart et al., 2001). First person accounts corroborate this (Windham, 2005, 2006), as does an EDUCAUSE study that reveals, among the Millennial cohort there is a strong movement toward universal ownership of information technology, access to broadband connectivity, and increased technical mobility – trends that are expected to increase (Caruso and Kvavik, 2005). The study also discusses corresponding changes in Millennials' educational expectations: they assume an educational experience that utilises technology for their convenience as well as the prospect of enhanced communication, time savings and improved presentation techniques. Expertise with gaming technology and virtual reality products also distinguishes the upcoming learner generation from its predecessors (Storey, 2005). Experienced with Xbox, Wii, and Playstation, 'gamers' are more resilient, sociable, motivated and analytical than older cohorts, a factor that predicts upcoming student cohorts' learning behaviours and pedagogical requirements.

Recent publications on higher education recognise and affirm the need to create and redesign educational environments that appropriately address the cultural characteristics, expectations, and learning styles of Millennials. In *Educating the Net Generation*, Oblinger and Oblinger (2005) summarise 'Net Gen' sensibilities and show how they align with specific learning preferences: working in teams, the desire for structure, a predilection for engagement and interaction. Net Gen students, they argue, are interested in what technology enables – customisation, convenience, collaboration and connectedness – and use technology for participatory learning, to construct their own meaning, to enhance the interaction of experiential learning. Because of their lifelong immersion in multiple media, the Net Generation prefer learning modes that are visual and kinesthetic.

Dede carries the multiple media theme further and describes 'Neomillennial' mediated immersion as resulting in a fluency in multiple media and virtual settings; communal learning involving diverse experience across a community, expression through nonlinear webs of representation; learning experiences personalised to individual needs and preferences. Today's and tomorrow's students, he asserts, learn by 'seeking, sieving, and synthesising rather than assimilating a single authoritative source' (Dede, 2005; 7).

And what are the implications for libraries as they plan and implement Learning Commons for Millennials, Neomillennials and beyond? Many campus stakeholders have pondered this question in the light of Millennials' facility with technology, comfort with multitasking, and interaction while learning – producing characteristic 'interchange and energy' (TerHaar et al., 2000; 30). It naturally follows that, in order to appeal to Millennials and thereby enrich their educational experience, libraries must overcome present and potential users' assumption that libraries are primarily 'a place to borrow print books', and not the first choice for information (De Rosa, 2005; section 2.1). To gain visibility and relevance, Joan Lippincott and others suggest that libraries create new learning environments that resonate with Millennials, that recognise Net Gen preferences for simple, responsive interfaces, global searching of resources, spaces that are comfortable, relaxed, 'celebrate technology' and 'promote community among students' (Lippincott, 2005; sections 13.3 and 13.11). The library – the Learning Commons – must be 'a place of interaction, learning and experiencing' (Boone, 2002; 392). In addition, Learning Commons must address more than Millennials' preference for comfort, convenience and interaction; they must explicitly attend to Millennials' learning modes (Bailey, 2005).

Encouragingly, there is evidence that libraries are taking heed of Net Gen preferences and learning expectations as they design and develop new learning spaces. Some Learning

Commons planners explicitly base project outcomes on formal student surveys. They gather data, not just from library measures, but from studies of learner constituencies across campus thereby ensuring that project drivers are student-centred (Mountfield, 2005). The literature also illustrates that Commons advocates periodically conduct post-implementation surveys to determine whether student characteristics and preferences continue to correspond to pre-implementation predictions and measures (Gardner and Eng, 2005). However, Learning Commons practitioners face a greater challenge. Beyond analysing Millennial pre-implementation preferences and evaluating post-implementation services and space utilisation, they must assess how the Learning Commons environment impacts learning outcomes.

This leads, quite naturally, to consideration of unbounded learning space considerations, as 'learning spaces' convey an image of the institution's philosophy about teaching and learning. A standard lecture hall, with immovable chairs all facing the lectern, may represent a philosophy of 'pouring content into students' heads'. An active, collaborative teaching and learning philosophy is often manifested in a different design. Space [utilisation] can either enable – or inhibit – different styles of teaching as well as learning (Oblinger, 2005). In contrast to traditional patterns for designing 'spaces for learning' on campus, most higher educators readily decry traditionally configured classrooms or laboratories as optimal learning environments (Forrest and Hinchliffe, 2005). In turn, educators recognise that 'Net Gen students, using a variety of digital devices, can turn almost any space outside the classroom into an informal learning space' (Brown, 2005; section 12.3). So learning space designers must now consider the instructional implications of these campus spaces – e.g., building hallways, plazas, and courtyards; dormitories; food service areas; and faculty offices including the library – in re-imagining the purpose of libraries and the institutions of which it is a part. With that explicit intention, at San José State University, instructional design consultants, academic technology leaders, campus facilities managers, student government representatives, faculty senate advisers, and university outreach librarians have collaboratively administered and interpreted an EDUCAUSE learning spaces survey instrument, which collected both narrative text and digital images from campus student populations. Intended to build upon the campus Learning Commons (named the Academic Success Center), findings from this rich data set will inform campus-wide reconsideration of campus learning spaces' (re)design (Somerville, 2007).

What seems most important in advancing systemic change is that the team identifies a set of principles that promotes learning within a context that is meaningful to the institution (Johnson and Lomas, 2005). In 'leading the transformation from classrooms to learning spaces' (Oblinger, 2005), Web 2.0 innovations for teaching and learning (Alexander, 2006) must move beyond the comfortable 'one-stop service centre' to become the 'heart of the university' teaching and learning environment that brings together students, faculty, technologists, librarians, writing tutors, instructional designers, and other key stakeholders (Duncan and Woods, 2004).

As the need for technology-enhanced spaces for service delivery, teaching and learning, and multi-media production are increasing, institutions are re-purposing or renovating spaces for expanded unit partnerships. These campus units include but are not limited to information technology, instructional technology, information and research services, and media services (Coalition for Networked Information, 2003; Brown et al., 2004). In addition, because thinking about the library as a social space, rather than as space primarily for undisturbed reading and individual study, involves some recasting of ideas about what makes for success in library planning – and beyond, sustainable learning spaces are reliant on the concerted effort of the library organisations in coordination with various institutional partnerships that share enthusiasm about the promise of new technology, new spatial designs and increased collaboration. Across campuses today, the shared goal might most appropriately be described as 'supporting collaborative learning by which students turn information into knowledge and sometimes into wisdom' (Bennett, 2003).

Learning assessment principles

Demands for increased accountability in higher education have furthered interest in outcome-based education. Professional organisations have long recognised the need for assessment standards and programs, of course. For instance, responding primarily to changes in accreditation requirements, the Association of College and Research Libraries (ACRL) formed a task force in 1998 to consider a 'philosophical framework for assessing libraries' and to develop 'prototypes for such assessment'. Underlying the Task Force's final report is the recognition that libraries must somehow determine whether their programs and services improve the academic performance of students. Such 'learner-centred' assessment approaches provide a valuable means to improve learning and, when 'intimately linked to an institution's missions and goals' (Palomba and Banta, 1999; p. 3), can transform institutional culture

(Angelo, 2007). Many assessment theorists favour measures that include students' broader educational experiences – i.e., out-of-class learning and development such as occurs in Learning Commons and other campus learning spaces. Commonly, guidelines advise that assessment needs to: (1) be client-centred; (2) integrate with the campus's overall assessment efforts; (3) include a variety of methodologies; (4) gather information conducive to improvement strategies; and (5) embody a continuous, adaptive process. Experience has also shown that 'authentic assessment...is iterative' and should be part of 'a continuous improvement cycle and not just a one-shot experiment' (Sonntag and Meulemanns, 2003; pp. 6, 20). As information literacy assessment efforts have shown, this is challenging: 'assessing student learning is extremely difficult because learning is complex and multidimensional' and will require 'multiple instruments/ methods...to capture learning from different dimensions' (Gratch-Lindauer, 2003; p. 26).

Assessment advocates also realise that assessment initiatives must be organisationally and institutionally grounded to be effective, and they encourage strategies that solicit wide support for measuring outcomes. For example, Lakos and Phipps (2004) argue that assessment efforts benefit from an organisation-wide buy-in, and that to engender positive long-term results from outcomes measures, they must emerge from an organisational 'culture of assessment'. Jenkins and Boosinger (2003) reflect and promote an even broader perspective; they assert that assessment endeavours require campus-wide collaborative planning and support to be truly effective.

National Science Foundation (NSF) cyberinfrastructure discussions also encourage thinking well beyond campus boundaries and urge measuring the 'cognitive implications of virtual or web-enabled environments' (Computing

Research Association, 2005; Foreward). Relatedly, various higher education and academic library publications explore the technological possibilities of measuring the impact of web-based instruction on student participants (Dugan, 2001), providing a means of evaluating web-based learning environments (Sheard and Markham, 2005), and assessing information and communication technology (ICT) literacy (Rockman, 2005; Rockman and Smith, 2005; Somerville et al., 2007).

National leaders suggest a range of methodologies: the observation of students and faculty in the learning environments; interviews or focus groups; the study of use patterns over time; and surveys that ask students to rate impact of space on their learning (Oblinger, 2005; 18). Statistical and qualitative data collection should be guided by the mission and goals of the learning environment in a coordinated assessment program that measures change over time in terms that address instructional and programmatic issues (Lippincott, 2006). Learning space and Learning Commons needs extend still further in requiring 'person-environment interaction models...[to]...help focus learning spaces assessment' in terms of 'student engagement' – because students learn by becoming involved (Hunley and Schaller, 2006; sections 13.4 and 13.5). One novel approach to assessing this dimension is the use of photographic studies as a 'direct observational method' that can 'capture observational data across time and in multiple settings with minimal intrusiveness' (Hunley and Schaller, 2006; section 13.7).

Another fascinating but problematic dimension is the 'informal learning' factor. Informal learning represents an important part of the overall learning environment, so 'a comprehensive assessment of learning space' must include the use of space 'that accommodates formal as well as informal and technology-based learning' (Hunley and Schaller, 2006; section 13.3). Such an assessment program acknowledges that learning 'takes place in a much wider variety of settings than formal education or training' and 'recognises the social significance of learning from other people' (Eraut, 2004; 247). This raises questions about informal learning, including 'what is being learned' and 'how it is being learned' through such activities as (1) 'participation in group activities' including teamwork on a common outcome and (2) 'working alongside of others [which] allows people to observe and listen to others...and hence to learn some new practices and perspectives' (Eraut, 2004; 266–267). Clearly, those interested in the measurement of formal and informal learning in university learning environments face especially intriguing and challenging research opportunities which require campus-wide conversation among learning and teaching stakeholders – suggesting that conversation is 'the new paradigm for librarianship' (Bechtel, 1986; 219).

References

Albanese, A.R. (2004) 'Campus library 2.0: the Information Commons is a scalable, one-stop shopping experience for students and faculty', *Library Journal*, 129(7): 30–3.

Alexander, B. (2006) 'Web 2.0: a new wave of innovation for teaching and learning?', *EDUCAUSE Review*, 41(2): 33–44.

Angelo, T.A. (1999) 'Doing assessment as if learning matters most', *AAHE Bulletin*, May.

Association of College and Research Libraries (1998) *Task Force on Academic Library Outcomes Assessment Report*. Available at *http://www.ala.org/ala/acrl/acrlpubs/*

whitepapers/taskforceacademic.htm (accessed 29 June 2007).

Bailey, R. (2005) 'Information Commons services for learners and researchers: evolution in patron needs, digital resources and scholarly publishing', presented at INFORUM 2005: 11th Conference on Professional Information Resources, Prague, 24 May 2005. Available at *http://www.inforum.cz/inforum2005/pdf/Bailey_Russell.pdf* (accessed 29 June 2007).

Bailey, R. and Tierney, B. (2002) 'Information Commons redux: concept, evolution, and transcending the tragedy of the Commons', *Journal of Academic Librarianship*, 28(5): 277–86.

Beagle, D. (1999) 'Conceptualizing an Information Commons', *Journal of Academic Librarianship*, 25(2): 82–9.

Beagle, D. (2002) 'Extending the Information Commons: from instructional testbed to internet2', *Journal of Academic Librarianship*, 28(5): 287–96.

Beagle, D. (2004) 'From Information Commons to Learning Commons', presented at Leavey Library 2004 Conference – Information Commons: Learning Space Beyond the Classroom, Los Angeles, CA, USA, August 2004. Available at *http://www.usc.edu/isd/libraries/locations/leavey/news/conference/presentations/presentations_9-16/Beagle_Information_Commons_to_Learning.pdf* (accessed 29 June 2007).

Beagle, D. (2006) *The Information Commons Handbook*. New York: Neal-Schuman Publishers.

Bechtel, J.M. (1986) 'Conversation: a new paradigm for librarianship?', *College & Research Libraries*, 47: 219–24.

Bennett, S. (2003) *Libraries Designed for Learning*. Washington, D.C.: Council on Library and Information Resources.

Bennett, S. (2005) 'Righting the balance', in *Library as Place: Rethinking Roles, Rethinking Space*. Washington, D.C.: Council on Library and Information Resources; pp. 10–24.

Boone, M.D. (2002) 'Library design the architect's view: a discussion with Tom Findley', *Library Hi Tech*, 20(3): 388–92.

Brown, J.S. and Duguid, P. (2000) *The Social Life of Information*. Boston, MA: Harvard Business School Press.

Brown, M. (2005) 'Learning space design theory and practice', *EDUCAUSE Review*, 40(4): 30.

Brown, M. (2005) 'Learning spaces', in D.G. Oblinger and J.L. Oblinger (eds) *Educating the Net Generation*. Boulder, CO: EDUCAUSE; 12.1–12.22.

Brown, M.B., Dewey, B.I. and Lippincott, J.K. (2004) 'Planning collaborative facilities: creating new opportunities and spaces', presented at EDUCAUSE Annual Conference: IT from a Higher Vantage Point, Denver, 19 October 2004. Available at *http://www.educause .edu/E04/Program/1663?PRODUCT_CODE=E04/ SEM04P* (accessed 29 June 2007).

Brown, M.B. and Lippincott, J.K. (2003) 'Learning spaces: more than meets the eye', *EDUCAUSE Quarterly*, 26(1): 14–16.

Bruce, C.S. (1998) 'The phenomenon of information literacy', *Higher Education Research & Development*, 17(1): 25–43.

Bundy, A. (2004) 'Beyond information: the academic library as educational change agent', presented at the 7th International Bielefeld Conference, Germany, February 2004. Available at *http://www.library.unisa.edu.au/ about/papers/beyond-information.pdf* (accessed 29 June 2007).

Caruso, JB. and Kvavik, R.B. (2005) *ECAR Study of Students and Information Technology, 2005: Convenience, Connection, and Control.* EDUCAUSE: Center for Applied Research. Available at *http://connect.educause.edu/library/abstract/ECARStudyofStudentsa/41159* (accessed 29 June 2007).

Church, J. (2005) 'The evolving Information Commons', *Library Hi Tech*, 23(1): 75–81.

Church, J., Vaughan, J., Starkweather, W. and Rankin, K. (2002) 'The Information Commons at Lied Library', *Library Hi Tech*, 20(1): 58.

Coalition for Networked Information (2003) 'Planning collaboration spaces in libraries: background', presented at Planning Collaboration Spaces in Libraries: An ACRL/CNI Preconference, Toronto, 20 June 2003. Available at *http://www.cni.org/regconfs/acrlcni2003/background.html* (accessed 29 June 2007).

Computing Research Association (2005) *Cyberinfrastructure for Education and Learning for the Future: A Vision and Research Agenda.* Washington, D.C.: Computing Research Association.

Cowgill, A., Beam, J. and Wess, L. (2001) 'Implementing an Information Commons in a university library', *Journal of Academic Librarianship*, 27(6): 432–9.

Crockett, C., McDaniel, S. and Remy, M. (2002) 'Integrating services in the Information Commons: toward a holistic library and computing environment', *Library Administration and Management*, 16(4): 181–6.

Dallis, D., and Walters, C. 'Reference services in the Commons environment', *Reference Services Review*, 34(2): 248–60.

Davis, H.L., and Somerville, M.M. (2006) 'Learning our way to change: improved institutional alignment', *New Library World*, 107(3/4): 127–40.

Dede, C. (2005) 'Planning for Neomillennial learning styles', *EDUCAUSE Quarterly*, 28(1): 7–12.

Demas, S. (2005) 'From the ashes of Alexandria: what's happening in the college library?', in *Library as Place: Rethinking Roles, Rethinking Space*. Washington, D.C.: Council on Library and Information Resources; pp. 25–40.

De Rosa, C. (2005) *Perceptions of Libraries and Information Resources*. Dublin, OH: OCLC.

Dewey, B.I. (2004) 'The embedded librarian: strategic campus collaborations', *Resource Sharing and Information Networks*, 17(1/2): 5–17.

Dugan, R.E. (2001) 'Managing technology in an assessment environment', *Journal of Academic Librarianship*, 28(1): 56–8.

Duguid, P. (2005) "The art of knowing': social and tacit dimensions of knowledge and the limits of the community of practice', *The Information Society*, 21: 109–18.

Duncan, J., and Woods, L. (2004) 'Creating the Information Commons: connection, community, collaboration', presented at Pace University 5 June 2004. Available at *http://www.pace.edu/library/pages/ootul/infocommons/ pacelib-creating_the_information_commons.pdf* (accessed 29 June 2007).

EDUCAUSE Learning Initiative (2006) 'New learning ecosystems', *EDUCAUSE*, available at *http://www .educause.edu/NewLearningEcosystems/2608* (accessed 29 June 2007).

Eckel, P., Green, M., Hill, B. and Mallon, W. (2000). *Taking Charge of Change: A Primer for Colleges and Universities*. Washington, D.C.: American Council of Education.

Eraut, M. (2004) 'Informal learning in the workplace', *Studies in Continuing Education*, 26(2): 247–73.

Forrest, C., and Hinchliffe, L.J. (2005) 'Beyond classroom construction and design: formulating a vision for learning spaces in libraries', *Reference & User Services Quarterly*, 44(4): 296–300.

Freeman, G.T. (2005) 'The library as place: changes in learning patterns, collections, technology, and use', in *Library as Place: Rethinking Roles, Rethinking Space*. Washington, D.C.: Council on Library and Information Resources; pp. 1–9.

Gardner, S., and Eng, S. (2005) 'What students want: Generation Y and the changing function of the academic library', *Portal: Libraries and the Academy*, 5(3): 405–20.

Garriock, B. (2004) 'Intention and perception: the Information Commons at Manukau Institute of Technology', *New Zealand Libraries*, 49: 352–64.

Gillette, D.D. and Somerville, M.M. (2006) 'Toward lifelong 'knowledge making': faculty development for student learning in the Cal Poly Learning Commons', in Orr D. (ed.) *Lifelong Learning: Partners, Pathways, and Pedagogies: Keynote and Refereed Papers from the 4th International Lifelong Learning Conference, Yeppoon, Central Queensland, Australia, 13–16 June 2006*. Rockhampton, Queensland, Australia: Central Queensland University; pp. 117-123.

Gratch-Lindauer, B. (2003) 'Selecting and developing assessment tools', in Fuseler Avery, E. (ed.) *Assessing Student Learning Outcomes for Information Literacy Instruction in Academic Institutions*. Chicago, IL: Association of College and Research Libraries; pp. 22–39.

Haas, L. and Robertson, J. (comps) (2004) *The Information Commons*. Washington, D.C.: Association of Research Libraries, Office of Leadership and Management Services.

Halbert, M. (1999) 'Lessons from the Information Commons frontier', *Journal of Academic Librarianship*, 25(2): 94.

Holmes-Wong, D., Afifi, M., Bahavar, S. and Liu, X. (1997) 'If you build it, they will come: spaces, values, and services in the digital era', *Library Administration and Management,* 11(2): 74–85.

Howe, N. and Strauss, W. (2000) *Millennials Rising: The Next Greatest Generation.* New York: Vintage Books.

Hunley, S. and Schaller, M. (2006) 'Assessing learning spaces', in Oblinger, D. (ed.) *Learning Spaces.* Washington, D.C.: EDUCAUSE; sections 13.1–13.11.

de Jager, K. (2004) 'Navigators and guides: the value of peer assistance in student use of electronic library facilities', *VINE: The Journal of Information and Knowledge Management Systems,* 34(3): 99–106.

Jenkins, J. and Boosinger, M. (2003) 'Collaborating with campus administrators and faculty to integrate information literacy and assessment into the core curriculum', *The Southeastern Librarian,* 50(4): 26–31.

Johnson, C. and Lomas, C. (2005) 'Design of the learning space: learning & design principles', *EDUCAUSE Review,* 40(4): 16–28.

Keating, S. and Gabb, R. (2005) 'Putting learning into the Learning Commons: a literature review', working paper, Victoria University, Melbourne, Australia. Available at *http://eprints.vu.edu.au/archive/00000094/01/Learning %20Commons%20report.pdf* (accessed 29 June 2007).

Kuh, G.D. and Gonyea, R.M. (2003) 'The role of the academic library in promoting student engagement in learning', *College & Research Libraries,* 64(4): 256–82.

Lakos, A. and Phipps, S. (2004) 'Creating a culture of assessment: a catalyst for organizational change', *Portal: Libraries and the Academy,* 4): 345–61.

Latour, B. and Woolgar, S. (1979) *Laboratory Life: The Social Construction of Scientific Facts.* Beverly Hills, CA: Sage.

Lenhart, A., Rainie, L. and Lewis, O. (2001) 'Teenage life online: the rise of instant-message generation and the internet's impact on friendships and family relationships', *Pew Internet & American Life Project*, June 20. Avialble at *http://www.pewinternet.org/pdfs/PIP_Teens_Report.pdf* (accessed 29 June 2007).

Lippincott, J.K. (2005) 'Net Generation students and libraries', in Oblinger, D.G. and Obliner, J.L (eds) *Educating the Net Generation.* Boulder, CO: EDUCAUSE; sections 13.1–13.15.

Lippincott, J.K. (2004) 'Co-location, cooperation & collaboration within the Information Commons', presented at Leavey Library 2004 Conference: Information Commons: Learning Space Beyond the Classroom, Los Angeles, CA, August 2004. Available at *http://www.usc.edu/libraries/locations/leavey/news/ conference/presentations/presentations_9-16/Lippincott .ppt* (accessed 29 June 2007).

Lippincott, J.K. (2006) 'Linking the Information Commons to learning', in Oblinger, D. (ed) *Learning Spaces.* Washington, D.C.: EDUCAUSE; sections 7.2–7.18.

Lynch, C., Murray, J.H., Springsteen, A., Karis, C., Callison, D., Goodman, J., Donzelli, D. (2004) 'The future of libraries: six perspectives on how libraries, librarians, and library patrons will adapt to changing times', *Threshold*, Winter: 13–17. Available at *http://www.ciconline.org/c/ document_library/get_file?folderId=35&name=W04- futurelibraries.pdf* (accessed 29 June 2007).

MacWhinnie, L.A. (2003) 'The Information Commons: the academic library of the future', *Portal: Libraries and the Academy*, 3(2): 241–57.

Malenfant, C. (2006) 'The Information Commons as a collaborative workspace', *Reference Services Review*, 34(2): 279–86.

Marcus, James W. 'From information center to discovery system: next step for libraries?', *Journal of Academic Librarianship*, 27(2): 97–106.

McKinstry, J.M. and McCracken, P. (2002) 'Combining computing and reference desks in an undergraduate library: a brilliant innovation or a serious mistake?', *Portal: Libraries and the Academy*, 2(3): 391–400.

Miller, M. (1998) 'Anticipating the future: The University of Michigan's media union', *Library Hi Tech*, 16(1): 71–83.

Mirijamdotter, A., Somerville, M.M. and Holst, M. (2007) 'An interactive and iterative evaluation approach for creating collaborative learning environments', *The Electronic Journal of Information Systems Evaluation*, 9(2): 83–92.

Misencik, K.E., O'Connor, J.S. and Young, J. (2005) 'A learning place: ten years in the life of a new kind of campus center', *About Campus*, 10(3): 8–16.

Mountifield, H. (2004) 'The Kate Edger Information Commons: a student-centred environment and catalyst for integrated learning support and e-literacy development', presented at the Third International Conference on eLiteracy, St. John's University, New York, June 2004. Available at *http://information-commons.auckland.ac.nz/ content_files/publications/kate_edger_elit.pdf* (accessed 29 June 2007).

Mountifield, H. (2005) 'Learning with a latte: the Kate Edger Information Commons – providing student-centered learning support', *EDUCAUSE Australia,* available at *http://www.information-commons.auckl and.ac.nz/content_files/publications/educause_article.pdf* (accessed 29 June 2007).

Moyo, L.M. (2004) 'Electronic libraries and the emergence of new service paradigms', *The Electronic Library*, 22(3): 220–30.

Nikkel, T. (2003) 'Implementing the Dalhousie Learning Commons', *Feliciter*, 49(4): 212–14.

Oblinger, D. (2005) 'Leading the transition from classrooms to learning spaces', *EDUCAUSE Quarterly*, 28(1): 14–18.

Oblinger, D.G. and Oblinger, J.L. (eds) (2005) *Educating the Net Generation.* Boulder, CO: EDUCAUSE.

Palomba, C.A. and Banta, T.W. (1999) *Assessment Essentials: Planning, Implementing, and Improving Assessment in Higher Education.* San Francisco, CA: Jossey-Bass Publishers.

Rockman, I. (2005) 'Editorial: ICT literacy', *Reference Services Review*, 33(2): 141–3.

Rockman, I. and Smith, G. (2005) 'Information and communication technology literacy: new assessments for higher education', *College & Research Libraries News*, 66(8): 587–9.

Selzer, D. and Woodbridge, S. (2004) 'Collaborative learning: building bridges to lifelong learning', presented at the 3rd Lifelong Learning Conference, Yeppoon, Queensland, Australia, 2004.

Sheard, J. and Markham, S. (2005) 'Web-based learning environments: developing a framework for evaluation', *Assessment & Evaluation in Higher Education*, 30(4): 353–68.

Somerville, M.M. (2007) 'Participatory co-design: a relationship building approach for co-creating libraries of the future', in *Libraries for the Future: Progress, Development and Partnerships - Proceedings of the 73rd International Federation of Library Associations (IFLA) Conference, Durban, South Africa, 2007.* Available at *http://www.ifla.org/IV/ifla73/papers/122-Somerville-en .pdf* (accessed 29 June 2007).

Somerville, M.M. and Brar, N. (2006) 'Collaborative co-design: the Cal Poly digital teaching library user centric approach', in *Information Access for Global Access: Proceedings of the International Conference on Digital Libraries*. New Delhi, India: ICDL; pp. 175–87.

Somerville, M.M., and Gillette, D.D. (2008) 'The California Polytechnic State University Learning Commons: a case study', in Tierney, B. and Bailey, R. (eds) *Information Commons Case Studies: Academic, Community College and Public Libraries*. Chicago, IL: American Library Association (in press).

Somerville, M.M., Huston, M.E. and Mirijamdotter, A. (2005a) 'Building on what we know: staff development in the digital age', *The Electronic Library*, 23(4): 480–91.

Somerville, M.M., Lampert, L.D., Dabbour, K.S., Harlan, S. and Schader, B. (2007) 'Toward large scale assessment of information and communication technology literacy: implementation considerations for the ETS ICT literacy instrument', *Reference Services Review*, 35(1): 8–20.

Somerville, M.M., Mirijamdotter, A. and Collins, L. (2006) 'Systems thinking and information literacy: elements of a knowledge enabling workplace environment', in *Proceedings of the 39th Annual Hawaii International Conference on Systems Sciences, Los Alamitos, California, 2006*. Available at *http://csdl2.computer.org/comp/proceedings/hicss/2006/2507/07/250770150.pdf* (accessed 29 June 2007).

Somerville, M.M., Rogers, E., Mirijamdotter, A. and Partridge, H. (2007) 'Collaborative evidence-based information practice: the Cal Poly digital learning initiative', in Connor, E. (ed) *Case Studies in Evidence-Based Librarianship*. Oxford, UK: Chandos Publishing; pp. 141–61.

Somerville, M.M., Schader, B. and Huston, M.E. (2005b) 'Rethinking what we do and how we do it: systems thinking strategies for library leadership', *Australian Academic and Research Libraries*, 36(4): 214–27.

Sonntag, G. and Meulemanns, Y. (2003) 'Planning for assessment', in Avery, E. (ed) *Assessing Student Learning Outcomes for Information Literacy Instruction in Academic Institutions*. Chicago, IL: Association of College and Research Libraries; pp. 6–21.

Spencer, M.E. (2006) 'Evolving a new model: the Information Commons', *Reference Services Review*, 34(2): 242–7.

Starkweather, W. and Marks, K. (2005) 'What if you build it, and they keep coming and coming and coming?', *Library Hi Tech*, 23(1): 22–33.

Storey, T. (2005) 'The big bang', *OCLC Newsletter*, Jan–Mar: 7–8.

Swarz, N. (2006) 'Libraries replacing books with bytes', *Information Management Journal*, 39(4): 13.

TerHaar, L.K., Campbell, J.D., Stoffle, C., Stroyan, S., Lombardi, J., Kaufman, P. and Pape, S. (2000) 'The fate of the undergraduate library', *Library Journal*, 125(18): 38–41.

Wedge, C.C. and Kearns, T.D. (2005) 'Creation of the learning space: catalysts for envisioning and navigating the design process', *EDUCAUSE Review*, 40(4): 32–8.

Whitchurch, M., Belliston, J. and Baer, W. (2006) 'Information Commons at Brigham Young University: past, present, and future', *Reference Services Review*, 34: 261–78.

Windham, C. (2005) 'Father Google and Mother IM: confessions of a Net Gen learner', *EDUCAUSE Review*, Sep/Oct: 43–58.

Windham, C. (2006) 'Getting past Google: perspectives on information literacy from the Millennial mind', in Oblinger, D. (ed) *EDUCAUSE Learning Initiative*. EDUCAUSE; p. 10.

Additional reading

Bazillion, R.J. and Braun, C. (2001) *Academic Libraries as High-Tech Gateways; A Guide to Design and Space Decisions.* Chicago, IL: American Library Association.

Beatty, S. (2002) 'The Information Commons at the University of Calgary: strategies for integration', presented at the 1st International Conference on IT and Information Literacy, Glasgow. March 2002. Available at *http://www.iteu.gla.ac.uk/elit/itilit2002/papers/ppt/06.ppt* (accessed 29 June 1007).

Conway, P. (2004) 'Deep infrastructure supports digital library services', *Syllabus*, May. Available at *http:// campustechnology.com/article.asp?id=9362* (accessed 29 June 2007).

Council on Library and Information Resources (2005) *Library As Place: Rethinking Roles, Rethinking Space.* Washington, D.C.: Council on Library and Information Resources. Available at *http://www.clir.org/pubs/reports/pub129/pub129.pdf* (accessed 29 June 2007).

Fliss, S. (2005) 'Collaborative creativity: supporting teaching and learning on campus', *College & Research Libraries News*, 66(5). Available at *http://www.ala.org/ala/acrl/acrlpubs/crlnews/backissues2005/May05/colcreativity.htm* (accessed 29 June 2007).

Fox, D., Fritz, L., Kichuk, D. and Nussbaumer, A. (2001) 'University of Saskatchewan Information Commons: reconfiguring the learning environment'. University of Saskatchewan, Canada. Available at *http://www.usask.ca/university_council/library/reports/ic.pdf* (accessed 29 June 2007).

Fullerton, A. (2002) 'Davis Centre Information Commons project: Information Commons – notes from many sources'. University of Waterloo, Canada. Available at *http://www.lib.uwaterloo.ca/staff/infocommons/reports/annesnotes.html* (accessed 29 June 2007).

Hughes, C.A. (2000) 'Information services for higher education. A new competitive space', *D-Lib Magazine*, 6(12). Available at *http://www.dlib.org/dlib/december00/hughes/12hughes.html* (accessed 29 June 2007).

Hunt, G.A. (2004) 'Ohio University Alden Library Learning Commons fact sheet', available at *http://www.cni.org/tfms/2004b.fall/abstracts/handouts/CNI_learning_stuart.pdf* (accessed 30 June 2007).

Joint Information Systems Committee (2006) *Designing Spaces for Effective Learning: A Guide to 21st Century Learning Space Design.* Bristol, UK: JISC.

King, H. (2000) 'The academic library in the 21st century: what need for a physical place?', in *Proceedings of Virtual Libraries: Virtual Communities: 21st IATUL Conference, Brisbane, Australia, July 2000.* Available at *http://www.iatul.org/doclibrary/public/Conf_Proceedings/2000/King.rtf* (accessed 29 June 2007).

University of Calgary (unknown) 'Learning Commons: strategic plan 2004–2006', University of Calgary, Canada. Available at *http://commons.ucalgary.ca/ documents/LC_StrategicPlan04-06Final.pdf* (accessed 29 June 2007).

Library Administration and Management Association (2001) *Building Blocks for Planning Functional Library Space.* Lanham, MD: Scarecrow Press.

Lippincott, J.K. (2004) 'New library facilities: opportunities for collaboration', *Resource Sharing & Information Networks*, 17(1/2): 147–57.

Long, P.D. and Ehrmann, S.C. (2005) 'Future of the learning space: breaking out of the box', *EDUCAUSE Review*, 40(4): 42–58.

McKinstry, J.M. (2004) 'Collaborating to create the right space for the right time', *Resource Sharing & Information Networks*, 17(1/2): 137–46.

Orgeron, E. (2001) 'Integrated academic student support services at Loyola University: the library as a resource clearinghouse', *Journal of Southern Academic and Special Librarianship*, 2(3). Available at *http://southernlibrarianship. icaap.org/content/v02n03/orgeron_e01.htm* (accessed 29 June 2007).

Pierce, J.B. (2004) 'Grassroots report: next stop, Information Commons', *American Libraries*, 35(4): 87.

Raspa, D. and Ward, D. (eds) (2000) *The Collaborative Imperative: Librarians and Faculty Working Together in the Information Universe.* Chicago, IL: Association of College and Research Libraries.

Stringer, J. (2006) 'Supporting the Learning Commons concept in the real world', presented at the California Academic & Research Libraries Annual Meeting 2006 Pre-Conference, May 2006. Available at *http://lane .stanford.edu/contacts/jenn/CARL_LearningCommons 2006SJennStringer.pdf* (accessed 29 June 2007).

Stuart, C. ' Georgia Tech's Learning Commons: an epicenter for student success', *EucauseConnect*, available at *http://connect.educause.edu/library/abstract/GeorgiaTechs Learning/39416?time=1183233159* (accessed 30 June 2007).

2

Circle of service: a collaborative Information Commons planning model

Barbara I. Dewey (Dean of Libraries, University of Tennessee, Knoxville, Tennessee, USA)

Introduction

Library space transformation is exploding across colleges and university campuses, specifically with the development of collaborative Information Commons spaces. This chapter will focus on a collaborative planning process for developing these new spaces to support the changing needs of twenty-first century students and scholars. The planning process model is structured so that it can be used to develop a variety of spaces and services that incorporate partnerships. The development process for creating the University of Tennessee Libraries' Commons will be used as an example. This newly created, service-intensive space is a partnership with the Office of Information Technology (OIT) and several colleges. A general checklist is provided at the end of the chapter (see Appendices) and may be used as a planning tool for any collaborative space.

The Commons is based on the 'circle of service' model and embraces the notion of connecting students to the information, assistance, and services they need to be successful. The circle of service model will be outlined in detail along with accompanying tools that can be customised for individual projects. I will discuss the importance of library as intellectual, social, and cultural space in the physical and virtual sense and explore selected examples of emerging 'new' spaces that connect students and/or faculty to collections and services in innovative and effective ways. Indicators of success and next steps for library transformation in the digital age will conclude the chapter.

Scenario for change

The current wave of library transformations and collaborative Commons development is based on a number of factors. Our highly-networked, digital, hyper technological environment, combined with the emergence of born digital students and faculty, set the stage. The digital revolution in its broadest sense is the primary driver. Students, in particular, have embraced the digital world, socially and intellectually. They have radically different ways of interacting, seeking and processing information. They have special interests and skills in social computing and collaboration.

Libraries are developing and purchasing digital collections, databases, and services to help people access digital resources and at least try to be in the same digital if not physical spaces as our users. Library physical spaces, built for legacy print collections, are ripe for transformation. College and university case-based curriculum require more teamwork. Spaces, hardware, software, and networking to achieve these group assignments are in demand. New standards of accountability demand that we, as educators, ensure use of our expensive collections and services in ways that specifically advance intellectual, cultural, and social development of students and support the process of knowledge creation for all. We are unable to achieve these goals unless we are in the same space. Thus, students or faculty should be co-creators of new spaces to ensure relevance and usability. Specific environmental factors illustrating the imperative to change and transform include:

- the changing nature of libraries and the need to repurpose spaces built for the print era;
- student and faculty reliance on digital scholarship and its supporting technology;
- the need to create effective learning spaces and services for net gen students;
- attracting and retaining the best and brightest students who have choices;
- the desire to access, 'remix', and share digital resources and rich media in new ways;
- addressing the imperative for 'always on' 24/7 services, collections, and environments.[1]

Planning for new spaces should be accomplished within the context of addressing the different needs of our user communities – undergraduates, graduate students, and faculty. Although this chapter discusses planning specifically for an Information Commons environment, a more holistic process will be necessary to successfully create the variety of library physical and virtual spaces needed for student and faculty success.

Commons emerging from larger transformation processes

Planning for Commons spaces should be undertaken in conjunction with broader planning efforts to look at the institution's library spaces and services in terms of user needs. Libraries still function in many areas with nineteenth century processes and space configurations. Students and faculty operate in the twenty-first century and the library should mirror the current environment in all regards.

The Commons,[2] located in the University of Tennessee Hodges Library, came out of a larger library transformation process to strategically address our services, collections, and spaces to meet the needs of twenty-first century students and faculty for a campus of 27,000 students, 1,350 faculty, and 6,900 staff. Hodges Library, a relatively new facility, opened in 1987. Although well known for innovative application of technology and strong service orientation, we were increasingly confined and constrained by space configuration in a 1980s building. We also had to consider how we were going to transform nineteenth century practices and reallocate staff and spaces to align with activities, programs, and operations relevant to the twenty-first century. Study groups were developed around six areas we knew were changing radically, especially because of digitally-based factors – more digital, less print collections, students bypassing library resources altogether, and faculty using our virtual space more than our physical space. The six study groups dealt with:

- services and spaces;
- digital production;
- access to content – user interfaces/user awareness;

- periodicals management;
- collection management/technical processes;
- special collections and archives.

Libraries can determine specific areas for review based on their unique needs and specific projects like Information Commons development will emerge. These types of holistic transformation processes, given the reality of constant change, should be seen as ongoing.

Surfacing the Commons concept

The Services and Spaces Study Group provided the initial focus for Information Commons planning at the University of Tennessee. The group's charge was to conduct an analysis of Hodges Library public service points in terms of the needs of twenty-first century users and the most effective use of human resources and space. The report proved to be our transformational breakthrough. The group's work centred on answering the question of how to make a 1987 library building more relevant, functional, and user friendly. When opened the building featured 'wow factor' grand marble staircases, huge hallways, and spacious atria. Service desks were numerous but invisible from the massive hallways. Large areas, such as the Reserve Book Room and the Periodicals Room, needed repurposing, as these collections are now largely digital. Additionally, the library had experienced positive collaborations with the Office of Information Technology (OIT) through creation of the Digital Media Service,[3] a drop-off production facility to digitise faculty course-related materials in all formats, implementation of VolPrint,[4] a system of pay-for-print, and development of innovative strategies for integrating scholarly resources and library services within the University's course management system Online@UT using The Teaching Library@UT website and the virtual reference website AskUs.Now.[5] Additional collaborations with OIT were needed and desirable.

Recognising the implications of the new digital context, as well as the key characteristics of net generation students and faculty, the Services and Spaces Study Group recommended that an Information Commons be developed in partnership with OIT initially in the high-profile space occupied by the Reserve Book Room (7,788 sq. ft) and extending throughout the entire second floor (47,000 sq. ft). A ground floor computer lab operated by OIT would be absorbed into the Commons. Complimentary services and spaces already existed on this heavily used floor including a 24-hour Starbucks Cybercafe, The Studio[6] (a multi-media authoring and production lab), and the Welcome Center, containing the main entrance to the library and the circulation desk. Other recommendations included moving periodicals and microforms to the first floor enabling the Information Commons to encompass the entire floor. Further phases would include renovation of the Media Services area to expand multimedia computing and other technologically and media rich user space.

General issues

Making an Information Commons happen requires addressing several general issues:

- process and actual installation must be flexible to meet changing needs and technologies;

- phased approaches should be considered given time and budget constraints inherent in the college/university environment;

- different 'partner' cultures must be recognised (library, IT, institutional administrators);

- sustainability of staff, equipment, and space maintenance should be considered;

- different funding strategies could be employed including bootstrapping, start-up, and recurring sources brought together by different partners;

- campus buy-in is a must;

- legal or policy issues should be noted.

Key planners should review these and other institutional issues to come up with the most efficient and effective strategy for making the project happen.

Preliminary planning (or getting the party started)

Once the need for a Commons is confirmed, key planners should identify champions at the earliest possible stage. Typical champions could include Provost, President, Deans, and campus budget officers. Commitment for and resources needed to initiate the planning need to be identified. Key planners then need to bring together a core planning group to begin the process realising that this group may change over time and also selecting membership in terms of expertise needed. Facilitation and initial idea support by consultants can be considered at this stage. The UT Information Commons steering committee, formed in April 2005, invited Joan Lippincott (Associate Executive Director,

Coalition for Networked Information) to spend the day with staff from the library and OIT presenting on collaborative learning space development and advising on important aspects of implementation. Members of the committee included the library associate dean (as facilitator), assistant dean of libraries and head of media services, dean of libraries, CIO, head of reference and instructional services, manager of OIT customer support, executive director of OIT customer support, system administrator for OIT Labs, coordinator for OIT educational technology, electronic services librarian, coordinator of library instructional services, library web designer, manager of OIT customer support, head of the digital media service and manager of OIT customer technical support.

Creating a vision and guiding principles

Key components of early planning include creation of a vision for the facility as well as guided principles for planning that form the basis for planning. Leadership for the planning team is identified and initial project definition and timeline should take place.

The vision: The Commons is a collaborative partnership between the Office of Information Technology and the University Libraries to connect students and faculty with the tools and information they need to be successful learners and teachers in the twenty-first century.

Guiding principles for the Commons were formulated and continue to be valuable as we develop new services and renovate additional areas.

The Commons guiding principles – The Commons:

- is a true partnership of the Libraries and OIT;
- is a physical and virtual environment;

- leverages joint expertise of Libraries/OIT faculty and staff;
- focuses on the needs of undergraduates (but also serves graduates and faculty);
- will increase services, access to content and technology for users;
- will be a 24/7 environment;
- will be developed in a phased approach;
- will be flexible, innovative, and appealing;
- will be developed with advice from students and other key campus groups.

Vision and guiding principles keep planners on track and disciplined to remain focused on the users' perspective.

The circle of service model

The circle of service philosophy emerges out of the vision and guiding principles. It incorporates the 'one-stop shopping around the clock' imperative that, in particular addresses twenty-first century needs and expectations of web intensive users. For the Tennessee project, initial services in phase one included information/reference, laptop checkout, technical assistance with logins, 24-hour book retrieval from the stacks, printing/copying/scanning, statistical consulting, wireless access, Digital Media Service pick-up point, presentation practice room, and computer technical support. All funding came from within the library and the OIT budgets, and staffing from reallocation and/or relocation of existing library/OIT positions.

Proof of concept budgetary strategy

A proof of concept strategy should be considered in institutions with lean budgets and competing priorities that describe nearly all of today's colleges and universities. Key planners can forge a strong partnership each bringing to the table a set of human and other resources needed to bootstrap development of the Information Commons. The circle of service concept can be presented to campus administrators and champions underscoring the project's high impact and relevance to student success. A phased approach is useful in discussing funding strategies. At the University of Tennessee the Dean of Libraries and the Chief Information Officer proposed funding from three sources: the Chancellor, Libraries and OIT. Graphical representations help make the pitch more effective because they can efficiently show sources of funding in a multi-year display even if planners are unsure of the cost in future phases (Figure 2.1). Statistics demonstrating success of existing Commons spaces further supports the case for significant campus investment.

Creating the buzz

Marketing the Commons concept at the earliest point is important in order to create excitement and thus, support. The Dean of Libraries and CIO wanted to create additional support for the Commons and gave presentations to the Deans and the Vice Chancellors early in the autumn semester right after phase one opened. More presentations were given to student groups and committees encouraging students to let their peers know of the new services and to obtain feedback on how the Commons was working for them. Students continue to provide valuable advice for space and service adjustments. The presentations helped create support and

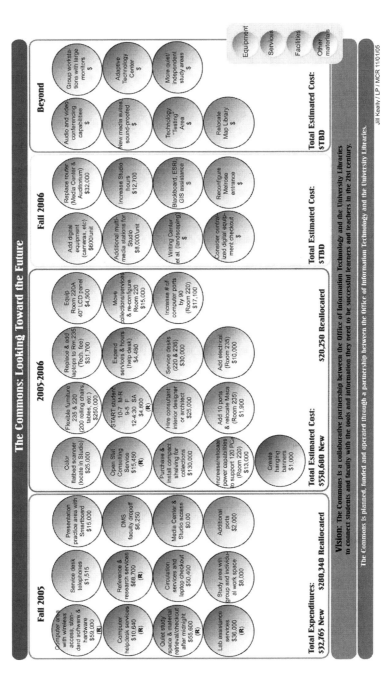

Figure 2.1 Bubble financial chart

excitement. A loud and distinctive 'buzz' was created combined with publicity generated by the Commons public relations subgroup in the form of news releases, a website, and large banners describing the Commons. The marketing plan at this stage was modest and pointed – Computer Help, Research Assistance, Fully Loaded Computers – but it worked. Students immediately embraced the facility (Figure 2.2).

Early indicators of success

Indicators of success, even at early stages of a project, can be helpful. For example we experienced dramatic increases in gate count (December 2005 gate count was up 46 per cent from December 2004), circulation (up 79 per cent), and room count (over 400 students midweek at midnight in the Commons). The student perspective at the onset was well represented by two quotes. Kristen, a sports management student, noted that 'every time I have been in the library after hours, the Commons has been packed full of students. Some students were finishing assignments, some were doing group projects, and some were just relaxing with friends. The group study areas are of the perfect number and size, and the computers have all the programs I could need on them. I cannot wait until the whole Commons project is complete'. Mark, a business major adds, 'The Commons is a great addition to the library. Students can study in groups or study alone, check our laptops, use computers, get help and find all the information they need in one room. The Commons has become the one-stop shop at the library making it user friendly'.

The Commons – phase two

The Commons, phase one, was initially developed without additional funding or professional designers but through

Figure 2.2 Marketing banner

The Commons
Collaborating. Learning. Creating.
Office of Information Technology & University Libraries
235 Hodges Library
commons.utk.edu

Computer help.
Research assistance.
Consultants.
Fully-loaded computers.
Wireless network.
Loaner laptops.
After-hours book retrieval and checkout.
Printing, copying, scanning.
Group work and study space.

reallocations, modest one-time investments, and existing furnishings. Once proof of concept was visible and successful the Dean of Libraries and CIO secured funding from the Chancellor and Vice Chancellors to expand the Commons into the Periodicals Room (10,171 sq. ft). Designers were hired to develop plans and a more accurate budget estimate for the expanded Commons. More specific project definition emerged including explicit timelines and budget. An ambitious design resulted, incorporating flexible furnishings for group and individual work, counters and stools for quick email, soft furnishings for more comfortable study and collaboration, and areas for tutorial and instructional purposes. The IT help desk, computer triage service, expanded laptop checkout, newly configured information/research service area, mobile audio/video conferencing services, additional presentation and group work rooms, and tutoring services were installed and ready for autumn semester 2006. The 'circle of service' expanded and partnerships increased (Figure 2.3).

Focused planning

The circle of service collaborative planning model provides a way to execute focused planning incorporating expertise of all parties in every stage of the Commons development. Subcommittees of the original planning committee can be formed to focus on different elements such as furnishings, specific programming areas, personnel and training, and technical specifications making sure that subcommittee work is brought back to the larger group.

Agreements and policies

Collaborations bring acknowledgements of cultural differences, expectations, and approaches. Trust is the single greatest asset in the circle of service planning model. However, some facilities will benefit from a memorandum of understanding (MOU) signed by the appropriate administrators outlining such things

Figure 2.3 Circle of service handout

Vision: The Commons is a collaborative partnership between the Office of Information Technology and the University Libraries to connect students and faculty with the tools and information they need to be successful learners and teachers in the 21st century.

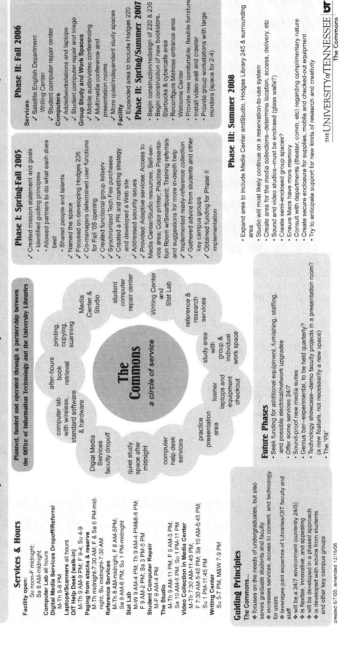

Planned, funded and operated through a partnership between the Office of Information Technology and the University Libraries

The Commons
a circle of service

- Media Center & Studio
- student computer repair center
- Writing Center and Stat Lab
- reference & research services
- study area with group & individual work space
- loaner laptops and equipment checkout
- computer help desk services
- practice presentation area
- quiet study space after midnight
- Digital Media Services faculty dropoff
- computer lab with wireless, standard software & hardware
- after-hours book retrieval
- printing, copying, scanning

Services & Hours

Facility open:
Su noon–F midnight;
Sa 8 AM–midnight

Computer Lab all hours

Digital Media Services Dropoff/Referral
M–Th 5–8 PM

Laptops/Scanners all hours

OIT Help Desk (walk-in)
M–Th 9 AM–9 PM, F 9–4, Su 4–9

Paging from stacks & reserve
M–Th midnight–7:30 AM; F & Sa 6 PM-midnight; Su midnight–7:30 AM

Reference Services
M–Th 8 AM–midnight; F 8 AM–5PM;
Sa 9 AM–6 PM; Su 1 PM–midnight

Stat Lab
M–W 9 AM–4 PM; Th 9 AM–4 PM&6–8 PM;
F 9 AM–2 PM; Sa 3 PM–5 PM

Student Computer Repair
M–F 9 AM–4 PM

The Studio
M–Th 9 AM–11 PM; F 9 AM–5 PM;
Sa 10 AM–5 PM; Su 1 PM–11 PM

Video Collection in Media Center
M–Th 7:30 AM–11:45 PM;
F 7:30 AM–5:45 PM; Sa 10 AM–5:45 PM;
Su 1 PM–11:45 PM

Writing Center
Su 5–7 PM; M&W 7–9 PM

Guiding Principles

The Commons...
❖ focuses on the needs of undergraduates, but also serves graduate students and faculty
❖ increases services, access to content, and technology for users
❖ leverages joint expertise of Libraries/OIT faculty and staff
❖ will be a 24/7 environment (currently 24/5)
❖ is flexible, innovative, and appealing
❖ will be developed in a phased approach
❖ is developed with advice from students and other key campus groups

created 5/7/05; amended 12/18/06

Phase I: Spring-Fall 2005

✓ Created mission statement and goals
✓ Identified guiding principles
  • Allowed partners to do what each does best
  • Named the space
✓ Focused on developing Hodges 235
✓ Co-managers determined user functions for Fall '05 opening
✓ Created functional group listserv
✓ Synchronized Tech Fee purchases
✓ Created a PR and marketing strategy and developed a Web site
✓ Addressed security issues
✓ Provided: Adaptive services; Access to Media Center/Studio resources; Self-service area; Color printer; Practice Presentation Room w/Smartboard; Training referrals and suggestions for more in-depth help
✓ Implemented ready-reference collection
✓ Gathered advice from students and other key campus groups
✓ Obtained funding for Phase II implementation

Phase II: Fall 2006

Services
✓ Satellite English Department Writing Center
  • Student computer repair center

Computers
✓ Added workstations and laptops
  • Student computer repair and fridge

Group Study and Work Spaces
✓ Mobile audio/video conferencing
  • Multimedia conference and presentation rooms
  • More quiet/independent study spaces

Facility
✓ Expanded area to include Hodges 220

Phase II: Spring/Summer 2007

  • Begin construction/redesign of 220 & 235
  • Begin construction of new bookstore,
  Starbucks & cybercafe area
  • Reconfigure Melrose entrance area
  • Provide new comfortable, flexible furniture
  • Install video wall and crawler
  • Provide group workstations with large monitors (space for 2-4)

Phase III: Summer 2008

  • Expand area to include Media Center andStudio, Hodges Library 245 & surrounding area
  • Studio will most likely continue on a reservation-to-use system
  • Create area for the media collections—determine location, access, delivery, etc
  • Sound and video studios—must be enclosed (glass walls?)
  • Create semi-enclosed group spaces?
  • Ensure Macs have more memory
  • Consult with departments (theater, comm, etc) regarding complimentary nature
  • Create secure enclosure for supplies, mobile and checked-out equipment
  • Try to anticipate support for new kinds of research and creativity

Future Phases

  • Seek funding for additional equipment, furnishing, staffing, and possible electrical/network upgrades
  • Offer some services 24/7
  • Sound-proof new media suites
  • Genius bar–experimental, to be held quarterly?
  • Technology showcase–demo faculty projects in a presentation room? (a new feature, not necessarily a new space)
  • The Pit

THE UNIVERSITY of TENNESSEE
The Commons

as the length of the agreement, governance, location, compatibility issues such as furnishings, signage, hours of operation, service philosophy, referral guidelines, and length of agreement (subject to renewal). Policies may need to be developed for use of specialised facilities commonly found within Commons facilities such as classrooms and presentation practice rooms. A review of existing policies and practices such as Acceptable Use Policies, Intellectual Property Practices, and access policies needs to occur to ensure compatibility. Service philosophies and expectations can also be confirmed.

The circle of service spreads

The existence of a commons space implies appropriate adjacent support services including appealing social spaces and opportunities for refreshment in a 24-hour model. These facilities should be planned and installed in the spirit and look of the Commons. This was an important goal even before the Commons was developed. Aramark Food Services installed a Starbucks Café in 2001 on the second floor of Hodges Library adjacent to a small convenience store developed earlier, years before the Commons was developed. Starbucks was an immediate, if not resounding, success, providing appealing social spaces for students and faculty to meet, and also provided a safe venue for late night snacking without going outside. A study area behind the coffee shop was developed into a Cybercafe, with walk up workstations to check email or surf the Internet. Now reconfiguration of these spaces as part of the Commons is in the planning stages. More phases are also underway incorporating the current Media Services and Studio area. A media wall is planned for the busy entrance of Hodges Library. These additional plans prompt thought to expanding partnerships to include the University's food service and communications groups. After all, multiple partners are also potential funders.

Research and inspiring spaces

Circle of service planning works great for a Commons development. And, at the University of Tennessee, the Commons turns out to be a wonderful spot for undergraduates to gather, work, socialise, and be part of a crowd. However, we hear, especially from graduate students and faculty, about the need for quiet, inspiring study spaces. A growing number of research libraries have developed or are planning physical and virtual library spaces especially for graduate students and/or faculty. Examples include research Commons, reading rooms, labs, and spaces for collaborative as well as virtual research.

Other libraries have renovated grand, historic spaces specifically for quiet, contemplative study. The University of Tennessee has a 75-year-old library building, Hoskins Library, in desperate need of renovation. We are exploring designating it as a humanities centre with research space contiguous with a grand reading room, the Digital Library Center,[7] and Special Collections.[8] Boston College,[9] the University of Southern California,[10] and University of Oklahoma[11] have recently transformed buildings from similar eras, featuring inspiring reading rooms meant for quiet study. Commons development spurs on the imperative to improve spaces for other audiences expanding the circle of service even wider.

Planning for the virtual Commons

Creating spaces for advancing intellectual, social, and cultural development in the digital era includes exploring new possibilities for virtual spaces. We are in the process of developing a robust virtual Commons.[12] Other universities such as Vassar,[13] the University of Michigan,[14] and Washington University[15] have developed virtual collaboration spaces including for faculty. The University of Minnesota[16] and North Carolina State University[17] libraries feature integrated social communication spaces as part of their services.

Extending the circle of service

Extending the 'circle of service' concept to the rest of the campus advances universities' goals of integrating expertise, technology, and environments needed to support teaching, learning, and the creation of new knowledge. Students and faculty now have experience planning, building, and using the circle of service-based Commons. They want it in their department, at least a smaller version. Even if the service philosophy itself was extended, progress would be made. The circle of service implies slashing bureaucracy and providing uncompromising service in a user-centred environment. Extending the circle of service further underscores the imperative for immersing the campus in rich research and teaching environment, twenty-first century communication options, and deeper interdisciplinary collaborations. And, this brings us full circle to why we plan a Commons in the first place.

Notes

1. Lippincott, J.K. (2005) 'Net generation students & libraries', *EDUCAUSE Review*, Mar/Apr: 56–66.
2. The Commons, University of Tennessee Libraries and Office of Information Technology (OIT), *http://commons.utk.edu/* (accessed 21 February 2007).

3. Digital Media Service, *http://digitalmedia.utk.edu/* (accessed 21 February 2007).

4. VolPrint, University of Tennessee, *http://volprint.utk.edu/* (accessed 21 February 2007).

5. AskUs.Now, *http://www.lib.utk.edu/refs/askusnow/* (accessed 21 February 2007).

6. The Studio, University of Tennessee Libraries, *http://www.lib. utk.edu/mediacenter/studio/index.htm*l (accessed 21 February 2007).

7. University of Tennessee Libraries. Digital Library Center, *http://diglib.lib.utk.edu/cgi/b/bib/bib-idx* (accessed 21 February 2007).

8. University of Tennessee, Special Collections Department, *http://www.lib.utk.edu/spcoll/* (accessed 21 February 2007).

9. Boston College, Babst Library, *http://www.bc.edu/libraries/ centers/bapst/* (accessed 21 February 2007).

10. University of Southern California, Doheny Memorial Library, *http://www.usc.edu/libraries/locations/doheny/* (accessed 21 February 2007).

11. University of Oklahoma Libraries, Bizzell Memorial Library, *http://libraries.ou.edu/* (accessed 21 February 2007).

12. University of Tennessee Libraries and OIT Commons, *http://commons.utk.edu/* (accessed 21 February 2007).

13. Vassar College Media Cloisters, *http://mediacloisters. vassar.edu/* (accessed 21 February 2007).

14. University of Michigan Libraries, Faculty Exploratory, *http:// www.lib.umich.edu/exploratory/* (accessed 21 February 2007).

15. Washington University Olin Library, Washington University Digital Gateway, *http://www.lib.umich.edu/exploratory/* (accessed 21 February 2007).

16. University of Minnesota Libraries, UThink: Blogs at the University of Minnesota, *http://blog.lib.umn.edu/* (accessed 21 February 2007).

17. North Carolina State University Libraries, WolfWikis and WolfBlogs, *http://www.lib.ncsu.edu/community/* (accessed 21 February 2007).

Appendix A

Planning checklist

Preliminary planning

- ☐ Need/rationale
- ☐ Project scope
- ☐ Key champions – project sponsorship
- ☐ Key administrators
- ☐ Partners for implementation
- ☐ Partners for operation

Project kick-off

- ☐ Method (team, committee, departments)
- ☐ Required team skills
- ☐ Resources, commitments for planning
- ☐ Assign roles
- ☐ Team formed

Project definition

- ☐ Project tracking, outcomes
- ☐ Accountability and reporting

- ☐ Refine mission, goals
- ☐ Confirm service philosophy with partners
- ☐ Preliminary timeline
- ☐ Preliminary budget
- ☐ Basic ground rules

Space

- ☐ Identify requirements
    - ☐ programmatic
    - ☐ physical
    - ☐ technical
    - ☐ strategic
- ☐ New construction or remodeling?
- ☐ Identify potential sites
- ☐ Assess sites based on requirements, cost, etc.
- ☐ Recommend site to champions

Research/assessment

- ☐ Conduct focus groups, interviews
- ☐ Refine mission/goals
- ☐ Consider ongoing evaluation/assessment plan

Personnel

- ☐ Determine personnel needed
    - ☐ Identify available personnel from partners
    - ☐ Identify need for new personnel, HR requirements

- [ ] Acknowledge/plan for cultural differences between partners
- [ ] Training needs for current, new personnel
  - [ ] Address expertise needs
  - [ ] Address cultural needs

Budget – building, infrastructure

- [ ] Seek 'players' for building budget
- [ ] Develop building, remodeling budget

Budget – operations

- [ ] One-time costs (hardward, software, training, launch)
- [ ] Recurring costs (minimum 3 year period)
  - [ ] Personnel
  - [ ] Technology, software, equipment refresh
  - [ ] Marketing costs
  - [ ] Software, hardware refresh

Collaboration/partnership agreements

- [ ] Identify need for agreements
- [ ] Develop agreements – Memo of understanding (MOU)
- [ ] Get sign-off from apprpriate partners, administrators
- [ ] Determine name of facility
- [ ] Problem resolution process
- [ ] Integrate into partners' strategic plans and planning process

Service considerations

- ☐ Hours of operation
- ☐ Staffing requirements
- ☐ Integration strategies with adjacent units, partners (i.e referral system, plan)
- ☐ Security considerations
- ☐ Access to facility

Marketing

- ☐ Marketing plan
- ☐ Outline methods of communicating service (web, email, brochures)
- ☐ Integrate information about facility, service with partners, campus outlets
- ☐ Develop launch plan (soft opening, opening event, etc.)
- ☐ Determine key participants for opening
- ☐ Consider dissemination of experience (presentations, publications)

Pre-launch analysis

- ☐ Basic components in place
- ☐ It works
- ☐ Training completed
- ☐ Staff from collaborating departments aware of new service
- ☐ User support in place
- ☐ Initial assessment plan

Launch

☐ Invite staff first

☐ Role of early adopters, key faculty

☐ Demonstrations, examples of service

☐ Timing of opening

Post launch

☐ Successes

☐ Outstanding issues, problems

☐ Strategies to resolve issues

☐ Implementation of post launch strategies

Communications

☐ Ongoing communication plan (reports, meetings)

☐ Ongoing assessment of operation, goals, mission

Prepared by Barbara Dewey for Planning Collaborative Spaces in Libraries: An ACRL/CNI Preconference. ALA Annual Meeting, Toronto, Canada, 20 June 2003.

Appendix B

Planning collaborative spaces in libraries I.Q. (institutional quotient)

This 'I.Q'. test is designed to help you determine the readiness of your library to plan collaborative spaces. Respond to each statement by circling True, False, or NA (for not applicable/don't know). Total the number of true statements you have circled and compare your rating with the chart on the reverse side.

Recognition of the importance of collaboration

- Collaboration is evident in our library planning documents such as strategic plans   True   False   NA

- Collaboration is a campus priority   True   False   NA

- Administrators are committed to supporting collaborative ventures   True   False   NA

- Staff sees value in and accepts responsibility for collaboration   True   False   NA

Library environment

- Library policies and funding are designed to enable collaboration   True   False   NA
- Collaboration exists among individuals and departments in my library   True   False   NA
- My library considers collaborative initiatives when allocating resources   True   False   NA
- My library actively cultivates partnerships with other campus units   True   False   NA
- My library supports and rewards those who engage in collaborative ventures   True   False   NA
- Collaboration leads to positive results in my library   True   False   NA

Collaborative spaces

- Space is (or will be) available in mylibrary for collaborative initiatives   True   False   NA
- A shared vision for collaborative space has been articulated   True   False   NA
- Funding is available for collaborative spaces   True   False   NA
- Library staff have experience in planning collaboratively   True   False   NA
- My campus has adequate space planning resources and expertise   True   False   NA

■ My campus is committed to the
realisation, maintenance, and
renewalof collaborative spaces   True   False   NA

Total number of true responses = _____

Your I.Q. score (sum of all the statements you marked true)
provides you with a relative ranking of where your library
may be planning in collaborative spaces. The following
listing suggests strategies you may wish to undertake based
on your I.Q. score.

If your score is:

1–3   You are taking 'first steps':

Why not initiate a local discussion about the value of collaborative spaces?

■ Invite someone from an institution with model collaborative
spaces to assist you in beginning the discussion.

■ Identify and share some articles.

■ Check out selected websites.

■ Identify what's being done already at your institution.

■ Seek out partners on your campus.

■ Identify collaborative space as a top library priority.

4–6   You are 'on your way':

Why not form a group or utilise an existing committee to begin structuring an approach?

■ Create a vision for collaborative spaces.

■ Develop a proposal for collaborative space in your library.

- Identify funding opportunities.
- Engender local expertise in collaborative planning.

7–9   You are experimenting':

Why not implement a pilot project?

- Examine 'best practices' at institutions similar to your own.
- Pilot the use of collaborative space.
- Consider scalability.
- Develop cost models.
- Publicise the lessons you learn.

10–12   You are 'full speed ahead':

Why not consider expanding collaborative space in the library?

- Provide an evaluation of the pilot project.
- Clearly articulate the goals of fully developed collaborative space.
- Construct a mechanism for continual evaluation and renewal.
- Develop a memorandum of agreement for the collaborative space.
- Establish and/or reallocate permanent resources and staffing.

13+   You are a 'model for planning collaborative spaces':

Why not consider sharing your approach?

- Present a paper at local and national venues.
- Write an article on both your successes and failures.

- Submit your project to the CNI/Dartmouth Collaborative Facilities website (*http://www.dartmouth.edu/~collab/*).
- Publicise your success and share your experiences.

Designed by Betsy Wilson, University of Washington (betsyw@u. washington.edu), and based on the I.Q. (Institutional Quotient) concept developed by Cerise Oberman and Betsy Wilson. June 2003.

3

The Information Commons at the University of Calgary: building on collaboration – a case study

Susan Beatty

The University of Calgary Information Commons opened in 1999 with collaboration between the University Library and Information Technologies in the provision of user-centred services as its foundation. Throughout the ensuing years, this unique collaboration has yielded many interesting and successful outcomes related to learning support. This chapter will update the reader on the steps taken, issues, and outcomes of the combined efforts to create and support learning opportunities. Finally, the chapter will look ahead to the potential of new collaborations within the new Taylor Family Digital Library.

Introduction

The University of Calgary Information Commons is a learning space supported by a unique collaboration between the University Library and Information Technologies (*http://library.ucalgary.ca/services/informationcommons/*). It is designed to provide space, support, and access to information resources in an integrated service environment. Opening in the library in 1999, the Information Commons has continued to evolve and develop its collaborative service model in response to the changing academic learning and research needs. This chapter will review the process undertaken to create a new learning space for students, some of the many forms in which collaboration has taken place in this space, and outline a few of the key initiatives, successes and lessons learned as the service developed over time.

Background

Towards the latter part of the 1990s, it was clear that the digital world was fast taking over the academic environment. Students and faculty were encountering more challenges in acquiring the skills to access, use, and create information within the new integrated digital learning environment. Many universities and their libraries were undertaking reviews of their current situation in order to develop strategies and solutions to meet the learning demands created by this new digital environment. The University of Calgary was one of those universities.

The University of Calgary is a medium sized doctoral university situated in a city approaching a population of 1,000,000. Most of its students commute daily to the university from the city and its surrounding communities. The city population itself is generally described as well-educated and keen users of technology. They have been and continue to be early adapters of technology. The latest Canadian Internet Use Survey, 2005 (*http://www.statcan.ca/*) indicates that in Calgary over 77 per cent of adults over the age of 18 are active Internet users. While in the late 1990s this number was lower, the trend indicators were there and it was concomitant on the university to meet the expectations of the user.

In 1998–99, the university had a student population of about 25,000 and a faculty of about 1,600. During the 1990s, the university and the library had experienced challenges because of reduced financial support over a number of years and growing demand for an increase in resources and access to information. In response, three academic reports were produced that focused on the student, technology and learning: the Library of the Future Task force report (1998), Technology Task Force Report (1997), and Learning Support Needs (1999). These three initiatives as well as others prepared the University for the need to change and to take advantage of any opportunity.

In 1998, the Alberta provincial government made money available to assist post-secondary institutions in making use of information technology. The University of Calgary successfully applied for a grant and directed $2.2 million to the University Library to create an Information Commons in renovated space in the library. It was to be a new type of integrated learning facility.

Lesson 1: review and preparation pay off

Project development and implementation: first steps

Because the grant came with a deadline, the library had only 1 year to complete its planning and implementation of the commons. And in reality because of the academic year, there were only 4 months available (May–August) when renovations could take place. Rapid planning and good project management were essential to ensure the project deadline was met.

Three major steps were taken that led to the success of the project. Firstly, the library established a nine person broad-based planning committee that included three members from Information Technologies (IT) and six from the library. While the library had received the money, it was clear that IT would be a valuable collaborative partner. Membership of the committee was from across the library (public and technical services), and included the Director of Information Technologies as well as two other IT service heads. The purpose of the Planning Committee was to develop a mission, vision, and a planning document (Appendix A), which would form the basis for the design principles and the creation of a relevant design for the new Information Commons.

Lesson 2: include all partners from the beginning of planning

A key transformation for the committee occurred when the members of the committee, very early on, changed their focus from what each wanted to see in this new facility, to what the user would want. This change in focus came about in the initial discussions when it became clear that better service outcomes could be described if the user's needs were the focus. This change in perspective lessened the political/territorial debates. The committee was then able to focus on the learner/user outcomes and develop a planning document that reflected the needs of the user. The committee used the information from the previously mentioned reports to frame the user outcomes. A significant outcome of the planning process was the development of a strong mutual understanding and working relationship in addition to a commitment to the vision and the service model among the collaborators. This did not come easily but it did come over time. Members of the committee report that a transformational moment occurred when, after much discussion and apparent problems in mutual understanding of operational procedures, the members from IT took the initiative to explain their culture (how they do things) and invited the members from the Library to reciprocate. This sharing of cultures and testing of assumptions cleared the air and set the stage for ongoing open and honest communication.

Lesson 3: focus your planning on user needs

Lesson 4: take time to build relationships

The mutual understanding and the intent to foster collaboration is apparent in both the vision and mission statements and user outcomes for the Information Commons included in its planning document (Ritchie et al., 1999).

The vision for the Information Commons is:
To provide the space, technology and expertise needed to support the scholarly use of information resources and act as the focal point for information services.

The mission for the Information Commons is:
To be the core facility for the provision of information resources and information technology for scholars at the University of Calgary.

The desired user outcomes are:

- Skill: Acquire the skills I need to identify, locate, retrieve and manipulate information.
- Information: Acquire the information I need.
- Support: Acquire the help I need.
- Access to facilities: I can use the various spaces and workstations to complete my scholarly work.

The four user outcomes framed the design and service model decisions. These four outcomes continue to guide the service decision making for the Information Commons.

Implementation of the renovation

The second and third major components to the planning process were the formation of an implementation committee and the hiring of a project manager. Once approval for the project was received, an 11-person Implementation Committee was formed with nine members from across the Library, and two members from IT. At the same time, a project manager, with expertise in communication, was hired to work with the committee, to deal with the architects and contractors and campus infrastructure, and to develop and roll out the communication plan. Notably, the project manager's main priority was to keep the project on schedule and on budget.

The deadline for opening the commons was the first day of classes in September 1999. With such a short deadline, coordination of the renovation and construction and continuous communication became the cornerstones of the project. The project manager was successful and the project was completed on time and on budget.

Lesson 5: hire the expertise you need to get the job done, do not try to do it all yourself

The Implementation Committee was responsible for renovation and service logistics. Primary concerns during renovation were sequencing of service and location changes, staff location changes and ensuring movement of public and staff within the building. As with most library renovations, service continued throughout the renovation, albeit in reduced or relocated circumstances.

The project manager had as one of her primary responsibilities continuous communication with interested and involved parties. The concept of the commons was unique and the library needed buy-in from the students to the president in order for the concept to gain interest and wide support and acceptance. Having a communication plan that was inclusive of all interested parties was a key element of the successful implementation. The results of good communication were a positive buy-in and ownership from all interested parties. For more information on the communication plan see *http://www. ucalgary.ca/IR/infocommons/*. Key elements in this plan included presentations to the deans, press releases, and regular communication and updates with staff via email and face-to-face presentations. No one was forgotten or excluded.

Lesson 6: communication, communication, communication

Design

Every renovation has its constraints and parameters. For this project there were a number. Design options and decisions were limited by the space and money available. Key elements of the design were identified to ensure a safe, warm, welcoming environment where learning can occur. There would be a single service desk for delivery of integrated reference and technical services, the reference collection would remain on the floor but would be significantly reduced in size to fit the space available. Because instruction was one of the goals, classrooms would be a part of the design. Workstations would be ergonomic and would have enough room to accommodate at least two students if necessary. There would be enough aisle space to allow for students with backpacks, bags, coats, and other paraphernalia to walk through unimpeded. Collaborative workrooms, (including an adaptive technology workroom and video viewing workrooms) would be safe and visible. Office area for IT personnel would be created and office area for support staff would not be renovated. The maps collection, air photos collection, GIS, statistical service desk, and the document delivery service would remain on the floor and become part of the Information Commons. This decision was taken because these services already existed on the floor and to move them elsewhere would be too cost prohibitive. It was also felt by the Implementation Committee that these services fell within the broad-based mandate of the plan to include a variety of elements related to information resources.

Ultimately, some extremely useful and creative features were implemented. For example, the workstations in the commons have proven to be a popular design. While commercially available workstations were considered, none seemed to meet the needs and approval of the committee. The architects' team created a unique curvilinear design, which has proven to be ergonomic, aesthetically pleasing, practical and well suited to the users of the commons

(Figure 3.1). The Library has shared the design of the workstations with many visitors and many versions of it can be seen throughout the world.

The collaborative workrooms were designed to be safe, comfortable and welcoming. Because Ethernet connections were available in the workrooms, no PCs were installed. While this has changed over time (three rooms now have a PC), whiteboards have proven to be the collaborative tool of choice by the students. Business office tables and chairs, natural lighting, and interior glass walls allowing for good visibility into the rooms have combined to create an extremely desirable workspace where 8–10 or even more students can comfortably work together (Figure 3.2).

The two classrooms each seat 25. A folding wall between the rooms allows for large class instruction up to 50 (or up to 100, if two people sit at each terminal), or 25 or less if

Figure 3.1   Desk design

Figure 3.2   Workrooms

only one section is needed. The design, featuring a vertical instead of horizontal seating alignment, plus an excellent projection system and interior windows looking into the rest of the commons, allows for good sight lines and comfortable seating. The classrooms are a flexible workspace and are some of the better classrooms on campus. The classrooms are reserved for information literacy instruction and software instruction where either a librarian or a member of the IT staff in the commons is involved. They are not available for academic instruction. Control of instructional spaces allowed the Library and IT to focus on information literacy and technical literacy instruction and to thereby expand their instructional role with the students. The classrooms are, however, available for student use when there is no instruction. Because the rooms are more controllable, this has also provided an additional feature as a naturally quiet study zone (Figure 3.3).

Figure 3.3 Classroom

Lesson 7: if you can't find what you want, create your own

Lesson 8: make the space comfortable, do not cheap out

Lesson 9: keep control of the features of your space that will allow you to meet the goals of your plan

The design supports learning, both formal and informal. Classrooms, workrooms and workstations combine comfortably with study space, lounge spaces, the reference collection, the service desks, additional office space, and allow for the flow through of traffic to and from other floors of the library. Students and staff mingle comfortably within the environment. The Information Commons is across the second floor of the library through three different spaces in two connected buildings. The three different spaces allowed for a variety of design elements throughout, thereby making the scale of the commons less grand and more comfortable. Workrooms, study space, workstations are distributed but still visible and accessible to all. The users choose where to sit and work. One can choose to sit in the busiest or quietest part of the commons. One can choose to use a workroom or sit at a study table, the lounge area or the workstations. Space limitations and features allowed for some creative solutions and some creative interactions. On any given day, it is possible to see students moving from group work at a table to solitary work at a computer or in combination with others who have a laptop. The Information Commons has become a social learning centre.

Lesson 10: allow the users to choose their own space for their own use

Implementation and collaboration

How did we manage the collaborative relationships during planning and implementation? Firstly it is important to note that relationships are a two way street and both parties must be involved in the management of the relationship and committed to its success, otherwise it will not be successful. Because of the previous and long standing working relationship between the Library and IT, there was some confidence by both parties that the collaboration would be successful, but it still took work to make it a success. The recently appointed directors of both the library and information technologies were highly motivated to make this project a success and they led by example. They were actively involved in the project and their expectation was that their staff would collaborate and make the project a success. While a library representative chaired both the planning and the implementation committees the members from IT were involved as equals. It is also fair to say that all levels of staff actively supported and worked towards the successful realisation of the commons. The energy and excitement were maintained throughout the project by the active leadership of all concerned.

Lesson 11: leadership is necessary at all levels

Service decisions

Each collaborator had different experiences with service delivery prior to the commons. The move to provide technical support from a highly visible public desk and offer direct assistance and instruction to the students was a goal of IT. However, IT had no experience with the library service model of face-to-face service at point of need. The Library wanted an integrated service desk, but it had no experience with students delivering assistance while working alongside reference staff. The library convinced IT that a single service desk was the way to go. IT convinced the librarians that the best way to provide technical assistance was to use students. In the end, each learned from the other. The student navigator position was created to provide direct technical assistance (see Appendix B for job description for the student navigator). IT learned how to deliver service from a public desk and in the students' own space and developed a new service model for direct student support, which included free software instruction for the students. The most positive service outcome for the Library was the successful integration of service and the creation of learning space within the library, which included classrooms for instruction. The Information Commons marked the beginning of a new phase of service for IT and the Library at the University of Calgary.

Lesson 12: be prepared to change and to create new service models

Technology decisions

A technology sub-committee was established as part of the implementation planning with a mandate to evaluate, acquire and install the best hardware available with the money available. A budget was set and the six-person committee (once again with members from the Library and IT) set about deciding the priorities. The committee was chaired by the chair of the Implementation Committee and the members were from Information Technologies Services (Library) and IT. The advice of the committee chair: get the best you can afford because it will need to withstand thousands of hours of use. Rather than being a high-tech facility the decision was made that the Information Commons would be a general use facility. Users would have access to the Internet as well as productivity software. Software decisions were made based on the principle that the software would be what the majority of students would need to use. This meant, for example, that Microsoft Office was available to all. The same download would be on all the computers with the exception of the specialised download on the computers in the MADGIC section (maps, academic data and geographic information).

Printing would be networked with students using their campus cards as debit swipe cards to release and pay for the print job. Technical support was divided between the Library and IT. The Library would support the hardware and software and IT would support the printers and the printer network.

Lesson 13: technology is not the driver of the service model but rather reflects the service goals

Staffing decisions

The Library and IT had to make some decisions on staffing. Because the service was integrated, the decision was taken to prepare all library reference staff by providing them with software training. IT developed and delivered the software training to all the reference staff while the renovation was underway. Once the commons was opened, it was clear though that reference staff providing reference assistance would deliver the best reference service just as the student navigators and IT support staff would provide the best technical assistance. The one-stop service became also one-step referral with each service provider referring to the appropriate expert as needed.

Staffing complements have changed over the years. The University of Calgary Library had had a mix of librarians and para-professionals providing reference service and this continued with the commons. Added to the mix were IT support staff, including instructors and a supervisor for the student navigators, student navigators for technical assistance, and night assistants (for overnight service). The number of full time employees (FTEs) has changed with the demands of the service, but the mix remains the same.

Lesson 14: be prepared to evaluate and change your plans once operations have begun

Continuing the collaboration

It should be noted that there is no written memorandum of understanding between the Library and IT. Nor is there a written level of service agreement. All issues and problems related to implementation and service delivery were either worked out beforehand (such as support responsibilities) or are discussed among the decision makers as issues occur. Primary among the decisions was who would pay for what. While the project money allowed for purchase of equipment and renovation of space, ongoing staffing was an item of concern. Initial first year costs for IT staff (four FTEs) were covered by the grant money. After the first year, this staff complement (currently two FTEs) has been paid for by IT. The library had no additional money for staffing for the first year, but managed to add two new positions in the second year: Head of the Information Commons and a 0.6 FTE reference librarian for night and Sunday service. IT and the Library share the cost of the student navigators. Staffing for 24 hour/5 day coverage (two FTEs during autumn and winter term) was paid by an anonymous donation for the first 4 years. The library continued to pay for this very popular student service once the donation ran out. The hardware has been refreshed twice and IT and the Library have shared the costs. Printers and scanners have been added, refreshed, and paid for by the Library.

As part of the ongoing management of the Information Commons, an operational management team was formed. The sponsors for the team are the Associate University Librarians for Client Services and Information Technology

Services, both of whom were involved in the initial planning and implementation of the commons. The chair of the team is the Head of the Information Commons. Members of the team are those people who represent units that have an interest in the commons. The team is made up of representatives from the Information Technology Services, Access Services, Liaison Services, Client Services, MADGIC, the Health Sciences and Law Library Information Commons, and IT. The team meets bi-weekly as required. The purpose of the team is to review issues related to operations, and make recommendations for action. Issues of concern can range from selection of software, to use policies, service improvement decisions, and printing issues. It is extremely valuable to have all interests at the table so that common concerns can be addressed, discussed and decided. Issues that are beyond the scope of the team to decide are referred to the appropriate decision makers – normally either or both of the Associate University Librarians. It is a useful tool to assist in the continuation of the collaboration and thereby continue the development of the service model.

Lesson 15: have a collaborative operational process in place that includes the opportunity for problem solving and decision-making

Today's commons: collaboration for learning

Because the commons is a learning space, it is more than a computer lab and more than a reference service. It is a vibrant space that is energised by the learning activities taking place. Formal and informal learning occur daily.

Integrated service delivery means that the student is assisted in his or her learning in a way that is suitable. Classroom instruction combined with in-person assistance at point of need ensure active learning. On any one day, any student may attend an information literacy session, get help with a PowerPoint problem, get help with finding information, collaborate with other students, and create and finally print a finished document. The student moves in and out of formal and informal learning with ease and according to need.

Partnerships and collaborations

The Library and IT have formed a partnership when it comes to instruction and formal learning support. The IT specialists in the commons deliver productivity instruction to the students. Over the years, there has been a shift from basic instruction to more applied uses with an ever-increasing variety of software. See *http://library.ucalgary.ca/services/informationcommons/hardware&software.php* for a current list of hardware and software. The classrooms are also used by IT for integrated classroom instruction, e.g. Access for management students, SPSS for graduate sociology students. For a look at the current library and productivity instruction schedule, see *http://library.ucalgary.ca/services/schedule/*.

Information literacy has also taken a big step forward assisted by the availability of the IC classrooms. The first few years after the commons opened saw IL instruction take off and over the following years the numbers have stayed level. True collaboration and integration occur when the IT instructor and the librarian collaborate in a subject related class to present all elements of information needed at a time when the student needs it. For example, data research skills and SPSS instruction, combined with charting, within a graduate research methods course will allow the students to move forward in their learning. The opportunities for enhanced learning presented by experts working together in the same space are multiple and are gradually being explored over time.

Face-to-face service

Face-to-face service in the Information Commons is delivered at the service desk, on the floor, and in one on one consultation by both library and IT staff. At the desk, reference experts work alongside technical experts. The library staff are not expected to provide technical assistance and the technical staff are not expected to provide library help. One-step referral is our motto. At the times when the library staff are not on the desk, the student navigators and night assistants answer technical assistance and directional questions. Library related questions are referred to the librarians for the next day response.

There is continuous training for both the library and IT staff. Upgrades in software skills are offered to the library staff and the technical support staff. Library orientation is part of the technical support training. A Blackboard site ensures ongoing communication and supports the learning among all technical support staff as well as their supervisors. There are continual postings on how to solve service problems posted either by one of the student assistants, the night assistants or one of the supervisors. All staff post news of the day as well as service issues and solutions, and questions. Staff training is primary to quality service delivery.

The users of the commons benefit from this service model in many ways. Primarily of course, they benefit by receiving help when they need it. This is in fact the reason that students come to the commons. They come not only because it is a great facility, they come just in case they need help. And, they know they will get it. Just as students are stopped in their research if they do not know how to find what they need, so too are they stopped in their academic endeavours if they do not know how to proceed in the next step – whether it is making a table in Microsoft Word, creating an Excel chart or printing a PDF document. Microskill learning is incremental in the commons. Without an integrated mix of expertise, continuous training and communication, and responsiveness to solving service issues, service delivery would not be of a high quality, the students would not come and the learning would not occur.

Lesson 16: ensure continuous learning among staff and students alike

Consultations

Sometimes students need more help than can be offered on the floor by the service people available. This is when service consultations are arranged. Of course, librarians have always had this service as part of their repertoire. With the commons, the librarians are able to meet students either in their office or at the service desk and continue with a lengthy service interview in the commons at one of the additional computers at the desk. Previous to the commons, IT staff had offered consultations (mostly data related) for graduate students and faculty at a cost, but with the commons came the opportunity for students to access more in-depth technical assistance when they needed it. For example, such assistance is offered by IT support staff in the commons to graduate students who need help formatting their thesis, or for students who are having problems with software such as FrontPage or Access. Normally the IT support specialist occupies about 10–15 per cent of his or her time during autumn and winter terms with this special service. This service simply grew out of the instruction that the specialist was offering.

Lesson 17: pay attention to the service, be ready to change

Changes in the service model

So, what has changed in the commons? The basics remain the same. IT and the Library work together to support learning in an integrated facility. Other partners for learning support appear as the opportunity occurs. Staffing complements for reference support and technical support have been reduced and yet we were still able to extend the hours of reference service. A special media area has been added to the commons. Specialised software such as Adobe Photoshop is available to the users. The specialised software is provided in response to student demand. Laptop docking stations and wireless access enhance the hardware mix in the commons. Staff are comfortable in their collaboration and seek and offer assistance from each other. Collaborative problem solving occurs on a daily basis.

Collaborative relationships

Library and IT services extend beyond the boundaries and services offered in the Information Commons. For example, the Library and IT work with the Teaching and Learning Centre (TLC), together and separately to support other learning opportunities for the faculty. The Teaching and Learning Centre has a mandate to support faculty learning and improved instruction. One of our initial and most successful collaborations has been an annual series of workshops and instructional sessions for faculty focusing on the mix of technology, learning and information. These workshops are called Faculty Technology Days (FTD) and have been held annually in May, hosted by the Library, since the commons opened. Specialists from the Library, IT and TLC combine their expertise to offer learning opportunities related to technology and instructional improvements to faculty and graduate students. The latest and most successful FTD offered sessions on such tools as concept mapping, blogging, formatting your thesis, engaging students in large classes, bibliographic software, various library databases and more. For more information, see *http://www.ucalgary.ca/ftd/*.

The early efforts in integrated instruction have led to many more collaborative endeavours, in addition to highlighting the various ways that each unit supports learning in the academy. For example, a group of librarians applied for and received a TLC grant to create a new learning tutorial to support information literacy instruction. This was an innovative project wherein the librarians worked with instructional designers and technical experts from TLC to create the tutorial. For more information on the project, see *http://library.ucalgary.ca/wispr/*.

Since the commons opened, librarians have become more active in instruction. They have also become more engaged in the opportunities that technology offers to improve their instruction. A recent example was a pilot course using podcasting where the librarian was asked to provide podcasts on library instruction. The librarian worked with the IT support experts, an instructional designer from TLC and the faculty member to create a new learning experience for students. Not all collaborative learning activities are directly related to the commons, but as a result of the relationships built through the commons, there are more opportunities to create new learning scenarios.

This past year a number of the librarians signed up to complete the Faculty Teaching Certificate program offered by the TLC (*http://tlc.ucalgary.ca/teaching/programs/ftc*). Not only did the librarians benefit by acquiring more knowledge and instructional skills, the TLC instructor was also able to learn more about what librarians have to offer for learning support in the classroom. In turn, other instructors have been informed of the librarians' skill set and have been encouraged by the TLC to include information literacy instruction in their course. The more relationship building that occurs the more opportunities that are created for further learning.

Evaluation

As part of a continuous evaluation process, the Information Commons has always had an online feedback form *http://library.ucalgary.ca/ic_feedback.php* (see Appendix C). The form is based on the Service Quality model and has provided instant and ongoing feedback over the years on the perceptions of service in the commons. This tool has told us that the vast majority of our users are undergraduates, that they greatly appreciate our service and that they hate standing in line and not getting a collaborative workroom when they need it. From the comments, we have been able to glean the information needed to address service issues immediately if needed. For example, if a student sends in a complaint about noise in the commons, or another disruptive event, and it is during a normal weekday, it is not unusual for the Head to go out on to the floor to check on the problem. This feedback tool has been very effective until the link was moved to a different location on the library web pages as a result of a library web page redesign. Use of the feedback form has dropped off, and we are currently considering other avenues for gathering feedback.

The Library has also participated in the LibQUAL+ (*http://www.libqual.org/*) survey in 2002 and 2004 and plans to participate again in 2007. While LibQUAL+ does not allow for a direct focus on the Information Commons, comments received from the participants have aligned with the results from the feedback form.

Future of the commons: the Taylor Family Digital Library

In 2006, the sod was turned on the site of a new concept in collaboration at the University of Calgary. This new facility is more than just an extension of the library. It will serve as a new space for learning on campus. The new Taylor Family Digital Library will bring under one roof Libraries and Cultural Resources, some of the services from Information Technologies, Teaching and Learning Centre, and Student and Enrolment Services (*http://www.ugcalgary.ca/tfdl*). This is a facility that will be designed for learning. The mission of the new collaboration is to support the quest for knowledge, understanding, creativity and innovation. Within Libraries and Cultural Resources, this means that The Nickle Arts Museum, Archives and Special Collections, the Visual Resources Centre will combine with the University Library to offer a mix of digital, print and three-dimensional resources to support the twenty-first century learner. With the opportunity for further collaborations still being explored, I took the opportunity to speak with the recently appointed Vice Provost for Libraries and Cultural Resources and University Librarian, Tom Hickerson, on his thoughts on what the future might hold. The following is a summary of our discussion.

> The focus of the collaborators in the new building is on students becoming empowered, autonomous agents through learning support in the virtual environment, through face-to-face instruction, and with point of thought assistance. It is clear that we have to extrapolate from the success of the commons as a satisfying and engaging learning environment for today's learners and apply our knowledge and understanding to designing the service and environment of the new building. Libraries are no longer the empty libraries of old. We provide what learners need. We provide a secure, welcoming environment where social learning spaces and opportunities abound. We provide reliable access to information. The future learners will continue to need a social space as well as a learning space. The future learners will be autonomous and will expect to get what they want when and however they need it. The value of bringing all resources together in one location cannot be underestimated. Our future learners will be using primary resources, digital resources and will be working in a digital environment that none of us can specifically imagine. With the faculty more intrinsically involved in direct learning through the spaces and services of the new building, students, instructors, librarians, experts in technical support and instructional support will have an even greater opportunity to create new knowledge. The

biggest question and perhaps the most thought provoking is to ask ourselves what are we prepared to do, and to think more collaboratively than ever, before we answer the question. It is clear that we can be real instigators in learning support for the future.

Conclusion

The University of Calgary Information Commons has become a benchmark facility for collaboration in learning support. Successfully designed for learning it has proven that the concept of the commons is valid for the twenty-first century. Learners will come to the library when and if the service, space and tools that they need are provided. Not only will they come, they will consider the space their own and change it to their own purposes. The key is to be prepared to change, seek like-minded partners, and embrace the transformation.

References and further reading

Beatty, S. (2003) 'The information commons: strategies for integration', in Martin, A. and Rader, H. (eds) *Information and IT Literacy; Enabling Learning in the 21st Century*. London: Facet Publishing; pp. 151–60.

Kearns, J. and Scharnau, K. (1999) 'Learning support needs: what University of Calgary students need to be more effective learners'. Joint research project. Calgary, Canada: University of Calgary.

Library of the Future Task Force (1998) 'Library of the Future Task Force: accelerating the transformation of information resources. Final report'. Calgary, Canada:

University of Calgary. Available at *http://www.ucalgary.ca/lib-old/lftf/index.html* (accessed 28 June 2007).

Ritchie, L., Clarke, H., Esche, H., Morrall, M., Neary, S., Thrasher, R., Warren, D., White, P. and Wilson, M. (1999) *Information Hub Planning Document.* Calgary, Canada: University of Calgary. Available at *http://www.ucalgary.ca/IR/infocommons/conceptdoc.htm* (accessed 28 June 2007).

Technology Task Force (1997) *Technology Integration Plan.* Calgary, Canada: University of Calgary. Available at *http://www.ucalgary.ca/~ispage/TIP* (accessed 28 June 2007).

Appendix A

Below is a copy of the Information Commons Planning Document. Please note that minor changes to style and some headings have been made to avoid confusion and better integrate it with the present work.

Information Commons

Planning Document

Information Commons Planning Committee

Chair: Lorin Ritchie

Helen Clarke

Harold Esche

Mick Morrall

Sharon Neary

Ross Thrasher

Darlene Warren

Peggy White

Morven Wilson

Vision

The Information Commons presents a redesigned and refocused infrastructure for information services that supports the delivery of customised, comprehensive, and convenient services reflecting the transformation of information resources now and in the coming millennium.

The Information Commons includes a redesigned space accommodating individual and group activity, integrates new technologies with services, and establishes dynamic and innovative partnerships with other information service providers on campus.

The Information Commons is an integrated learning environment for all members of the University Community. It provides the space, technology, and expertise needed to support the scholarly use of information resources and acts as the focal point for information services.

Mission

To be the core facility for the provision of information resources and information technology for scholars at The University of Calgary.

The Information Commons provides a focus for the provision of services and technology to support the effective identification, acquisition and use of information resources by members of the University Community. The facility provides all members of the University Community with timely access to the technology and expertise needed for the successful exploitation of information resources. The commons staff have expertise in research consultation, information navigation, and technological support, and work in an integrated and open environment. The physical environment of the Information Commons accommodates many types of scholarly activity. The commons serves as a central place for members of the University Community to meet and explore information and exchange ideas. The commons includes group work areas, private study spaces, open consultation and service points, and adaptive workstations. Spaces are equipped to support the use of information technology. The space is also planned to support a high level of use.

The development of information literacy skills in the University Community, especially undergraduate students, is a key mission of the Information Commons. Competency in the identification and evaluation of information, the extraction and manipulation of data, analysis, and presentation, are core research skills. The facility has been designed to give instructors and students the opportunity to effectively integrate information resources into individual and group learning activities. The staff in the Information Commons integrate opportunities for training into all aspects of service. The Information Commons will seek collaboration with faculty, the Learning Commons, and other University units to develop effective learning and teaching opportunities for students.

The Information Commons is part of Information Services ongoing commitment to innovation and improvement that provides the University Community – students, faculty, and staff – with the highest level of access and support in achieving the integration of information resources and technology into research, teaching and learning.

Physical setting

The Information Commons will be designed to accommodate access to information resources, information technology and supporting services, in a single integrated facility. The layout and design will clearly direct scholars from a central entrance to all elements and services. Spaces will be designed to be flexible, supporting a variety of activities, and capable of being modified with minimal effort as needs and priorities change. The facility will be designed and wired to provide access to workstations throughout the facility and to accommodate substantial increases in the amount and capacity of computers, printers, and other equipment over that present at opening. Finally, the Information Commons will be designed to be a pleasant, safe, and comfortable environment, which conveys a sense of activity and purpose.

Desired outcomes

The service outcomes and consequent service goals and implementation elements described give specific, concrete descriptions of the Information Commons' facilities and operation, and will provide the basis for design and planning.

Desired outcome: skills

User goal

Acquire the skills I need to identify, locate, retrieve, and manipulate information.

Service goal

Provide a suite of instructional services and facilities for individuals and groups.

Implementation elements

- Provide spaces for instruction:
  - An Instruction Lab. A large space that can be sectioned off when necessary and that is adequately equipped and configured so that products can be easily loaded and has workstations that can be tailored to individual instruction

session requirements. The areas must be flexible and securable, capable of seating 50 users comfortably for hands-on instruction sessions, and readily available for general use as and when appropriate.

- Consultation Spaces that can be used for point-of-need individualised instruction.

■ Provide instruction in the identification, retrieval and manipulation of information.

■ Ensure that skilled staff, in sufficient number, are available to deliver instruction and maintain the facility.

■ Provide a comprehensive array of guides and self-paced tutorials, both print and on-line.

■ Build on user skills by providing instruction as well as assistance during user transactions.

Desired outcome: information

User goal

Acquire the information I need.

Service goal

Provide the information resources, technologies, and expert staff to support the University's learning and teaching activities.

Implementation elements

■ Provide information resources to support curriculum and research in a multitude of formats.

■ Ensure timely access to needed information resources.

- Provide facilities for and assistance with:
    - remote access to information resources including technical trouble-shooting and explanation of any access restrictions;
    - viewing and retrieval of numerical information including the use of necessary specialised software (e.g. Excel, SPSS);
    - searching and use of all databases to which the Library has established access, including bibliographic and full-text databases;
    - searching for and use of information available through the Internet/World Wide Web;
    - timely document delivery.
- Provide collections that serve the needs of on-site and remote users for immediate access.
- Provide printing, downloading, capture, and scanning capabilities to allow users to take information away in useful and convenient formats.
- Provide mediation and referral that gives follow-through to point of user satisfaction via a precise and direct system of referral and verification by staff of the usefulness of referrals before providing them to the user.
- Provide information concerning any programs, activities, and operations of the University either directly or through referral.

Desired outcome: support

User goal

Acquire the help I need.

Service goal

Deliver quality information resource and information technology services that enable interaction with and use of information.

Implementation elements

- Provide assistance in identifying and requesting resources available through document delivery.

- Provide assistance in the search and retrieval of information from a variety of resources, both print and electronic.

- Provide information resource and information technology consulting service points for both face-to-face and remote service.

- Collaborate with other University information technology service points and facilities to identify resources and expertise that will compliment the activities of the Information Hub.

- Provide advice in configuring the scholar's personal workstation.

- Provide assistance with capture, transfer, scanning, manipulation, and output of information.

- Ensure availability of trained staff.

- Ensure quality service on the part of all staff (pride in outcome, knowledge of what's out there, curiosity, collegial problem-solving, interest in learning).

- Provide self-paced learning modules.

- Provide ongoing active learning programs for staff. This requires continuous professionally delivered training as part of the job.

- Provide an expertise base that is broadened and interconnected rather than fragmented or individualised.

Desired outcome: access to facilities

User goal

I can use various spaces and workstations to complete my scholarly work.

Service goal

Provide a variety of easily identified and conveniently located spaces and workstations that support different scholarly needs.

Implementation elements

- Provide securable flexible workstation areas.
- Provide workstations that allow users to capture, transfer, scan, manipulate, print and download data and information:
  - For example, workstations should be equipped with standard browsers, plug-ins, sound and video cards.
- Provide group study spaces that are fully wired and equipped.
- Provide spaces for laptop users.
- Provide multimedia preview space.
- Provide presentation practice space that is fully wired and equipped, including video playback facilities (this might be done through partnership with the Learning Commons).

- Provide printing, downloading, and file transfer capabilities.

- Provide adaptive technologies adequate to the needs of scholars with disabilities.

Planning document appendix: background

The Library of the Future Task Force report, *Accelerating the Transformation of Information Resources* (*http:// www. ucalgary.ca/library/lftf/index.html*), delineated a clear understanding of the future of information resources in the research and teaching environment of the University of Calgary.

In this future, the traditional role of information services – focused on the identification, distribution and use of local print information resources – will undergo a radical change.

Drivers of this change are:

- increased access to electronic information resources;

- growing number and complexity of searching and retrieval tools;

- growing importance of non-print media and non-text information in the research process at the undergraduate level;

- increased dependence on a technologically sophisticated environment;

- increased need for information literacy.

Changes in the nature and use of information resources will fundamentally affect the means by which research will take place, be recorded, and be retrieved. Information Services must be capable of assisting all categories of users in access to and use of (streamed and non-streamed) audio and video, numeric and spatial data, imagery in both digital and print forms, and multi-media and virtual learning experiences. Information Services needs to incorporate these changes fully if it is to properly serve all scholars including undergraduates.

Consequently, Information Services plans to use a major portion of the money granted through the Knowledge Networks Grants to create transformational information facilities in the University of Calgary. Creation of these facilities will involve:

- redesign of primary physical spaces, including access to an large number of properly equipped workstations and consultation spaces;

- expansion of services to fully include new media, non-text and networked information;

- in-depth consultation concerning the use and integration of new and traditional formats into the research process;

- instructional spaces for teaching information literacy skills;

- technology to support the delivery of content and services to users at remote locations;

- a program of continuous staff training to develop the skills needed to work in the changing information environment assisting scholars in the retrieval and use of information regardless of location or format. In this new environment, no individual public services staff member will find his or her current level of expertise sufficient.

As an integral part of this redesign, Information Resources will also seek partners from within the University, especially Information Technology, whose co-location in the 'Information Commons' would provide scholars with centralised access to the services and expertise needed to use information resources and information technology.

Information Services articulates, through the Information Commons, a clear understanding of the profound changes taking place in information for research and scholarship, and its commitment to creating a place where all members of the University Community will have access to the technology and expertise needed to learn about and take advantage of these changes.

Planning document further reading

Library of the Future Task Force (1998) *Library of the Future Task Force: Accelerating the Transformation of Information Resources Final Report*. Calgary, Canada: University of Calgary. Available at *http://www.ucalgary.ca/library/lftf/index.html*.

Government of Alberta (1998). *Government of Alberta News Release, July 9, 1998: Adult learning institutions to receive $20 million in Knowledge Networks grants*. Available at *http://www.gov.ab.ca/pab/acn/199807/6516. html*.

Technology Taskforce (1997). *Technology Integration Plan*. Calgary, Canada: University of Calgary. Available at *http://www.acs.ucalgary.ca/~ispage/TIP/*.

Appendix B

Below is a copy of the Information Commons Student Navigator Position. Please note that minor changes to style and some headings have been made to avoid confusion and better integrate it with the present work.

Information Commons Student Navigator Position

The Information Commons is an integrated service facility. Staff at the Information Commons work collaboratively with Information Resources and Information Technologies. This position is available to current students only. The successful candidates would be hired for the autumn and winter semesters.

Computer competencies required

Strong working knowledge of the following software:

- All Windows platforms
- All Internet Browsers
- Microsoft Office Suite (Word, Excel, PowerPoint, Access, Publisher, FrontPage)
- In depth knowledge of the Internet
- Telnet, WS-FTP, SSH

- Adobe Acrobat
- Data recovery software (Norton Utilities, Lost and Found, FinalData)

Strong working knowledge of the following hardware:

- PCs
- Printers
- Scanners
- CD/DVD readers and writers
- Laptops (PC and MAC) (Ethernet and Wireless)
- Network and server knowledge

Knowledge of the following software applications and hardware would be and asset:

- Blackboard
- Webdisk
- SIS (InfoNet)
- myUofC (UofC Portal)
- Unix (AIX), DOS
- Adobe Photoshop
- McAfee VirusScan
- Media Players (QT and WMP)
- Digital cameras, USB keys, Mac computers

Other competencies required

Customer Service Experience:

- Strong communication and customer service skills.

- Respectful behaviour and appropriate appearance.
- Must have strong trouble shooting skills. Able to analyse problems and provide the user with the solution in a timely fashion.

Self motivated and responsible. Able to be trusted to work creatively and effectively without direct supervision at times.

Teamwork and collaboration are integral to this position. Must be comfortable referring questions to others and not be afraid to do so.

Knowledge of the University of Calgary campus and environment.

Able to enforce University and Library policies.

Able to navigate the library catalogue and the library web pages including the article indexes.

Open to learning new skills and sharing knowledge.

Technical writing is an asset.

Appendix C

This is a copy of the online form – text entry windows and radio buttons are represented here as images to give an impression of what the user would see when using the real form online.

Information Commons feedback

University of Calgary

The following statements relate to your feelings about the service provided at the **Information Commons.** For each statement, please show the extent to which you believe this facility has the feature or service described by the statement.

- Choosing a 1 means that you **strongly disagree** that the Information Commons has that feature or provided that service.
- Choosing a 7 means that you **strongly agree**.
- You may choose any of the numbers in between to show how strong your feeling is.

There are no right or wrong answers. We are only interested in the numbers that best show your perceptions regarding the quality of the Information Commons service.

1. **I did not have to wait more than 20 minutes for a computer.**

   (strongly disagree) 1   2   3   4   5   6   7 (strongly agree)

2. **I was able to book a collaborative workroom when I needed it.**

   (strongly disagree) 1   2   3   4   5   6   7 (strongly agree)

3. **Staff at the Service Desk are helpful and friendly.**

   (strongly disagree) 1   2   3   4   5   6   7 (strongly agree)

4. **Staff at the Service Desk are able to answer my questions.**

   (strongly disagree) 1   2   3   4   5   6   7 (strongly agree)

5. **The facility is welcoming, safe and clean.**

   (strongly disagree) 1   2   3   4   5   6   7 (strongly agree)

6. **Signs within the Information Commons are clear.**

   (strongly disagree) 1   2   3   4   5   6   7 (strongly agree)

7. **How long did you have to wait for a computer?**

   - ○ 10 minutes or less
   - ○ 10 to 20 minutes
   - ○ 20 to 30 minutes
   - ○ 30 to 45 minutes
   - ○ more than 45 minutes

8. **Please choose one of the following categories:**

   - ○ Undergraduate Student

○ Graduate Student

○ Faculty

○ Staff

○ Alumni

○ Community Reader

9. Please comment on your experience in the Information Commons. Please enter any questions you have here. For an immediate reply please include your email or contact information.

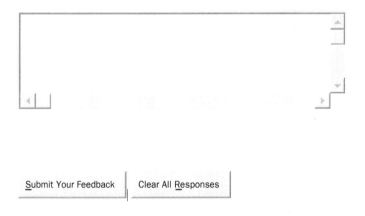

Submit Your Feedback | Clear All Responses

Thank you for taking the time to complete this survey. Your responses will help us to improve the service and the facility to better meet the needs of all of those using the Information Commons.

4

Building for learning: synergy of space, technology and collaboration

Susan Thompson and Gabriela Sonntag

Overview of Cal State San Marcos

The California State University San Marcos (CSUSM) celebrated 'Fifteen Years of Excellence' in autumn 2004. Located in North San Diego County in a once rural but quickly developing suburban area, CSUSM is one of the newest of the 23 campuses belonging to the California State University (CSU) system. One of the state of California's public higher education systems, which also includes the University of California system and the California Community College system, the CSU is the largest system of postsecondary education in the United States that does not include community colleges. It bestows about half of the Bachelor's degrees and a third of the Master's degrees awarded annually in California, and prepares about 60 per cent of the teachers in the state.

A comprehensive university of over 8,500 students taught by about 500 faculty, Cal State San Marcos is composed mainly of undergraduate students from the local area, with about 60 per cent transferring from local community colleges. As a result, CSUSM is primarily a 'commuter' campus with our first residential facility for 475 students completed in 2003. Programs are divided among three Colleges (Arts and Sciences, Education, and Business Administration) and a new School of Nursing. Nine programs offer Masters Degrees. We also offer a Masters in Education, 20 different teacher credential programs, and have recently started an Ed.D. program in Educational Leadership. As a newer campus, CSUSM is ultimately expected to grow to over 20,000 students. Our enrollment increases roughly 6 per cent annually, although it has fluctuated drastically with some years as low as 1 per cent and others as high as 13 per cent. New degree programs are added every year.

The library

When the university moved to its permanent campus in 1992, the library was temporarily housed in a corner of the administration building. Due to state funding problems, our 'temporary' quarters lasted over a decade. During that time, the library was unable to increase its shelving or study spaces while enrollment increased by a factor of five, from 1,259 to 6,257.

As a result of the cramped facilities, over one-third of the 222,000 volume collection was stored off-site requiring a daily courier service. As a new campus, we had a relatively small collection and uncertain budgets have forced us to acknowledge that our collections might never be as robust as we would like. Fortunately, CSUSM developed strategic partnerships that early on provided access to a very large collection. Through the San Diego Library Circuit, a cooperative catalogue with online request and next-day campus delivery system, we access the libraries of San Diego State University, the University of California San Diego and the private University of San Diego. We also have very close ties to two local community colleges through a cooperative called the North County Higher Education Alliance that grants students reciprocal borrowing privileges.

With so much of the building taken up by the collection, very little space was left over for student study – less than a quarter of the recommended standard. We tried to maximise study space using two-storey cubicles with room for four students in a 10 x 5 ft footprint. Of the few rooms originally available for quiet studies, all but one had to be allocated for offices. The small reference area forced us to choose between a reference desk and public access computers. We preferred to use that space for computers. This gave rise to a model of tiered reference service with a research-consultation office, student information assistants roving the reference area, and librarians available for in-depth research appointments.

Rooms also had to be used for multiple purposes. The information literacy program, in particular, had to make do, sharing a dozen computers in a small room with the campus IT staff training program. As class sizes grew, the instruction program began to use the library staff room, already doubling as the university's teleconference facility.

Lack of space is one reason why teaching students to find information became a primary goal for us. The request 'Can you do a tour of the library for my class?' became 'How can you work with my class to give them what they need to successfully complete their class assignments?'. Each request was an opportunity for faculty/librarian collaboration in assignment design incorporating information competencies. Course guides and other online resources, which did not require library space, became extremely popular as they offered the just-in-time support the student sought while also providing a virtual 'gathering-place' for updated information during the course of a semester.

Planning for the new library began in March 1992 but was put on hold several times as a result of the problematic California state budget. When planning began in earnest in 1998, a small, administratively-heavy committee had only the Library Dean to channel all library concerns. Within the library, ample opportunities for input were provided via both library-wide and unit meetings, and focused meetings to discuss specifics, such as technology planning. Additionally, the Library Dean met with numerous faculty groups, and the planning committee organised two campus-wide forums to present information and to seek input. Two consultants were asked to provide comments to the library planning documents in 1999 and again in 2001. Their input was invaluable as we anxiously planned for the future.

Objectives for the new library

Building the new library (Figure 4.1) was a big event for the whole campus as well as for the library itself. With its central location between existing and new growth facilities, the massive $48 million building was literally expected to reshape the campus. It promised to enhance student life by adding places to study, a coffee/sandwich shop, and exhibit spaces. It would augment the academic program by adding media production facilities, more computer stations, and more room for storage of University archives. Everyone was excited at the promise of seeing the whole collection in one place.

Three core principles guided library planning and were used to 'sell' the building to various constituencies. These

Figure 4.1 Kellogg Library exterior

were: (1) the library as a teaching and learning centre; (2) the library providing access to collections in-house and beyond; and (3) the library providing services to facilitate 'anywhere, anytime' learning. Central to the design was the desire to build on the following unique aspects of a Cal State San Marcos education:

Study

San Marcos students balance work, school and family in a busy and challenging schedule. The library planned to provide greatly expanded space for quiet study with more than 1,500 reader stations, including a comfortable reading room. The goal was to enable students to combine traditional methods of study and research with new technology-based learning opportunities.

Collaboration

CSUSM's academic programs emphasise student collaboration. The new library building was planned with a large number of group study rooms to provide space for students and faculty to work in teams on research projects. Plans also called for some of these study rooms to feature high-tech equipment for creating group presentations and multimedia productions.

Instruction

A key component of academic requirements at Cal State San Marcos is computer and information competency. Classrooms designed to teach students how to find and critically evaluate information using both traditional methods of research and hi-tech resources were an important part of the building's design.

Technology

Technology was planned throughout the building to enable students to acquire and integrate new information. The technology was not only expected to put the myriad of library materials at the fingertips of students and faculty but it would support the entire research process, from initial information discovery to final paper. Planning for media was a major focus, from the Media Library collection to small-scale student multimedia projects to large-scale media studio production facilities.

Select partners

Libraries are often expected to share their building with other programs and ours was no exception. However, during our planning process we actively included specific programs whose proximity would create opportunities for strong partnerships. Three programs were specifically selected to be part of the new building. The Barahona Center for the Study of Books in Spanish for Children and Adolescents brought its comprehensive collection of Spanish language children's literature. The Academic Technology division of campus IT moved in with its student help desk, support for computer labs and instruction rooms, and management of the media production studios. The Faculty Center took advantage of the new library's central location to provide programming and support for faculty, as well as working closely with librarians to provide workshops on such topics as faculty use of e-resources, the integration of information competencies into class assignments, and library collaboration in teaching and learning. As planning evolved, we also added an office for University Police – to provide a security presence on the 'high tech' floor. To handle the everyday issues of different departments sharing a special-purpose building, the library established a 'homeowners association'. The group met regularly starting about a year before move-in to resolve issues ranging from locking doors and mail delivery to carrying food through the public library areas.

In addition to incorporating whole departments, the new library planned to provide significant support for two other university programs. While general ADA accommodations are provided throughout the library, we worked closely with Disabled Student Services to create an Assistive Technology Lab with a wide variety of devices specifically designed to adapt the format of information sources, including a Braille keyboard and printer, scanners, and cranktop tables. Besides the basic curriculum collection space to support the College of Education, we added a 'suite' that includes a workroom for creating curriculum materials, a classroom to teach and practice curriculum strategies, and extensive study space with two large study rooms, tackable walls, and enough seating for an entire class. The study space is open to all, but used primarily by the College of Education.

A *regional asset*

Beyond the university itself, the new library was also to be the intellectual centrepiece for the region, providing a valuable information resource for community members as well as students. In particular, CSUSM is the only federal government documents repository in North San Diego County.

Technology objectives

The library developed a strategic plan that articulated the role of technology in fulfilling each library function's vision of services in the new building. The plan guided all technology-related decisions during the building process. Appendix A has a more complete description of the technology planning process.

The technology planning process started by questioning 'just what was technology's role in the modern library building?'. Historically, computers were placed near the entrance of the library to act as a direct replacement for the card catalogue and journal indexes; but those days are long past. Technology has evolved to the point that it is so easy and convenient to work from home that users don't even have to come into the library to locate and use many of the library's resources. From a technology perspective, is there really any benefit to working in the library? These questions posed an interesting conundrum for planning technology in the context of a building project. In fact these questions can be expanded to include the library as a whole. Aside from access to non-electronic resources, is there any reason for a student to come to the library at all? It was when we looked at the role of the library as a learning space that we found our answers.

Rethinking our assumptions on library technology's role in terms of the student research process led us to consider the building as a partner in the student's learning process. Students often go to great lengths to find online resources rather than use a book or journal that requires a physical trip to the library. However, working in the library encourages use of traditional library resources and the expertise of library staff. Students are more likely to ask questions if the librarian is right there. It also creates an environment supportive of iterative research in which students use additional resources as they refine their topic. Therefore, rather than seeing technology's role as just locating library resources, we changed our vision to seeing technology as providing cradle-to-grave support for the entire research process – from topic development to initial resource identification to writing the paper to compiling the final bibliography.

Building a Learning Commons

Historically the Cal State San Marcos library has been a very active teaching and learning centre. Our campus has a computer literacy requirement that requires students in their first year to demonstrate basic computer competency. Since the university's beginning, students were required to use computer skills in all their courses. As a result of this requirement, the campus has always had a strong computer infrastructure, including an emphasis on technology in the library's services and collections. Another major impetus for library use is found in the university's writing-across-the-curriculum requirement that has students writing a minimum of 2,500 words in each course. Most courses meet this requirement by having students do library-based research. Both of these requirements, along with the early focus on teaching students to find information that could be delivered to them, gave rise to the Information Literacy Program and the importance of student learning as one of the driving goals of library services.

It was important to us that our new library building continue to enhance the library's teaching and learning role on campus. Early in the planning process we discussed centralising our technology and research support services following the Information Commons model. We ultimately abandoned the idea for two practical reasons. First, design constraints would require an Information Commons to be placed on the second floor, which would take reference services away from the library entrance located on the third floor. Second, we wanted enough room to place the Media Library close to Academic Technology's media production studios and student help desk in order to centralise media resources, in effect creating a 'media Commons'. As the Information Commons approach wasn't feasible, we had to reconsider how use of physical space could best facilitate student learning.

Looking at how to provide an Information Commons with technology supporting the entire research process led us to see the primary purpose of the *entire* library building as a space designed to foster student learning rather than to house a collection. Library literature for some years has positioned the library as the central learning space on campus moving us away from the 'warehouse of materials' model. Our design emphasised the educational and social aspects of study and collaboration throughout the building. Technology was seen as the way to enable all the library's public spaces to serve the learning role.

Based on this understanding of the learning role of the building, four goals were developed for planning the new library's technology:

- The primary purpose of library technology would be to assist students in their research.

- Rather than an end in itself, it was critical to use technology planning as a way to enable each library functional area to attain each of *their* visions of services in the new building.

- Students today are using a wide variety of formats in their research beyond books and journals, whether in print or online. Therefore, it was important to provide full technology support for all formats of library materials.

- More and more access to technology will be needed by students throughout their research process. As a result, no matter how many computers we provide, demand will always outstrip physical units. Nevertheless, we wanted to figure out a way to provide ubiquitous computer access throughout the new library.

The new library

The new Kellogg Library (Figure 4.2 and Table 4.1) opened its doors in January 2004. We introduced the new library to our students as a place for knowledge, a place for technology, and a place for them.

> 'Think of the Library as a one-stop shop for all your academic needs: get expert research help, attend classes, work on a group project, see a writing tutor, grab a cup of coffee, watch a movie, write a paper'. (Kellogg Library brochure)

Figure 4.2 Kellogg Library interior floorplans

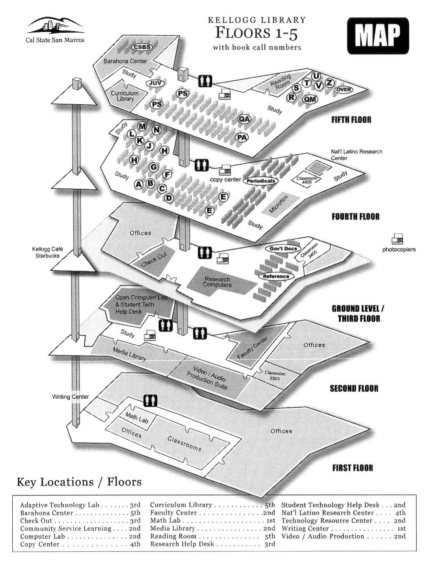

KELLOGG LIBRARY
FLOORS 1-5
with book call numbers

MAP

Cal State San Marcos

FIFTH FLOOR

FOURTH FLOOR

GROUND LEVEL /
THIRD FLOOR

SECOND FLOOR

FIRST FLOOR

Key Locations / Floors

Adaptive Technology Lab 3rd	Curriculum Library 5th	Student Technology Help Desk . . . 2nd
Barahona Center 5th	Faculty Center 2nd	Nat'l Latino Research Center 4th
Check Out 3rd	Math Lab 1st	Technology Resource Center 2nd
Community Service Learning 2nd	Media Library 2nd	Writing Center 1st
Computer Lab 2nd	Reading Room 5th	Video / Audio Production 2nd
Copy Center 4th	Research Help Desk 3rd	

The new library has had a huge impact. Illustrating the campus's excitement over the new library is the gate count of 30,290 people entering the new building the year it opened. In contrast, the year before the library's move (FY2002/03) the gate count was 8,265. After the first year,

Table 4.1   Contrast between old and new library facilities

	Old library	New library
Building size	28,000 sq. ft	200,000 sq. ft
Study spaces	263 seats	1500+ seats
Study rooms	1	37
Network connections	51	1200
Public computers	40	250 (plus IT computer lab)
Volume capacity of open stacks	115,000	400,000

traffic in the new library has settled down to roughly double that of the old facility with a count of 15,918 in FY2005–06. In-house use of materials has also doubled in the new building, from 16,038 in FY2002–03 to 33,441 in FY2005–06.

Library-wide technology and learning

Ubiquitous technology access throughout the library was the cornerstone of the library design supporting our principles of access to collections in-house and beyond and 'anytime, anywhere learning'. This was based on the premise that technology is essential to almost every action users take in the library. Taking notes, chatting with study buddies, finding resources, reading articles on reserve, writing papers – traditional research activities – all depend on technology to a greater or lesser extent. It is this goal that is at the heart of our library's philosophy that the entire library should function as a learning space.

However, determining how to provide technical access throughout the library revealed competing support needs. The most efficient way to deploy computers was in concentrated areas where staff constantly monitor and provide support. Placing students in a central location has the advantage of allowing them to benefit from proximity to reference materials early in their research process as they define and refine their topics – usually when the library gets the most use. Even more important, they have ready access to librarians who can directly support their research process.

However, the whole point was to provide technology where students want to use it. Traditionally, students did their research at cubicles, comfy chairs, sitting on the floor between the stacks. Herding students together in computer 'labs' leaves 90 per cent of the library unused, at least from a technological point of view. Why should students have to go elsewhere to do certain parts of their research process?

We dealt with these conflicting demands by choosing to do it both ways. We centralised technology in four of the learning spaces: reference, classrooms, the Media Library, and in the Academic Technology computer lab. But we also went wireless. Knowing we could never provide enough computers was, in a way, freeing. It moved us beyond trying to find the one best lab location or figure out how to support computers in a variety of locations. Instead, we would depend on students to provide the technology. We discuss each of these in detail below.

Support for learning: reference services

Adjacent to the library entrance, the new reference area includes the reference desk, study and computer workstations, an Assistive Technology Lab, the reference and government document collections, an instruction classroom, the research consultation office, copier and printing services and the reference/instruction librarian offices (Figure 4.3). Proximity of these related services has created a dynamic, bustling area

Figure 4.3 Reference services floorplan

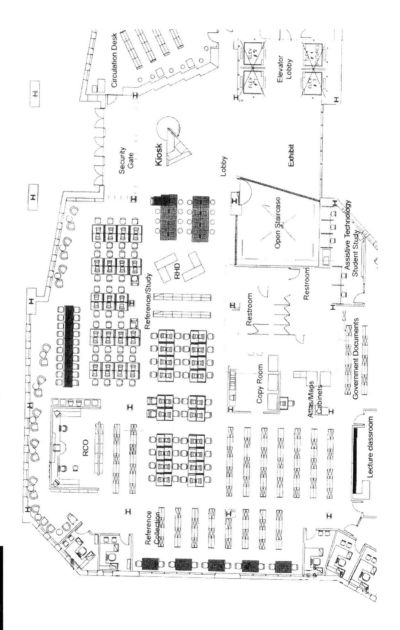

where students can find everything they need to start their research process.

Reference at CSUSM is multidimensional. Due to a history of tiered reference the new building has both a conventional reference desk, which we had not had before, and the research consultation office (RCO). A second service point is the Help Desk on the fourth floor located by the periodicals area, which includes microforms storage and the microforms workstations. Two reasons for having this second desk are student lack of familiarity with using microforms and the relative complexity of using the systems.

Reference provides one example of how old models don't always work in new spaces. The RCO, with two computer workstations, a large table and chairs, ample counter space and cupboards, is one feature brought over from the old building that did not work as planned. In the old library the office had been a busy place, the centre for research help, but clearly in the new building the action was at the reference desk. The librarians' offices, in close proximity to the reference area, replaced the RCO as the place where in-depth consultations occurred.

Research help desk

The reference or Research Help Desk (RHD; Figure 4.4) is the primary contact for students coming to the reference area. Because it was originally designed to have a student information assistant and a librarian on duty there are two seats with two computers. After about a year, a librarian no longer sat at the RHD. Instead the information assistant refers research questions to the librarian on-call. In the information literacy program librarians are working with students in the classroom collaboratively with faculty, are seeing students during office hours, are designing online

Figure 4.4   Research Help Desk

tutorials, and updating the library's web guides. Thus they are very aware of students' research needs and of the assignments in the various courses. Furthermore, statistics nationally show a marked decrease in the number of questions at the reference desk. The reference area as an open lab seemed to generate numerous technology-related questions and less of the actual research questions that would require a librarians' constant attention.

However the RHD, as the primary point of contact, sees heavy traffic. To answer the technology questions a second student employee with specialised technology training was added during heavy use times. This IT student was hired and trained by the campus IT department and then co-supervised by Reference and IT staff. After a year of testing this model we concluded that while having two assistants at the RHD was highly desirable, having them trained by and reporting to different areas created some confusion. Additionally, we felt that the library's RHD information assistant was very capable of handling most of the technology questions while providing a better overview or context for judging which questions were in reality research questions and referring them to the librarian. In the future we expect to have two RHD information assistants who will receive additional technology training to better understand the kinds of questions that need to be referred to the Library Systems help desk.

Statistics (Table 4.2 and Figure 4.5) provide evidence of the popularity of our program. While the number of questions answered by the students at the RHD is declining, the number of questions for the librarians has remained relatively steady and reference appointments have increased. Students ask for help at the fourth floor Help Desk much less frequently. However students take advantage of the opportunity to meet with the librarians in their offices. We meet and surpass student expectations, providing research assistance 'on-demand', using all the various options for reference – appointments, office hours, email, chat, live 24/7 reference, and individual librarians also provide reference via Instant Messaging (IM), and even social networks such as

Table 4.2 Reference usage statistics

	2003/2004	2004/2005	2005/2006
RHD questions – Information Assistant	12,064	10,920	8,760
4th floor questions – Information Assistant	0	1,000	874
RHD questions – Librarians	7,372	6,713	6,959
Librarian appointments	400	994	1007
Total	19,836	19,627	17,600
Questions referred by Information Assistant		127	575

Figure 4.5   Reference usage statistics

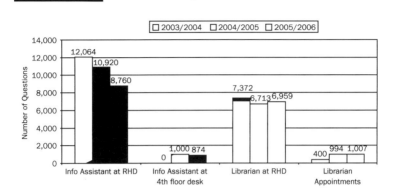

FaceBook and MySpace (Chu and Meulemans, in press). This technology-based research assistance coupled with a strong program of information literacy instruction provides a personalised, customised approach, tailored to each class, academic major, or faculty syllabus.

Student workstations

Planning the reference area workstations epitomised our technology goal of support for student research. Almost 100 workstations are located in this area making it the second largest computer lab on campus. Two conflicting needs drove the design – the need to ensure quick, ready access to library resources vs the desire to encourage extended research and study. We used furniture and layout to try to create the right environment for each need.

To provide quick and easy access to library resources, we developed walk-up stations that are configured as 'library catalogue' workstations (Figure 4.6). No login is required for these computers to provide fast access and to facilitate use by community members as well as the university. The catalogue workstations' highly visible locations and walk-up furniture design provide a 'McDonald's' feel to encourage users to move along quickly. Many features and applications are locked down by editing Windows' group policies to keep the focus on the library catalogue and databases and also to simplify support. In addition to the 16 in the reference area, catalogue workstations are also located at key points on each floor of the library building. Differences in the various library workstation capabilities are indicated by location and types of furniture for the most part. Students understand that the walk-up workstations do not require a login and also do not have all the features for doing research that the sit down research workstations do.

At the opposite end of the spectrum, we wanted the research workstations (Figure 4.7) to create an environment that encouraged students to stay a while and work on all aspects of their research project. The research computers are configured with a full suite of productivity applications including Microsoft Office, data viewers such as ArcView

Figure 4.6 Catalog workstation outpost on 5th floor

Figure 4.7 Research workstations in reference 'lab'

for geographical information, and campus statistical packages. Students and faculty can access and save documents on their campus network directories. The systems are generally restricted to university users and require a campus login.

An essential element in creating an environment conducive to research is adequate desktop space. It is important to get away from thinking about the amount of desktop space according to what is needed for the computer and instead think about what is needed for research. One of our biggest 'battles' was to convince the architects to make the work surface wide enough for books and writing materials as well as the computer components. We requested a 48-inch width but finally settled on 42 inches. Depth is also important. The 3 ft depth of the desktops was considered adequate with the older monitors originally specified and proved to be an ideal depth with the flat-screen monitors actually used.

Ergonomic and social needs were also considered important in the computer cubicle design. The cubicle walls are high enough to define individual work areas but low enough to let in light and provide an open atmosphere. A lightly textured surface was selected to balance between writing and mousing needs. By the time we moved in, mouse design had moved on and no longer required a special surface, but the desktop still works well for writing. We insisted on a relatively low 27-inch desk height to improve the ergonomics of extended keyboarding. The flat-screen monitor's height can also be adjusted, another ergonomic element. Finally, we specified an extended slot rather than individual grommet holes for cords to make it easy for students to move the keyboard and mouse, particularly important for left-handers (Figure 4.8).

Cubicle design also included features to facilitate technical support. The CPU hangs under the desktop on rails that make it easy to access the cords in back. The entire back

Figure 4.8 Research cubicle

wall under the desktop can be removed to access the wires. This space includes the power outlets so that only a single wire hangs to the floor. One problem became quickly apparent. The cubicles were made of high quality wood, which made the removable panel very heavy. The problem was aggravated by the lack of handles and the small screws upon which the panel hangs.

Since the new library opened in January 2004, we have conducted several studies looking at computer use. Throughout the 2004 spring semester we conducted a series of observations to discern how students were using the new research stations (Table 4.3). The results indicated that at least 60 per cent of the computer use was clearly related to

Table 4.3   Research workstation use

Applications	Total users	% use
MS Office programs	228	**39.04%**
MS Excel	14	2.40%
MS PowerPoint	22	3.77%
MS Word	189	32.36%
Web browsing	139	**23.80%**
Library or Campus applications	116	**18.15%**
Library catalogue	8	1.37%
Databases	26	4.45%
Online courses	36	6.16%
CSUSM Campus or Library website	36	6.16%
Email and other non-work	91	**15.58%**
Email	87	14.90%
Games	4	0.68%
Utilities and viewers	12	**2.05%**
Study only – computer not in use	8	**1.37%**
Total students observed	**584**	

educational goals, as defined by use of library or campus-related websites, utilities, and Microsoft Office applications. The most used application overall was Microsoft Word (32 per cent). Only about 5.82 per cent of the use involved the library catalogue or journal databases. Internet searching comprised 24 per cent of use. While general Internet browsing was not counted as either educational or non-educational, given the fact that students prefer the Internet as a research source it is likely that a significant portion of its use was research-related. Less than 16 per cent of use was something we definitely thought was not education-related, mostly email. An interesting, if minor, finding was that there was almost always someone using a computer cubicle for non-computer related studying.

In autumn 2005, the CSU system surveyed campus libraries on their number of computer workstations. Of the 14 campuses who responded, Cal State San Marcos' new Kellogg Library placed fourth in both the number of public workstations (186) and the number of classroom computers (76). In contrast, San Marcos' enrollment of 7,502 students ranked us as eleventh in size, with most of the 'top five' campuses having enrollments over 25,000.

During that same semester, we compared the use of the library's reference computer lab with the campus IT lab on the second floor of the library. During the sample week of 16 October 2005, the campus IT lab had 3,123 logins and the library's reference lab had 5,098 logins (or about two-thirds of the computer use in the library labs). As can be seen in Figure 4.9, the amount of time students spent on the library computers differed greatly as did the pattern of use with and without the catalogue computers. 20 per cent of the library computer usage was for 5 minutes or less. About half of this 'quick look-up' activity happened on the library's catalogue computers, which was the role we hoped they would play. Interestingly, the amount of activity on the

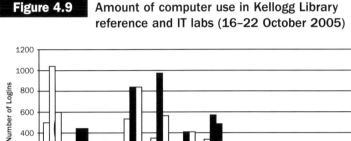

Figure 4.9   Amount of computer use in Kellogg Library reference and IT labs (16–22 October 2005)

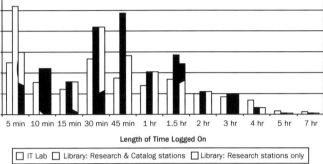

catalogue computers is almost non-existent for the other time periods with the exception of 45 minutes, when they again represent about half the library lab logins. One theory is that 45 minutes is about the length of time a student could use the library between classes. Overall, the research workstations represent about 80 per cent of the library computer use.

The median length of computer time for both the campus IT lab and the library's reference computers was 30 minutes. Use of the library computers was higher for the 5 minute and 45 minute categories. Almost 50 per cent of computer use was over 45 minutes. The campus IT lab computers had the highest per cent of extended use beyond an hour and a half at 29 per cent vs the library's 21 per cent.

Support for learning: the information literacy program

The university's computer competency and writing-across-the-curriculum requirements along with the library's early focus on teaching students to find information that could be delivered to them gave rise to the Information Literacy Program. This multi-tiered program teaches students the abilities needed for lifelong learning and the skills for college level research. In both general education and courses for majors, instructional librarians work closely with faculty to help students recognise a need for information, to learn how it is organised and how to find it, and to evaluate, analyse, and present it. Integrated throughout the lower-division General Education courses, this program includes a 9-hour module of librarian-led classes within the semester-long First Year Experience course where students work in the library to build a foundation of basic searching and evaluation techniques using a variety of resources as they gather information for a final project. Over 20 sections of this course will be offered in autumn 2007. Even without counting the intensive involvement in this First Year course, the number of information literacy instruction sessions have steadily increased. Changes in instruction such as those in 2005/2006 can be caused by various factors including, as in this case, staff changes (Figure 4.10).

Student evaluation of instruction similar to those occurring at the end of the semester in regularly offered courses is conducted in most of our information literacy

Figure 4.10 Annual instruction growth (1993–2007)

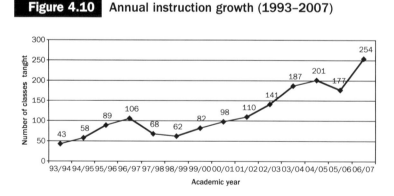

instruction session. Using various questions librarians measure four important categories of program strength and student satisfaction with the session. The categories are librarian respect for the student, their ability to facilitate learning, the match between the instruction offered and the assignment for the course that brought them to the library, and finally any changes in the students' attitude toward the library following the session. Individual librarians' scores are compiled to form a score for the information literacy program as a whole. Taking a combined score for 2 years, Table 4.4, shows students are very satisfied with the program with all four categories having a mean score very near the 5 (strongly agree) on a five-point Likert scale.

Wanting to know if the growth in demand for information literacy instruction could be simply due to a response in

Table 4.4 Student evaluations of instruction (overall average from 2003–2005)

Evaluation categories	Strongly disagree	Dis-agree	Neutral	Agree	Strongly agree	Total	Mean score (5 point scale)
Respect for students	13	5	30	153	627	828	**4.66**
Facilitated learning	12	5	27	145	683	872	**4.69**
Appro-priate to assign-ment/ class	11	7	29	142	673	862	**4.69**
Affective/ attitudinal changes	82	9	48	152	434	726	**4.08**

enrollment growth, we prepared the following graph (Figure 4.11) to compare the growth of enrollment and the growth of instruction as measured by the number of information literacy classes taught during the year.

Extending the idea of the library as a 'learning laboratory' the Context: Library Series brings exhibits and programming into the library to fuel research ideas and take students beyond the classroom, immersing them in academic literature, scientific studies and cultural critiques. These exhibits serve as a catalyst for discussion, an impetus for related research and a learning opportunity for students outside the classroom. For example, with Lynching in America (autumn 2004), instruction librarians collaborated formally with numerous classes and faculty in a variety of subject areas showing the impact of the exhibit across disciplines. Students attend the artist lecture, visit the installation and relate it to class discussion and research. Their feedback truly resonates with the Context mission — exposing students to new ways of understanding and experiencing the world, while engaging them in the research process and academia as young scholars.

Figure 4.11 Comparison of campus growth and growth of library instruction program

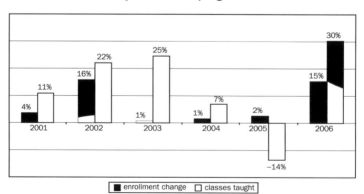

The second technology goal was to enable each library function area to achieve their vision for the new building. The development of the instruction facilities is an example of working together to determine how technology fit into our vision of information literacy instruction in the new library. We had three objectives in planning the instruction facilities. First was to make the rooms fit our instruction styles. Second was to put the latest technology at the instructor's fingertips. Third was to ensure that technology didn't get in the way of instruction.

Our plan for teaching spaces in the library building was not readily accepted. Shill and Tonner (2003; 138), in their article on academic library building projects, documented the significantly increased role that information literacy instruction had on new buildings and library renovations in the period between 1995–2002. Even though our design goals within the library were consistent with this trend, the space for the instruction program was a hard-fought battle. Many of the library planners, architects and administrators involved in the project considered even one dedicated library instruction classroom a luxury, much less the number we were recommending. The strength of our vision, along with the support of two key documents — the *Report of the Task Force on the CSU libraries of the 21st Century* (unpublished) and ACRL's *Guidelines for Instruction Programs in Academic Libraries* — and our own statistics, finally won the day. For a detailed explanation of how these documents supported our instruction plans, see Appendix B.

Instruction design goal 1: make the room fit the instruction style

To make the room fit the instruction style, we developed three instruction room designs; each calculated to meet specific pedagogical goals.

Computer-lab style classroom

Our computer-lab style classroom (Figure 4.12) is sized for the typical San Marcos class size with 42 computers. Instruction-friendly features of the room include recessed monitors that facilitate line-of-sight so students can see the instructor and projection screen while using their computer. A 6-ft width for each two-student desktop provides enough room for the students to take notes. They can even pile their papers on 'wings' that provide extra depth on either side of the monitor ledge. Ergonomics were accounted for with low 27-inch high desktops and adjustable office chairs. An important element specified by the library instructors is wide aisles between desks to allow instructors to walk between rows to observe and help students. Several types of lighting allow instructors to adjust the room brightness for screen projection. It helps that the room is on a lower level with limited windows.

Figure 4.12 Computer lab instruction room floorplan

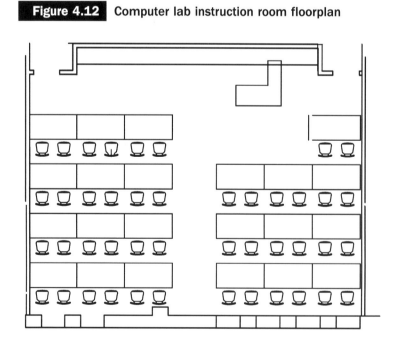

Ask any instruction librarian and they will tell you that our computer lab style classroom with a computer at every student's desk is excellent for fast interactive teaching (Figure 4.13). The focus is on technology-related, often demonstration-style instruction and hands-on student practice rather than lecture or group activities. Students are shown a concept or resource and then asked to mimic this to answer a question or create a product. We now have enough computers for all students, and therefore develop hands-on activities that can replace not supplement the basic instruction we provided. Leading the learner to self-discovery has proven to be much more effective than lecturing and demonstration alone. Use of the Vision software that allows the instructor to control student workstations has also been a long-awaited improvement that, if nothing else, has helped students focus their attention and, we hope, learn the lesson better.

Figure 4.13 View of computer lab classroom from student desk perspective

Lecture classroom

The third floor instruction room (Figure 4.14) is designed to facilitate both lecture and hands-on computer work. Tables in the middle of the room encourage students to focus their attention on the instructor and taking notes. Instruction sessions often start with students at the tables to listen to the introductory lecture. Students can then move to the computers lining the sides of the room to practice what they've just learned. As the computers face outward, it is easy for the instructor to see all student screens from the front of the room. An electric screen makes it easy for the instructor to move from using the white board to presenting on the screen (Figure 4.15).

The room is designed to support large groups (up to 70) and multiple configurations. The furniture is light and easy to move with additional tables and chairs in the room's closet. The tables have power and data ports. In addition to the 32 computers on the side tables, at least 28 laptops can be added for a total of 60 computers.

This room is especially important when a class is a mix of show-and-tell with hands-on activities and reporting out.

Figure 4.14 Lecture classroom floorplan

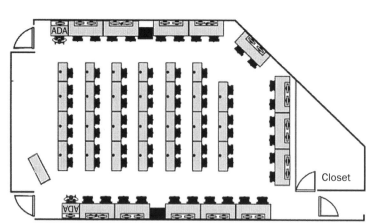

48 Student Capacity Center Seating
28 Student Capacity Perimeter Seating (2ADA)

Figure 4.15 View of lecture classroom from student desk perspective

One example is for a class where students are required to write a literature review. After leading them through a discussion of the process for writing a literature review, the Librarian demonstrates the various shortcuts to search the appropriate databases effectively. Students are then sent off to search the databases implementing these strategies as they begin searching for literature on their specific topics. In contrast, attempting to teach the same assignment is much more difficult in the computer lab classroom, where even recessed monitors can act as barriers that hinder open conversation and make it much more difficult to establish the give-and-take dialog in the initial phase of the instruction.

Collaborative classroom

The library's third classroom is designed to encourage collaboration (Figure 4.16). The room features round tables to accommodate 6–8 person groups. The table halves have wheels

Figure 4.16 Collaborative classroom floorplan

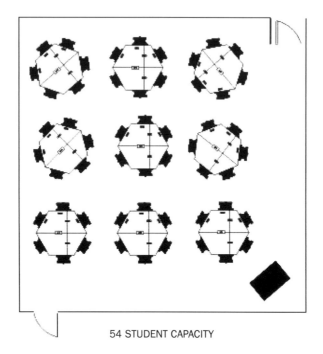

54 STUDENT CAPACITY

and can be separated and moved into new configurations. The room includes a variety of white boards, flip charts and bulletin boards for sharing ideas. Access to technology is not its primary purpose but laptops can be added as needed. The tables have power ports to allow extended use of laptops.

This third venue is geared to class sessions where the students are asked to work in groups. Students at these tables can share documents, laptops, and participate in conversation where everyone is easily heard. We felt that larger tables would cause breakdown into smaller groups rather than encourage a group conversation. One recent class had groups working through various 'learning stations' to come up with a research plan. These plans were later shared with the group as a whole and critiqued by the class. Having laptops readily available also enhances group research (Figure 4.17).

Figure 4.17 Collaborative classroom from student desk perspective

Instruction design goal 2: put technology at instructor's fingertips

The second technology goal for instruction was to put the latest technology at the instructor's fingertips. Careful design of the instructor's lectern was instrumental to meeting this goal. The lectern includes a computer, media players including DVD, VHS, CD and TV, and a document camera. Because the computer is linked to the campus network, faculty can access their own files for instruction materials.

The lectern furniture (Figure 4.18) was custom designed by campus IT's expert in classroom media. The lectern desktop has enough room for notes but is still streamlined. Putting the relatively small monitor (15 inch) on an articulated arm reduces clutter on the surface and allows the instructor to position it to see the class. The

Figure 4.18 Instructor's lectern

computer and media players are embedded in the main pedestals. A shelf on one side can be raised to accommodate a laptop with easy access to the network and use of the overhead projector. The document camera folds into a drawer on the other side. Mobile teaching devices to help instructors get out from behind the lectern are stored in a locked drawer. The devices include a wireless microphone, a PowerPoint presentation 'clicker', wireless mouse and keyboard.

The document camera was not part of the original design. Even after it was added, we weren't sure how much it would be used. It has, however, turned out to be essential for allowing us to bring the printed word to life for a room full of students. Using a document camera allows us to show students exactly how useful specialised reference sources can be. For example projecting pages from the *Encyclopedia of the American Constitution* convinced one particular student audience that looking up 'establishment clause' would catapult them forward in their research. Activities that allow students to review various resources have proven to be an excellent discussion starter about evaluating information. A key feature of the camera is its ability to fold so it can slide into the drawer when not in use (Figure 4.19). Originally the drawer side made it difficult to use with large books like atlases. Shortly after we began to use the new classrooms the drawer was redesigned so that the end panel can now be folded flat.

Figure 4.19 Document camera drawer

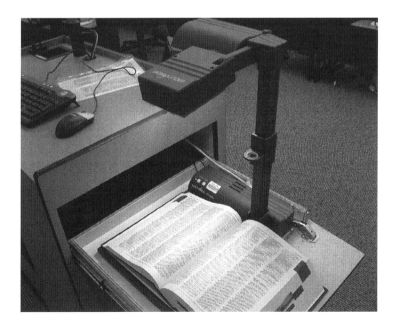

Instruction design goal 3: keep the instructor in control

The final goal for instructional technology was to make sure that it didn't get in the way – that the instructor was always in control. This goal influenced design of both the instructor lectern and the student stations. The lectern was designed to be relatively small and easy to walk around so that it didn't dominate the room and divide the instructor from the students. Unused equipment and controls disappear when they are not needed. For example, the monitor can be moved into a variety of positions including swinging out of the way altogether. The instructor has a choice of the embedded computer or their own laptop, which they can hook-up to power, network, and projection system.

The lectern allows the instructor to operate all the classroom's technology from one location via a custom application available at all times on the screen. Controls are easy to see and use (Figure 4.20). The 'buttons' can turn on the projector, select the device to be viewed whether computer, media or document camera, and adjust the speaker volume.

Altiris Vision is installed on all classroom systems to allow the instructor complete control over the student's computers (Figure 4.21). Vision can prevent any use of the computers, display the instructor's presentation on student screens, and monitor individual student online activities on the instructor's station. One of the more interesting features is the ability to project a student's work for the rest of the class to share. Additionally, a chat feature allows the instructor to ask questions of the class. A question is sent to each of the student screens. Their answers remain anonymous but are collated and projected for all to see allowing them to check their own learning and the instructor to see what concepts

Figure 4.20 Lectern control window

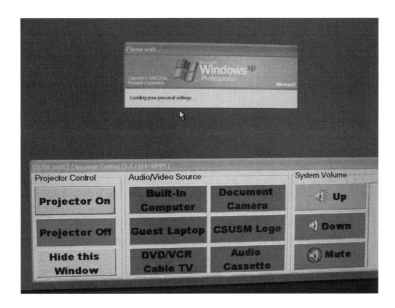

Figure 4.21 Vision instructor software showing six student screens

may need more time. This serves the same function as the now-popular but expensive personal response systems also known as clickers. Another application, Altiris MasterPointer, allows spontaneous markup on screen.

These three instruction labs allow us to teach in different ways. They also prompt us to look critically at how we teach and what we teach as we think of new components or different lesson plans that will better reach the students. Shill and Tonner's research proves that the quality of library spaces greatly impacts the amount of use that is made of them. (Shill and Tonner, 2003; 145) But we are convinced that our new space has had an impact far greater than merely increasing the number of classes taught. It has allowed us to reintroduce print sources, such as reference books, into the research process. It has seen students gathered around a project working collaboratively sharing and teaching each other, guided by the librarian instructor. It has helped us to provide true hands-on experiences so that students better grasp the concepts presented.

Whenever instructional activities allow it, we have opened up the instruction labs for use by other campus groups. During final exams the computer lab classroom is scheduled for proctored exams attached to the various online courses. During the weeks prior to finals and on Friday afternoons both Faculty Center and Academic Technology staff schedule training sessions in this same lab. Recognising that so far, the collaboration classroom has less use due to the advanced preparation needed to set up the laptops ahead of time we also agreed to allow computing staff to schedule faculty technology training sessions and new employee orientations in this classroom. These informal agreements are closely monitored.

Our *Policy for the use of Instruction Labs in Kellogg Library* (Appendix C) has allowed us to manage these various requests. Room scheduling is controlled by the Library's Information Literacy Program rather than the campus Curriculum and Scheduling Office. The library tends to have many short-duration classes, often with a very short notification timelines, that makes scheduling incompatible with the semester-long commitments of other university classrooms. Another factor influencing the extent instruction librarians use the instruction labs is that we have more instruction librarians – soon to have 8, which is three more than when we moved in. Eight librarians place a heavy demand on three labs as, at certain times in the semester, more than three librarians are teaching at the same time.

Therefore, it is important that the instruction program control access to these rooms. All library instruction is scheduled first and other users can be 'bumped' if an unexpected instruction request needs the space. The overall need for space on campus, the admitted beauty and functionality of these learning spaces, and our desire to be good citizens have dictated that we share our instructional space, but we do so on our own terms.

Support for learning: microforms and media library

With our third technology goal, we wanted to encourage students' use of a wide variety of information formats in all aspects of their research and with full access to the power of the building's new electronic environment. Key to this goal was providing students with the ability to use alternative formats, such as media and microform resources, in the full-spectrum of ways that we have come to expect for paper and online text-based sources. First, we wanted to expand the ability to save and transfer research results to a wider variety of information formats so that students could take advantage of the pay-for-print system, their campus network account, email, and storage media such as CDs and USB devices. In particular, the ability to save information electronically was considered desirable as both an alternative to the expense of printing to hardcopy and a way to facilitate working on a project in several locations. Second, we wanted to enable students to input any type of information into the computer, manipulate it electronically, create a variety of research projects, and output the final product in whatever format was appropriate.

Beagle, in his Information Commons as a new service delivery model, puts this in context. As earlier forms of library technology, such as microfiche readers and movie projectors, 'did not 'speak' to each other' (Beagle, 1999; 83) it was rare for a user to try to move content from one format to another. Today's digital environment is quite different. Not only do users combine different information formats but, according to Beagle, they are also more likely to stay at the same workstation from information discovery to project completion. In other words, unlike users of typical print products who usually take the results of their initial library search home to work on, users in the digital environment are more likely to stay and complete their research in the library.

Microforms

Planning for the microforms area typifies what we did to enable alternative formats to access the electronic environment. We replaced our old microform machines with equipment able to scan the fiche or film into electronic form with the help of an attached computer (Figure 4.22). Once in electronic form, specialised software allows the microform image to be manipulated – not just rotated or enlarged but also changed, for instance by minimising blemishes to improve readability. The ability to network the machines allows access to the pay-for-print system, email and the campus network. Information from microform documents can also be saved to storage media using the attached computer.

However, despite having equipment and software capable of making all these things happen, in the case of the microform equipment the technology is still on the 'bleeding edge'. The system is fragile and complex. While able to connect to a computer, the microform machine itself hasn't really been redesigned for the task. It still largely uses the traditional microform technology and simply hands off the data to the computer for electronic processing. Of the few applications that are available for manipulating this data,

Figure 4.22 Microform workstation

none of them are particularly well designed and they have not been updated for several years. We have chosen to use the application with the simplest end-user interface, which only provides some of the capabilities we were looking for. Even then, we have to provide supplemental documentation and hands-on help, requiring the Help Desk to be in the immediate area. Despite the difficulties, just the ability to network to the pay-for-print system has been a significant benefit.

Media Library

Going into the building project, we recognised that media is more important than ever in student learning and the use of multimedia in student research projects is exploding. We had two main goals in planning technology for the Media Library: (1) to facilitate electronic access and use of media, and (2) to provide support for student creation of multimedia research projects. The Media Library was designed with the idea that it would no longer just be a depository for non-print materials but that it would actively support student research using audio, video, and images from online as well as traditional media sources (Figure 4.23).

A great deal of consideration was put into the design of the A/V and computer media stations, resulting in a design that places equipment to one side and provides writing space for the student. We tried to procure AV equipment that combined functions in order to reduce clutter. The area includes a number of group study rooms to support students working together on projects. A larger room with a big-screen TV provides space for larger groups or small classes to work together.

Computer-based multimedia is now supported. There are as many computer stations as traditional AV stations.

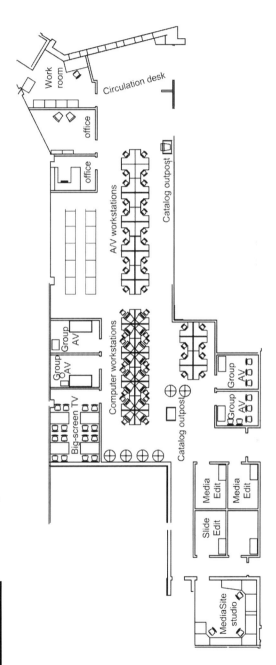

Figure 4.23 Media Library floorplan

The computers have all the capabilities of the research workstations plus a number of enhancements to better support multimedia. They include bigger hard drives and easily accessible inputs on the front for camera memory cards, Firewire, USB, and audio, including RCA. Utilities are installed to support online audio, video and images in a variety of formats. The media computers are equipped with software that can input non-electronic media, edit and create media-based projects, and output the final product in electronic, print or traditional media format (Table 4.5).

Two media edit rooms (Figure 4.24), in addition to the traditional AV group studies, facilitate collaboration and provide extended capabilities. The computers in the edit rooms have dual monitors, attached scanners, speakers, video cards (for analogue video), and the ability to input traditional media formats. One room has an attached

Table 4.5 Multimedia software applications

Audio editing	Post-production: video compositing
Adobe Audition	Adobe After Effects
Audacity	**3D animation**
Sound Forge	Blender
DVD authoring	**Video editing**
Adobe Encore DVD	Adobe Premiere Pro
Roxio Easy Media Creator Suite 9	Windows Moviemaker
Ulead DVD Workshop 2	**Web page creation**
Graphics editing	Adobe Dreamweaver 8
Adobe Photoshop CS2	Microsoft Frontpage
Adobe Illustrator	**Web animation**
Post-production: encode multiple formats	Adobe Flash 8
Cleaner XL	

Figure 4.24 Media edit room with cart

video/DVD player and the other has a media cart. The media cart provides equipment to input and output all the media formats in the library's collection, including VHS, DVD, DV video, and audio tapes. An example of a student project that uses the media edit facilities is a typical assignment from the business program. For this assignment, the student is expected to find an example of a leadership style in a movie and then download and include the movie clip in their presentation for the course. Students typically browse the library's collection to find an appropriate movie, play it on the DVD or VHS player attached to the media edit computer, and use an application such as Movie Maker or Premiere to pull-out their clip.

In order to support all this new technology, a multiphase support strategy was developed. A custom interface on the media workstations provides clear access to the different media applications available and provides links to online tutorials. Support by Library Systems and Media staff is provided to help the student identify the best application to use for their project, input media in traditional formats from the library collection, and to output the final project in an appropriate format. If the student wants to go beyond this basic level of support, detailed manuals on each of the major technologies are available on media reserve. We are also looking into sharing advanced support for media with Academic Technology's media specialists. Already the Media Library is working closely with Academic Technology on such projects as using video-on-demand and the new campus IPTV network to provide additional access to media reserves on and off campus. The Media Library has also provided the facilities for the campus's new MediaSite studio, which allows instructors to create their own web videos.

Distributed support for learning

In November 2003, Shill and Tonner (2003) published the results of their 1995–2002 survey of building projects at 354 academic libraries. Published shortly before our new library opened, the study's findings closely paralleled the new features we had included in our building project. In particular, they found there was a major change in study space with over 90 per cent of the new or renovated libraries adding collaborative study spaces, a feature that was provided in less than half of the older facilities. In addition, over 80 per cent of the new facilities provided study seating with wired network access. However, only a quarter of the new facilities provided wireless network access to all their study seating, a feature that might have also been lacking in our building if not for strong advocacy in early planning. We have found that ready network access throughout the study seating, combined with ready access to laptops, has a powerful synergy.

Shill and Tonner drew the significant conclusion that the emphasis placed on increasing seating capacity was a clear indication that we expect 'users will continue to come to the physical library' (Shill and Tonner, 2003; 450).

Study rooms

Creating study spaces designed to meet a variety of student needs was one of the most important aspects of providing learning support throughout the building. The Kellogg Library has over 1,500 study seats in a variety of configurations. Single-person cubicles line the windows with their spectacular views of North San Diego County. Tables and comfortable seating are scattered throughout the library, particularly in the stacks. We have special study spaces ranging from the elegant reading room with its sofas and fireplace to the practical collection of tables, group studies and tackable wall that supports education classes in the curriculum area.

Of all these types of study spaces, the most important to our vision of the new library were the collaborative or group study rooms. We initially requested over 40 group study rooms. Convincing the building planners that we really needed that many study rooms was a challenge, especially when even the library consultant questioned the large number. However, we felt this type of study space was particularly important for our students given the emphasis Cal State San Marcos programs place on collaborative learning. We ultimately settled on 35 general-purpose group studies in two sizes – 27 six-person small studies and eight

10-person medium studies. Shortly after the new library opened, we lost five studies as 'temporary' offices for another university program, but we've been able to retain the remaining 30 studies (Figure 4.25).

In looking at how our quantity of study space compared to other libraries in Shill and Tonner's survey, we fell into the one-third of libraries that provided 1,500 or more seats. Only 8 per cent provided more than 30 group study rooms (Shill and Tonner, 2003; 450). However, the level of use since the new library opened justifies our decision to have a large number of study rooms, particularly considering that the university plans to ultimately grow to over 20,000 students. A count was made of study room occupancy every Thursday during the spring semester in 2005 (Figure 4.26). The results showed that 60–70 per cent of the rooms are constantly in use throughout the semester.

Figure 4.25 Small group study room

Figure 4.26 Study room use, spring 2005

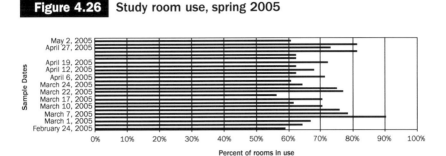

Percent of rooms in use

Wireless network

In considering how to provide ubiquitous technology access to our study areas, we ran into competing assumptions. One was that we assumed technology would be needed by most users most of the time. The other was the assumption that the library can never provide enough computers to meet user demand, especially given the fact we're a growing university. So, in addition to providing a number of on-site computers, we felt the real answer lay in creating a robust, building-wide network capable of providing laptops and other electronic devices with full access to the library's electronic capabilities.

Wireless networks are commonly accepted today but, in 1999, we had a hard time convincing campus IT, who were responsible for making the ultimate decisions in the building's technology, that it was a viable concept. They were interested, but felt the technology was too undefined and underpowered to rely on. They weren't sure wireless was likely to be used at all, much less that we could count on it as our primary network. Thus, the building was designed with over 2,000 wired network connections with power outlets and only included limited wireless capabilities in the main public areas. However, as we neared the end of the building process in 2003 the situation was quite different. The technology had matured and campus IT had gained a great deal of experience in retroactively installing wireless in other areas of the campus. By then, everyone was convinced wireless was the way to go.

Fortunately, we knew as we went into the building project that trying to predict the state of technology over a 5-year window was unrealistic, so we had built in plenty of flexibility in the technology planning and procurement process. The library had also established a close relationship with campus IT and communicated regularly on changes and possibilities. We were therefore able to work together to make significant changes to the library's telecommunication plan late in the building process. We upgraded and greatly expanded the wireless network to encompass the entire building and even some of the outside seating areas. At the same time, we greatly reduced the number of wired locations in the public areas. Staff areas, classrooms, and labs retained all of their wired connections but now had access to wireless as well. The resulting costs savings was in the tens of thousands of dollars that we were glad to put to use elsewhere in the project.

There was one interesting side-effect of the change. When the wired network was reduced, it was late enough in the building process that conduit with embedded power had already been laid in the floors. After we occupied the building we found this had a significant benefit – we have power to most of our study locations. As anyone who's ever worked on a battery-powered laptop knows, availability of power outlets is almost as valuable as the network itself.

Campus IT and Library Systems also worked closely to develop the network protocols, especially for wireless. It was important to the library that wireless users could access library resources, including its databases, in just the same way as someone using one of the catalogue workstations. We also wanted to provide access to printing in the library and enable access to the campus network for students and faculty using the wireless network. Basically, we wanted wireless to have all the same capabilities as the various wired workstations in the library. Campus IT developed creative solutions to our specifications that resulted in a two-part authentication scheme. When a laptop first connects to the network, the user is given an opportunity to login to the campus network. If the user does not login, they still have access to all library resources, including the databases. Users that do login have full network privileges including access to their campus account, network resources they are already authorised for, and access to the pay-for-print stations throughout the library.

Laptop checkout

In contrast to its cool reception to the idea of wireless networking, campus IT was very excited right from the beginning about the laptop checkout program the library proposed at early planning meetings. In fact, they quickly offered to take on responsibility for maintenance and ongoing costs for the program. Campus IT worked closely with the library to develop the laptop program protocols. Some policies were based on simple 'common sense'. For instance, laptops are not checked out with power cords, partly to reduce peripherals that have to be managed and partly as a theft deterrent. The laptop circulation period of three hours was determined by the average battery life. Appendix D has a copy of the Laptop checkout policy.

Academic Technology's student technology help desk serves as the laptop checkout point. A room behind the help desk houses banks of extra batteries and rechargers (Figure 4.27), which enable immediate turnaround of returned machines

Figure 4.27 Laptop battery room

to be checked out again. The library gave campus IT access to the Innovative media booking module and trained them on how to use it for circulation and fine collection.

The library instruction program also wanted to have laptops. Laptops would be used in the collaborative classroom, which did not have permanently installed computers, and they would also make it possible to teach larger classes in the other two classrooms. Funding for procurement of instruction laptops was available from a grant but Library Systems was concerned about long-term maintenance and refresh costs of the technology. It was also a new type of technology that Systems would have to support with no additional manpower. Finally, no one had experience with using laptops in an instructional situation. We weren't sure just how much they would be used.

As a result of these concerns, Library Systems developed a plan with the library's Information Literacy program and campus IT to house the library's instruction laptops with the checkout laptops. When not in use by library instruction, the laptops would be available for student checkout. Campus IT would be responsible for maintaining the computers. If instructors needed more laptops than the 28 funded by the grant, they would be able to reserve additional laptops from the checkout pool. This solution seems to be a win all around – more laptops for students, flexibility in number of laptops for instruction, more laptops for campus IT, and one less new responsibility for Library Systems.

The library has experienced several beneficial side effects from the synergies of study spaces, network saturation and laptop availability that we hadn't anticipated. Not too surprisingly, within a year of occupancy, the desirable research computer lab area would fill to capacity during busy times of the day and semester. We had planned the quick-turnover design of the catalogue workstations to compensate for just this type of situation and, indeed, even during the busiest times, at least a few catalogue workstations were almost always available to provide library resource access. However, students wanted to have access to computers with full research capabilities. We quickly figured out referring students to the laptop checkout program, along with other campus labs, took care of this need.

The popularity of the reference lab area combined with its proximity to the traffic in the entrance area had another side effect: noise. As we began to get more complaints about the noise, it occurred to us that the laptops could also solve this problem. With 200,000 sq. ft of space, 1,500 seats and 31 study rooms, students with laptops can always find someplace quiet enough to suit them. Finally, as students became familiar with the features of the new building, they began to ask to use the instruction rooms, particularly for practicing class presentations. Again the combination of a laptop and a group study room provided the answer with the perfect environment to practice mock presentations.

Technology support structure

In order to develop and support all the technology enhancements planned for the new building, we knew Library Systems couldn't do it alone. Library Systems had only gained one-half of a staff position for a total of four people to manage the more than fivefold increase in computer technology in the new building. We knew early on that we would need cooperation from campus IT to make it happen. The question then became, how could we take advantage of campus IT resources without losing the ability to customise technology to library needs?

Aside from providing more manpower, establishing a close working relationship with Campus IT also had other benefits. The Library didn't control key infrastructure areas, such as the network, but we had certain expectations of what we wanted campus IT to provide. We were adding technology in areas where previously there was none and needed help in designing configurations for the many new types of systems. Most important, during the planning process it quickly became apparent that, paralleling the reluctant response to the library requests for instructional and study space, architects and other planners didn't have much respect for the library's technology decisions. It was critical to have campus IT buy-in and help to successfully advocate for our technological vision.

Shared planning and good communication with campus computing staff was key to the successful development of technology in the new building. Early on, Library Systems shared their vision and ideas with relevant leaders in campus computing. Systems and campus IT were in many of the same planning meetings. If we were not, we made sure the other was aware of what was missed. Starting 9 months before the move, we established bi-weekly meetings where we dealt with initial deployment and configuration issues. We also identified support needs for all the planned technology and determined areas of responsibility.

We ended up developing a shared support structure. The complex but flexible relationship we developed maximised support and services although the division of support was not always clear. Library Systems gave up some of its direct control over library technology and campus IT agreed to customise certain campus configurations and protocols to the library's specification. However, as trust in the library's technical expertise grew; more access was provided to underlying campus systems for the library to directly manipulate. In one example, the student research computers are no longer completely built by Library Systems. To meet campus security standards, IT builds the basic image according to the library's specifications. However, Library Systems then has access to the image server to build custom add-ons for computers in different areas of the library.

The ability to successfully work in a shared support environment depends on an atmosphere of trust and excellent communication at all levels. We were fortunate to have a good relationship with campus IT going into the building project. The shared planning and development of ongoing partnerships for maintenance and support during the project has significantly strengthened that relationship. And, as time has gone by, it has become apparent that much of the success of this complex but informal support system is dependent on the personal relationships we've established with certain individuals in campus IT. A recent reorganisation within campus IT has put new players in many of our key relationships. As a result, we have had to spend more time explaining procedures and re-establishing reliable lines of communication. At a certain point, we may have to create more formal documentation of some of these shared support processes.

Changes and lessons learned

Clear vision of library objectives

One of biggest strengths of our project was that we went into the project with a clear vision of the new library and its services. From something as seemingly simple as lighting to something as complex as classrooms, the library knew what it wanted, had researched best practices, and was persuasive (or just stubborn) in seeing it carried out. This was particularly helpful in justifying the large number of study rooms and classrooms we felt were appropriate.

Importance of real-life examples

Most people can't really visualise three-dimensional objects based on flat plans. No matter how adept some of us became at reading the architectural plans, it was still very difficult to understand how the detail plans, such as built-in furniture, would look in real life. The most striking example of this problem was our kiosk.

The vision for the library entrance was that upon walking into the library the user would immediately see the circulation desk on the left, the research help desk rising above the computer workstations on the right and in front a striking view of the central core with its two-storey windows, glassed-in staircase and art exhibit area. In the middle of the entrance area was to be a small kiosk that could have staff to provide directional help and display basic library information. While the kiosk evolved during the design process to incorporate more capabilities, we could see on the plan (Figure 4.28) that the footprint was still appropriately small.

The reality was a disaster (Figure 4.29). The kiosk was huge! Almost touching the ceiling, it was like a small room in the middle of the entrance. It completely blocked the user's view of the windows and exhibits; circulation and reference staff couldn't see each other; and traffic had to split along two narrow channels on either side. As soon as we saw the kiosk going up, we realised our mistake but it took 2 years before we could get rid of it. The problem was our inability to visualise what a small triangle on the plans would look like in real life.

Figure 4.28 Kiosk floorplan

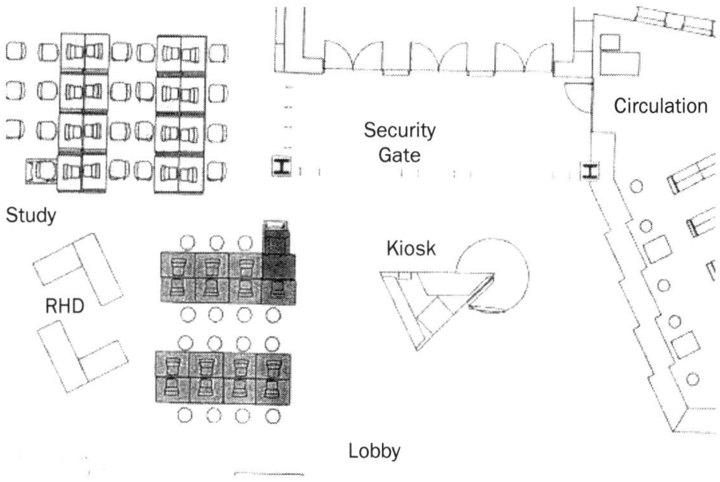

Study

RHD

Security
Gate

Kiosk

Circulation

Lobby

Figure 4.29 Kiosk, looking from circulation towards reference

In contrast, the design of the instructor lectern for the library classrooms was a particularly successful experience. The lectern furniture was custom designed by campus IT's expert in classroom media. After receiving our initial specifications, he designed a lectern that combined our needs with best practices he had learned in the field. To help us evaluate the design, he then built a cardboard prototype and had the librarians physically interact with it. Some of the changes that were made as a result of the prototype included reducing the size to make it easier to walk around, lowering the height so even our shortest librarians were comfortable using it, putting a smaller monitor screen on a multi-position arm to make it easy for the instructor to see around (and be seen), and creating a fold-down shelf for guest instructor's laptops and instructional materials. As a result of this concrete, hands-on design process, the lectern has been very successful in real world use (Figure 4.30).

Figure 4.30 Lectern prototype

Involve all staff in the building project

It is important to realise that no one knows what will work better in an area than the staff that uses the area. For example, the instruction librarians were intimately involved in every detail of the classrooms. As a result, the classroom spaces have been very successful.

Plan for flexibility and change

Several examples have been given of areas where we succeeded or failed to plan for change. The Research Office is one example of old methods that do not work in a new space. Could we have foreseen that the reference area would change the way students and librarians interacted? By contrast, the success of the wireless and laptop plans both benefited from the flexibility built-into the telecommunication and computer planning processes.

References and further reading

Association of College and Research Libraries (2003) *Guidelines for Instruction Programs in Academic Libraries.* Chicago: ALA

Beagle, D. (1999) 'Conceptualizing an Information Commons', *The Journal of Academic Librarianship*, 25(2): 82–9.

Chu, M. and Meulemans, Y.N. (2008) 'The problems and potential of Myspace and Facebook usage in academic libraries', *Internet Reference Services Quarterly*, 13(1): in press.

California State University San Marcos (2004) *Kellogg Library: Map brochure.* San Marcos, CA: California State University San Marcos.

Shill, H.B. and Tonner, S. (2003) 'Creating a better place: physical improvements in academic libraries, 1995–2002'. *College and Research Libraries*, 64: 431–66.

Sonntag, G., and Palsson, F. (2007) 'No longer the sacred cow – no longer a desk: transforming reference service to meet 21st century user needs', *Library Philosophy and Practice*, Feb. Available at *http://digitalcommons.unl .edu/libphilprac/111/* (accessed 17 April 2007).

Sonntag, G. and Ohr, D. (1996) 'The development of a lower-division, general education, course-integrated information literacy program', *College and Research Libraries*, 57(4): 331–8.

Task Force on Facility Planning for Library and Information Resources (1996) *Information Resources Facilities for the 21st Century: A Framework for Planning. Appendix A.* Long Beach, CA: California State University. Available at *http://www.calstate.edu/LS/Fnl_Rpt.shtml* (accessed 13 April 2007).

Appendix A

Cal State San Marcos Library's technology planning process

Library Systems worked closely with each library unit early in the building planning process to develop a strategic plan that articulated the role of technology in fulfilling their vision of services in the new library. The plan guided all technology decisions over the next 5 years, including those that were immediately implemented in the old building as well as those planned for the new building.

In order for the library's technology vision to be successfully integrated into all aspects of the building it was important for Library Systems to be involved in all aspects of building planning. In addition to the technology plan itself, Systems was heavily involved in the architectural planning and the furniture, fixtures, and equipment specifications and budgeting. The Media Library is one example.

The example of the media technology plan in Table 4.A1 shows some of the specific details that guided decisions during the building process. For each area of the building the type of equipment, the number of network connections, and total number of computer systems was specified. The specifications also accounted for existing equipment, as well as new equipment to be purchased with building funds. Finally, the plan indicated how we expected the systems to grow over a 5-year period after move-in.

Table 4.A1 Library technology plan – Media Library excerpt

Area	Equipment Type	Network Connections				Computer (other equip)				Current		Total new
		total	yr 1	yr 3	yr 5	total	yr 1	yr 3	yr 5	lease	non	
Counter 9.1	Staff computers (3 checkout stations)	10	10			5	3	1	1	1	2	2
Catalog 9.2	Catalog	4	4			2	2				1	1
Listening cubicles 9.6	Multimedia computers	60	60			15	5	5	5			15
9.6	TV monitors (w/close captioning)						(20)	(5)			(12)	
9.6	DVD/CD players						(10)				(2)	
9.6	video/audio tape players						(10)	(5)			(2)	
Instruction 9.7	multimedia computers, instructors station, audio/video cabinet	50	50			41	41					41
Equip 9.10	staff computers, copier, fax	6	6			2	1		1			2
Group study 9.11	wired student positions; multimedia presentation station	17	17			1	1					1

Table 4.A1 Library technology plan – Media Library excerpt *(Cont'd)*

Area	Equipment Type	Network Connections				Computer (other equip)				Current		Total new
		total	yr 1	yr 3	yr 5	total	yr 1	yr 3	yr 5	lease	non	
Offices 9.12, .13, .15	Complement computers, network printer	12	12			6	2	1	3	1		5
Group listen 9.25	multimedia computers with editing hardware	18	18			3	2	1				3
9.25	large-screen TV, DVD/CD, Video	12	12				(1)	(1)				
9.25	Go-Video dubbing machine	6	6				(1)				(1)	
9.25	multimedia cart						(1)	(1)				
Slide produc. 9.26	staff computer, slide scanner, possible photo lab equipment.	3	3			1	1					1
Total		198	198			76	58	8	10	2	3	(71)

Definitions

Catalog Computers   Web browser with access to PAC and electronic databases. Open login. Pay-for-print.

Reference Computers   Catalog setup plus standard 'lab' package including word processing and e-mail. Also, specialized research software such as ProCite, a citation organizer. User-specific login. Pay-for-print.

Multimedia Computers   Reference setup plus graphic and web editing capability (e.g., Photoshop, FrontPage). Some machines may have additional capabilities including writeable CD drives, video inputs, and advanced editing packages such as Premiere and SoundForge. User-specific login. Pay-for-print.

Laptop Computers   Reference setup. Possibly configured for wireless network. User-specific login. Pay-for-print.

Instructor Station   Reference or multimedia computer (depending on location), projector. Ability to hook up audio/video display. User-specific login. Room printer.

Multimedia Input Cart   Audio/video components such as DVD/CD player, VCR, and monitor with switch box and

	cabling to download information to multimedia computer.
Complement Computers	Employee computers with standard campus IT setup. User-specific login. Office network printer.
Staff Computers	Shared-use and student employee computers. May contain specialized applications, most will have standard complement software (and be purchased as lease machines). Login varies – some user-specific, some shared by function area.

All the cubicles in the media library are equipment cubicles (16 old and 24 new). Each cubicle should have one data, two power and one cable connection. Each study room should have six data, eight power, and one cable connection. At least two data, four power, and the one cable should be along the counter, the balance on the other two non-door walls. The equipment room, 9.10, has additional power requirements in order to handle 20 pieces of equipment plugged in at any one time (including 10 recharge stations).

The architectural plan then placed the technology into the actual library spaces. The media architectural plan (Figure 4.A1) shows the relation of the technology decisions with the physical layout of the new area. Technology planned for this area included 16 workstations and two media edit rooms. The architectural plans allowed us to see what the area might look like, how the technology would fit, and how use of the area might flow.

Table 4.A2 Media equipment, furniture, and fixtures specifications

Room	Room name	Item	Item description	Vendor	Units req.	Est total ($)
2110	Media Library Group Study	Cart – Multimedia			1	$400.00
2110	Media Library Group Study	Chair – Study Room		Brandrud-904	16	$5,463.68
2110	Media Library Group Study	Clock – Round Battery Operated		Seth Thomas	1	$34.00
2110	Media Library Group Study	DVD Player		Sony	1	$249.00
2110	Media Library Group Study	Monitor – Video Monitor PVM-20N5U		Sony	1	$1,000.00
2110	Media Library Group Study	Patchbay 2600		Switchcraft	1	$375.00
2110	Media Library Group Study	Plasma EDTV – 42"	Panasonic PT-42PD3-P	Panasonic	1	$5,000.00
2110	Media Library Group Study	Projection Screen – Da Lite 92722, 69"x92"		Troxell	1	$439.42
2110	Media Library Group Study	Stereo – Hi-Fi/VCR		Panasonic	1	$140.00
2110	Media Library Group Study	Table – 4 Seat Classroom		Steelcase Ellise	4	$912.00
2110	Media Library Group Study	White Board – 3 X 4 Dry Erase		Demco	0	$0.00
2110	Media Library Group Study	White/Marker Board 4 X 10		Demco	1	$400.00
2111	Media Library Catalog Area	Catalog Carrel (Stand-up) #6		Agati	1	$1,457.86
2111	Media Library Catalog Area	Computer – PC-NT Multimedia	Dell OptiPlex GX300	Dell	13	$33,800.00

Table 4.A2 Media equipment, furniture, and fixtures specifications (*Cont'd*)

Room	Room name	Item	Item description	Vendor	Units req.	Est total ($)
2111	Media Library Catalog Area	Media Storage Container		Checkpoint	1	$17,132.34
2111	Media Library Catalog Area	Monitor		View Sonic	1	$0.00
2111	Media Library Catalog Area	Talbot Chairs		Agati	42	
2112	Media Library Group Listening	Chair – Study Room		Brandrud-904	4	$1,365.92
2112	Media Library Group Listening	Clock – Round Battery Operated		Seth Thomas	1	$34.00
2112	Media Library Group Listening	DVD/VCR Player		Sony	1	$300.00
2112	Media Library Group Listening	Table – Small Classroom		Vecta Runner	1	$307.00
2112	Media Library Group Listening	TV – 32 inch		Sony	1	$630.00
2115	Media Library Group Listening	Cart – Multimedia			1	$9,230.00
2115	Media Library Group Listening	Chair – Study Room	Dell	Brandrud-904	4	$1,365.92
2115	Media Library Group Listening	Computer – PC-NT-Media Editing	OptiPlex GX300	Dell	1	$4,800.00
2115	Media Library Group Listening	Fast SCSI Interface Dual-Channel		Adaptec	0	$0.00
2115	Media Library Group Listening	Monitor		View Sonic	1	$0.00
2115	Media Library Group Listening	Table – Small Classroom		Vecta Runner	1	$307.00

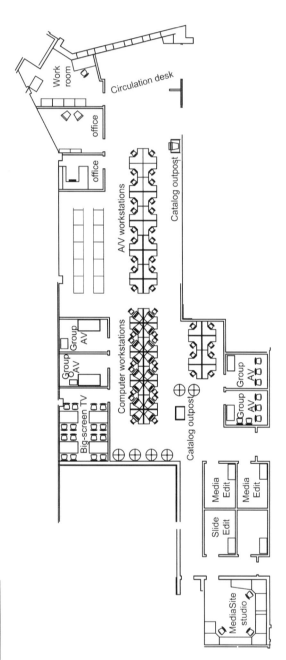

Figure 4.A1 Media architectural plan

Three years before we moved into the building, we began the process of specifying furniture, equipment and fixtures. It was important to make the specifications precise enough to develop a budget but flexible enough to adapt to the inevitable changes in technology. The media specification and budgeting plan was used to determine budget request, develop room layouts, and finally procure the actual items. Table 4.A2 has a sample of one page from this plan. Purchasing so much technology seems like a dream shopping spree, but the reality was that it was hard work to spend over half a million dollars just on technology alone.

Appendix B

Use of supporting documents to justify classroom design

Our plan for teaching spaces in the library building was supported by the Report of the Task Force on the CSU libraries of the twenty-first century that states that 'Training in the use of library collections and services (electronic and otherwise) will be an ever-increasing activity in the CSU libraries of the future. All new library building programs should include heavily networked and computerised facilities for such training'. However even this recognition that instruction programs are becoming more commonplace did not provide the justification needed to include instruction classrooms in the new library. In fact this space for the instruction program was a hard-fought battle. While the instruction librarians desperately try to find a place to teach, library planners, architects and many administrators consider dedicated library instruction classrooms a luxury.

Integral to the planning of any library space in the CSU are the formulas outlined in this Taskforce report (Appendix A in Taskforce, 1996) that describe four types of spaces, collections, non-book materials, reader stations, and technical processing/public service areas. Each of these four spaces has specific formulas. For example, an 'open stacks' area is to be planned at the 10:1 ratio (10 volumes per 1 assignable sq. ft) and non-book materials is to be calculated at 40 per cent of the space allocated for 'open stack' collections. While the number of readers stations is generally governed by ACRL standards, or at least, that is the ideal; the CSU also outlines three different types of reader stations. Each one is allotted very specific space. The CSU document recognises that it is using formulas to determine both technical processing and public service spaces that are 15 years old but retains these without changes. Thus we were still held to the original rate of 225 assignable sq. ft per projected staff member. Classroom space must be carved out from among and between these strictly defined types of spaces, with a battle on each front. Certainly we didn't want to take over collection space or staff space. Our only hope was in the fact that the number of staff didn't increase at the same rate as allotted. A campus with 8,000 students is allotted space for 67 staff members and it is from there we could negotiate teaching space.

Our plans were aided by the *Guidelines for Instruction Programs in Academic Libraries* (ACRL) where three sections that lend support to our call for space. In the section on Instructional Facilities the guideline calls for 'ready access to facilities of sufficient size and number' including at least one computer to demonstrate information systems and research practice. Additionally it states 'It is desirable that the facilities provide individual hands-on experience for those being instructed. It should be flexible enough to accommodate active learning and student collaboration when appropriate'. Another section targets instruction support, such as additional equipment and space for preparation and storage of instructional materials. And while library administrative support is by far the most important tool in the fight for space, some data also helps. At CSUSM instruction statistics have been kept fairly consistently since 1992 and as we have seen, the growth of the program has been much greater than enrollment growth alone would have predicted.

Appendix C

Policy for the use of Instruction Labs in Kellogg Library

This policy applies to the three Library Instruction Labs (4400, 3400, and 2303)

Primary use

A. The instruction labs are to be used primarily for library and information literacy instruction sessions taught by an Information Literacy Program (ILP) librarian.

B. The instruction labs are not available for semester-long scheduling of meetings or courses as this would block their availability for course-specific library instruction.

C. For instruction before or after regular library hours, refer to the 'Procedures for After-hours Use of Kellogg Instruction Labs'.

D. Library materials taken to the room should be removed immediately after the session has ended. Materials may be left on a book truck in the reference area for students needing to refer to them after class.

Secondary use

A. Library instruction requests cannot be predicted as they are dependent on professors' instructional needs throughout the semester. Therefore non-library sponsored events will not normally be scheduled in these rooms.

B. Secondary use must be instructional in nature. Current secondary uses include: orientations, campus/library training, non-library meetings, professional instruction, community instruction (e.g. National Latino Research Center), and outreach instruction.

C. Requests for exceptional uses should be made to the Dean of the Library through the Coordinator of Information Literacy Program or designee. Requests for library instruction labs must occur after campus instructional lab scheduling has been contacted.

D. The instruction labs will not be scheduled for any time the Library is not open.

E. Exceptional events should not conflict with potential instructional use of the labs. Events will not be scheduled more than 7 days in advance during the peak- use times. Secondary use will generally be scheduled during intersession and off-peak times.

F. Those requesting use of these labs must cover all Request for Use (RFU) related costs. In addition there may be a room charge to help cover the secondary costs associated with room usage.

Scheduling

A. Library instruction takes priority over any secondary uses; therefore, secondary uses may be displaced for instruction.

B. The use of the instruction labs must be reserved. ILP librarians can reserve the labs by indicating the date, timeframe, and following information on the Room Scheduling calendar located in the Outlook Calendar: course (e.g. GEL 101) or event name/last name of instructor-of-record/last name of librarian.

C. Instruction in the library labs will be scheduled following these guidelines:

1. Course-integrated library instruction directly related to the curriculum.

2. Open student workshops taught by library faculty.

3. Professional development workshops taught by library faculty.

4. Professional meetings sponsored by the library.

5. Library-wide meetings (e.g. Quarterly Staff Meetings)

6. Library staff training sessions.

D. If there is a scheduling conflict, individuals responsible for the classes should negotiate alternative dates and times. Otherwise priority is given to the earliest scheduled class.

E. Anyone who wishes to schedule an event in a library instruction lab should contact the Information Literacy Coordinator or designee. Alternatively the Library Administration Office can be contacted at (760)xxx–xxxx.

F. College Faculty who wish to lead their own sessions in the use of information resources may do so after consulting with their liaison librarian or, if that person is unavailable, with the Information Literacy Coordinator. ILP librarians may be present at these sessions to provide expertise in the use of the information sources and to assist with the equipment.

Other considerations

A. Those authorised to use the labs will be responsible for the space and the use of the equipment. Lab users must log-off all computers when finished. Users agree to make no modifications to the equipment configuration and ensure that the lab is as functional upon completion of the event as it was when they gained access to it. Violation of this policy may result in the loss of lab use privileges.

B. The labs are locked except when in use. Each ILP librarian has a room key. The labs may be opened before the scheduled time for preparation purposes. For secondary scheduled use, access to room must be arranged prior to event and event sponsors must be present once lab is opened.

C. Event sponsors are responsible for any damages to furniture or equipment during the event.

Food and drink

A. The library's food/beverage policy applies to the instruction labs. Beverages in approved containers must be placed away from computer terminals and keyboards.

B. Food or drink for special events must have prior approval as outlined in the Kellogg Library's 'Guidelines for Caterers'.

C. Event sponsor must provide copies of the RFU and of the Catering agreement to the Library Administration Office prior to the event.

Last revised: September 29, 2006.

Appendix D

Laptop checkout policy

Student Technology Help Desk

LAPTOPS AVAILABLE FOR CHECK OUT

The Student Technology Help Desk, located on the <u>second floor of the Library</u>, has laptop computers available for checkout by students.

These laptops are ready for use with the university's wireless network, include the Microsoft Office suite of applications, and let you access your home folder, printers, and Internet resources from anywhere in the Kellogg Library.

You'll need your **library barcode** to check out the computers. Don't have one? <u>Get a barcode</u>.

Checkout is for 3 hours and laptops may not be removed from the library. Please stop by the Student Technology Help Desk (KEL 2013) for more information.

Please review the <u>Laptop Checkout and Use Policy</u> before use.

STUDENT LAPTOP CHECKOUT AND USE POLICY

Borrowers

Laptops can only be checked out by CSUSM students, with a valid CSUSM Library card.

Limits and availability

- Laptops can be checked out from the Student Technology Help Desk (STH) located at Kel 2013.

- Laptops are only for use in the Kellogg Library and cannot be removed from the building.

- Laptops must be returned in person to the STH prior to library closing.

- Laptops will be available on a first come, first served basis. They cannot be reserved ahead of time.

- Check-out is for up to 3 hours. They can be renewed at the STH if no one is waiting.

- Laptops will not be checked out when there are less than 2 hours before the STH closes.

- If you have fines on your Library account you will not be allowed to checkout a laptop.

- If you have previously violated this checkout agreement, you will not be allowed to check out a laptop.

- You may not save your work to this laptop, but instead you must save it to a server or email it to yourself.

- You may not install software on the laptop or otherwise change its configuration.

Fines and liability

- Laptop late-return fees are $10 for each hour or portion of an hour the laptop is late.

- If you lose or significantly damage a laptop, you will be responsible for reimbursing the campus for the repair or replacement of the system. Replacement cost for the laptop computer is based on the retail price of equipment with similar specifications. Repair costs will be based on actual costs of parts and labor.

- You will be charged for necessary repairs if you tamper with security seals on the laptop.

- You must not leave the laptop unattended – you are responsible for replacing the laptop should it be stolen while checked out to you.

Taken from *http://www.csusm.edu/iits/policies/laptop.htm* (accessed 9 August 2004).

5

The Saltire Centre and the Learning Commons concept

Jan Howden

> The incredible unpredictability of the engagement of technology with culture is the lesson that comes out over and over again, which means you've got to be incredibly sensitive to the way technology and culture come together and ready to rethink assumptions, develop new experiments and transform the way you do things. You've got to be able to turn on the dime.
> Ludwig and Starr (2005)

This chapter looks at the Saltire Centre at Glasgow Caledonian University in Scotland (Figures 5.1 and 5.2).

The Saltire Centre opened in January 2006. This followed Glasgow Caledonian's first Learning Commons project known as the Real Learningcafé (Howden, 2003) in 2001. Both developments attract a lot of attention from schools, universities, colleges, public libraries and researchers; including a couple of anthropologists. In the UK, Learning Commons developments have various names. There is no one single model or any development that captures the range of possibilities (the Saltire Centre team are working on it!). More frequently used terms in the UK may be one-stop shops, learning café, learning cluster, social learning spaces, group

Figure 5.1 The Saltire Centre

study areas with technology or flexible space to meet a variety of learning styles. Recent reports include the Saltire Centre as an example of the kind of facility that those supporting

Figure 5.2 The Saltire Centre

learning should develop (Scottish Funding Council, 2006; Joint Information Systems Committee, 2006). Support services were key players with facilities managers in the project and led on the learning and teaching objectives. (Scottish Funding Council, 2006):

> The Saltire recognises the importance of flexible learning, supported self learning and similar learning concepts that are made possible by the electronic delivery of information. It goes further by making itself the starting point of the learning process and by encouraging 'deliberate socialising'. This includes accepting noise, combining learning environments with food and drink with the associated risk of damage to food and property. This approach places confidence in the students trusting them to identify what constitutes acceptable behaviour.

> The Saltire Centre could be seen as an unstructured 'educational soup' and, at nine times the size of the Learningcafe might not be easy to operate...the Centre offers a wide range of spaces to suit different people, learning methods and styles – from open and interactive to closed, structured study spaces. The large, open ground floor contrasts with the smaller scale top floor, and there is gradual shift from noisy front ground floor to quiet back top floor. The interior design, furniture, fixtures and fittings have been carefully selected to complement the range of spaces within the Centre.

The Joint Information and Systems Committee (JISC) supports 'education and research by promoting innovation in new technologies and by central support of ICT services'. JISC produced several reports on the design of learning environments including the development of Learning Commons. This work is culminating in the provision of a website using web 2.0 and multimedia content to provide data and case studies. The JISCinfokit was made available in early

2007 (JISC, 2007). What is particularly useful are the video comments from people who use the facilities and evaluations for each case study. This includes a detailed specification on a range of factors describing the Saltire Centre.

The Saltire Centre featured in the most high-profile report from JISC, 'Designing Spaces for Learning'. Like the SFC report it considers spaces that have high levels of tutor support, not just Learning Commons developments (JISC, 2006). Once again, the report concentrates on the social learning aspects of the Saltire Centre.

> The Saltire Centre is the social heart of the campus, a place where students meet and converse as well as study. The design of the Centre and the way in which it is administered recognise the social origins of learning and the need for interaction between learners on different levels and in different forms. It is also a self-regulating environment that places discussion on an equal footing with solitary learning – it is the policy of the University to give students responsibility over their learning environment as well as over the way in which they learn.

The concept of a Learning Commons is also defined:

> The Saltire Centre overtly encourages conversation as the basis for all learning, and seeks to engage the whole community as co-learners. Its social area is the hub of the campus where essential support services are also located. It is this supported approach to learning that Glasgow Caledonian University believes will lead to deeper understanding of concepts and ideas.

Most reports were in print before the Saltire opened; it was the scale of the project and the desire to consider how to put the student experience at the centre of the new building that attracted the attention. The Saltire Centre is a large-scale project, that took several years to open. The interest from the higher education sector in the Saltire Centre and the Learningcafe during the building and design process helped inform smaller Learning Commons developments in other organisations that we could then use for staff development and to inform our plans. Being reviewed by the research projects also helped us have conversations and start to embed a myriad of ideas into the development of the Learning Commons.

Background information on Glasgow Caledonian University

Glasgow Caledonian University is a post-1995 university with 1,700 staff and 15,000 students, of whom 5 per cent are research students, 25 per cent are postgraduate and 28 per cent part time. Students are mainly drawn from west and central Scotland, but there are around 90 different nationalities and non-European Union student figures doubled last year to just under 1,000. Courses are mainly vocational courses in health, built and natural environment, computing, engineering, business and law. Most of the University's income comes from the Scottish Executives higher education teaching grant. The University has a new Principal and a new vision to develop the University and diversify its roles and sources of income. The Vision of the University is:

To be a socially entrepreneurial institution, committed to:

- contributing to the social and economic regeneration of the communities we serve, by providing learning, teaching and research opportunities;

- creating civic minded, employable graduates, who want to use their skills to make a positive difference to society;

- focusing more on raising Glasgow Caledonian University's profile and involvement in learning, teaching and research around the world;

- helping more people to access the University, by getting more practically involved with the communities we serve.

The Saltire Centre first year review

So, after 1 year of operation, and 3 years development, this is a good point to review the initial response from the students, assess the success against the expectations and trends for new learning spaces, and mention what will happen next at the Saltire Centre.

Previous work has looked at how learning and teaching theory supported the development and described the building (Watson, 2006; Howden, 2007).

The Saltire Centre set out to:

- create a campus hub;
- integrate student services;
- create a variety of study places;
- store and access information in efficient ways;

Each of these aspects needs consideration. The main features of the building will be considered against the data and information available on the building to assess the impact on the student experience but first, some general feedback from students on the Saltire Centre.

The Student Experience Project at Glasgow Caledonian University is a longitudinal study reviewing the student experience. Its initial focus was various student retention issues, but it now reviews most aspects of student life to improve the experience for every student. Just a few months after the Saltire Centre opened the Student Experience Project conducted a survey of all students with a significant return rate (Figure 5.3).

The most used facilities/services by students is the Saltire Centre – 95 per cent use the Centre (always/regularly/sometimes). Satisfaction levels are also the highest – 79 per cent of students find the Saltire Centre very satisfactory/satisfactory. Other high scoring facilities include catering (78 per cent use it with a 78 per cent very satisfied/satisfied rating), social spaces (70 per cent use, 52 per cent satisfaction rating) and private study space (73 per cent use, 56 per cent satisfaction rating) (Student Experience Project, 2006).

Some of these facilities blur a little as most are visible within the Saltire Centre and in some cases the Saltire is the main provider.

Figure 5.3   **Student Experience Project survey results**

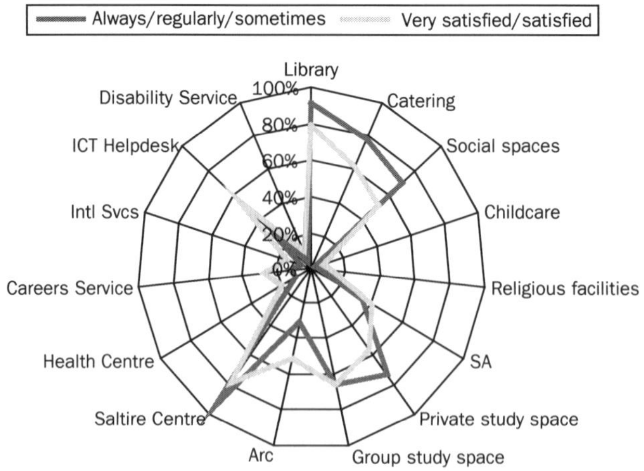

Reported use and satisfaction with facilities

Figure 5.4 Library facility survey results

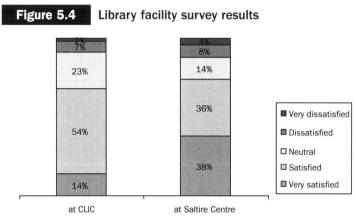

at CLIC   at Saltire Centre

Note: CLIC – Caledonian Library and Information Centre; the previous building.

The survey also asked about library facilities (Figure 5.4):

Satisfaction with library services

There has not been a significant change in other indicators of library services. Book issues, enquiries or information literacy evaluation and activities have not had an impact on this view. The main reason for this substantial rise in the very satisfied from 14 per cent to 38 per cent is probably to do with moving the library some 500 m closer to the teaching buildings and increasing accessibility to them (the Saltire Centre is attached to the two main blocks and the furthest main block is around 200 m away), the integration of services at the Base (the integrated services desk discussed in full later), plus the general improvement in the environment, the range of environments and the speed and form factor of the computing available to access information. It is therefore essential to maintain and develop the environment as well as the standard of computing and Internet access.

The neutral/dissatisfied/very dissatisfied number 32 per cent for CLIC (Caledonian Library and Information Centre), the old library, and 26 per cent for the Saltire Centre. In future surveys the old will probably not be compared with the new, but measures of satisfaction will still be sought. A more qualitative study amongst the dissatisfied might prove useful to determine issues but, again, as most indicators are remaining positive or stable it is likely to be around similar issues as those affecting the improvement in satisfaction levels: integrated support, environments, computer access; in effect Learning Commons developments, but ensuring a high proportion of quiet study area availablilty remains.

Create a campus hub

> 'The building is an architectural phenomena. The variety of space is well managed throughout...a warm and welcoming feeling.' *Comment from student survey*

The Saltire Centre aspires to embody the vision of the University and portray a dynamic social and intellectual hub for the University. This is created by the library, artwork, support of virtual and physical communication, architecture and interior design. The marketing opportunities for the University are extensive: for example, open events, school visits and in the use of images on the web and in prospectuses. It has also informed the development of similar facilities throughout Scotland and the rest of the world. Over 70 institutions have visited the Saltire Centre; this increases the University's standing with other stakeholders. The Saltire has hosted many high-profile events this year serving several academic departments. The mezzanine, which looks over the 2,500 m², with a 9 m high ceiling, group study area with 600 seats is adaptable for many events and exhibitions. The group study area has also been used for major events, such as degree shows for creative industry students including a fashion show catwalk. Most activities are less disruptive to routine activity and easily become part of the expectation of those visiting the area. For example, student clubs will set up stalls to raise awareness on issues beside people studying in groups. Many academics use the Saltire to promote the University to potential students and business guests, and will hold meetings alongside student groups.

All of this activity comes by basically saying yes to most requests and then working out the logistics. Requests come through the general enquiry system. It is likely that we will continue to explore the development of the Saltire Centre as a campus hub. It might be worth focusing more on how to make this a simpler activity for people and assisting more in the promotion, design and set-up of activities to encourage more events and stimulate the campus culture.

It is a specialist and complex space, used simply in a multitude of ways by different people at different times. It does not attempt to create its own brand, an obvious and inconsequential route pursued before, but rather support the concept of Glasgow Caledonian University and support whatever part of the University chooses to use it.

The idea of a campus hub adds to the Learning Commons value; this includes a very busy café providing food and drink to consume anywhere on level 0. Vicarious and accidental learning can take place alongside intended purposes. It also adds to the sense of place and encourages a variety of activities and freedom to use the technology and furniture to suit group and individual needs. The space is owned by the people, not the service providers. Having the Learning Commons as the campus hub is a positive coalition of activities.

Integrate student services

'Love it.' *Comment from student survey*

As the Saltire Centre developed, activities crucial to success, known as the 'Student Access to Service Project' were in progress. This reviewed all services and systems with a view to making them more student-focused and more available. A model of support relying on web services, as the basic mode for information and transactions, also formed the basis of a hierarchy of support within the Saltire Centre.

Step model:

- student homepage;
- quick information kiosks;
- plasma screen information;
- self issue and return points for books at all entrances;
- the base (the name of the support desk area); information and service reception, plus roving support and telephone support information appointments and drop-ins with specialist services;
- all interaction in a joint environment.

This encourages self service or mutual support in the Learning Commons with easy access to further support as it is needed.

The Base answers the basic questions that were previously answered by specialist services in different offices throughout the University. It also makes appointments and referrals to specialist services. The services available include: library services, IT systems (virtual learning environment, etc), registry, subject librarians, careers, effective learning service, funding, wellbeing advice, international student support, student disability service, research collections, ICT skills, counselling, nursery and chaplains. The Base is located on the large ground floor group study area. This location enables a supported collaborative environment within the group study area. The Base is supplemented throughout the building by Base staff roving around the different learning environments offering support.

Learner Support conducted a survey of students during the first week and repeated the survey a few months later. In both surveys, over 90 per cent of students were satisfied with the integration of services at the Base. All indicators declined slightly in the second survey but the Base maintained the best levels of satisfaction. There is very little feedback or comment on service provision from other sources such as 'Your Views', the online complaints, compliments and suggestions system. This is thought to be because the Base ran as a pilot project in the previous building and students regard the integration of all services in this way as a perfectly natural positive way to operate, rather than being referred to distinct enquiry desks.

Most of the specialists now work in the Saltire Centre using the shared consulting rooms and the seminar room. This is seen as an important aspect of student support. During the consultation with students on their experience of support services, there were several comments about feeling they were interrupting the service providers in their offices and they would prefer the space to feel like shared space and be in familiar territory. This formed the basis of the use of consulting rooms, with other administrative work performed in the open-plan office, which is not used for face-to-face support. Again there is little information on the effectiveness of this move other than an appreciation of the holistic approach offered by the Base; which is obviously there to support students as its soul purpose. There is no data available yet on how the changes have affected access to specialist services other than the increased number of enquiries that the Base answers for all specialist services operating over 72 hours a week.

Some new Learning Commons in the UK, such as the Learning Gateway at St Martin's College, Carlisle, place more emphasis on faculty and external trainers as well as students using facilities. Open-plan areas with technology are available, but rooms with collaborative technology are also provided. They have assistants dedicated to laying out rooms and ensuring people know how to use the technology. Saltire Centre support is not as focused as this mainly because we have kept the technology very much to devices that people have general access to; desktop computers, plasma screens, laptops, digital still and video cameras. More could be done at the Saltire Centre to signal how the technology could be used for group projects through more intense groupings of furniture and technology and experimenting with this is being considered. It is thought that this would necessitate some further review of how roving support is operating and what services roving support offer. For example, if we created a multimedia cluster; it would be good if all Base staff could be trained on using scanners and laminating rather than relying on a distinct team.

Create a variety of study places

'Love the beanbags – perhaps there should be more. On a busy day it will be difficult to get one free.' *Comment from student survey*

The Saltire Centre is the biggest provider of group and quiet study areas in the University (Figures 5.5 and 5.6). As

Figure 5.5 Group study area

already discussed, in the Student Experience Project survey the University meets expectations for group study but not for quiet study. The same survey asked about satisfaction

Figure 5.6 Group study area

levels with the course or programme. Group work opportunities and opportunities to mix socially are more or less satisfactory, but also not as important as other aspects of the course such as access to tutors. There are probably lots of positive and negative reasons for this perception and this needs further exploration to determine the main drivers and if more or better cooperative and collaborative learning environments would change this, or if it is related to cultural learning style factors or particular pedagogic plans.

Consultation on the building happened using various fora. A cross-campus group known as the 'creative academics' also looked at the building. This group had a series of 'creative lunches', brainstorming ideas by looking at symbols and metaphors to describe the intended ambience and values in the Saltire Centre. Various ideas were presented based on the idea of passports, lego, and broken chains; the idea leading to the most fruitful discussion centred around the idea of a village centre. This seemed to fit the ideas around a sense of place and the size of the Saltire Centre in relation to the rest of the campus. They had considerable input into the idea of a range of technology-assisted environments. Glasgow Caledonian is one of the first universities in the UK to provide high quality open access group study facilities. The students obviously welcome this provision and perhaps still regard it as innovative, as there is little to compare it with in their experience.

Learner Support repeated a survey on basic indicators of satisfaction with the Saltire Centre during the first year. The first survey acts as a week one benchmark when people just enthused about most aspects of the facilities. A similar picture emerges when you look at the data in association with comments received to that presented by the SEP survey. The demand for computers is not met, with a fall from over 90 per cent to 60 per cent being satisfied in the second survey; quiet study areas are perceived as not quiet enough, perhaps because occupancy rates and computer use within them are consistently high; and the group study areas are also popular but computer access for groups is not sufficient, with satisfaction falling from 98 per cent to 79 per cent. There is also a view amongst support staff that the initial promotion of these areas as silent did not aid this result. That satisfaction with quiet areas shifted from 72 per cent to 50 per cent. Despite increasing provision on all of these aspects compared to the previous library, the Saltire Centre has a problem of increasing demand putting pressure on the ability to deliver the service desired by different students.

Students are less happy with private study. Looking at this and other data, it would appear that private study is one of the main reasons for a lack of satisfaction with the Saltire Centre. The amount of quiet study space has not been reduced. The student consultation, during the design period, indicated a desire for larger desks with computer access and task lighting. This looks great and offers a high quality individual study environment, but in practice a large desk can also encourage wandering groups seeking out a computer to stray into the quiet areas. The quiet areas are generally kept quiet but this is also part of the problem. The odd heavy hand on a keyboard can be a major irritation. Silent keyboards might offer some respite. Some areas on each floor are now desktop PC free (although laptops can still be plugged in).

The survey reviewed various aspects of IT provision. Despite over 90 per cent claiming access to a computer at home or work, computer availability scores high with over 95 per cent indicating it was important/very important. Unfortunately, just over 53 per cent were satisfied/very satisfied. Occupancy rates for every environment and facility in the Saltire are much higher than in the previous library. There are more computers available too, but the demand is not met. There is a view that the faster computers and the well-designed environment are increasing demand and therefore frustration amongst students not able to log on whether they are cooperating, collaborating or studying alone with colleagues in a physical group or online. Most of the desk furniture in the Saltire Centre offers people the ability to plug in their own laptops and other devices, with a choice of wired or wireless networking. There are more people using their own devices in the building and sharing them with colleagues, so there is more demand for the full range of environments on offer, but this sets its own tensions as the previous seasonal peaks of activity are now high semester-long plateaus for all activities. The view that the space could be flexible, with more quiet individual study at exam time, has not proved to be achievable as the demand for group study or computers does not diminish. The building has excelled at providing opportunities for technology to be available no matter what the learning situation. Unfortunately, demand is also higher and the building is struggling to cope with the demand created.

Consequently, revision of using some of the upper floors flexibly is in progress; round study tables from the upper floors have been relocated to new group study locations on level 0 and 1, with more bench tables going onto the upper floors and more side screens being used.

Store and access information in efficient ways

'Most impressive building I have been in a while; loads of gadgets; could be a tourist attraction.' *Comment from student survey*

219

From the perspective of the Learning Commons view, the Saltire Centre has created a space for people rather than a space for collections but information resources are available online and physically in the immediate vicinity. Two thirds of the books and all the paper journals on campus are in open access compact storage. The remaining third of the most frequently used reading list books are on, mainly low level, open shelves. There are no major humanities collections and no large legacy paper journal collections. Two thirds of the library budget is spent on information accessed electronically. It seems natural to reduce the prominence of paper resources in the building to the benefit of the range and comfort of the environments for people. Like most universities in the UK, there are concerns over the prominence of Google and an over-reliance on the first few hits of an infinite list of results. As is well known, Google is also developing to support the academic community. The University needs to review its journal bundle deals and faculty support services. This could be by supporting students via informal support in the Learning Commons, by a member of the Base team or a subject librarian and via integration with the curriculum to work on the best value from purchased information and information evaluation skills.

Conclusion and next steps

The various sources of feedback and data available to us have led to a very active first year of reviewing our opening profile and planning for future developments. So in UK terms, the Saltire provides a leading example of a Learning Commons. Help is holistic but could develop to be more proactive and linked to pedagogy as well as general support. The technology available is mainstream and simple. Some more challenging technology clusters could help support specific pedagogic aims but again the Base would have to

Figure 5.7 Examples of Saltire Centre interior design

(a)

change and develop in this direction. Delivery of services online is fully exploited to support the individual or the group working in the Learning Commons; again more

Figure 5.7 *(Cont'd)*

(b)

proactive support could increase the effectiveness of resources and this should be explored. Further studies should analyse how each academic department uses the building, the

Figure 5.7 *(Cont'd)*

(c)

base and the various environments with technology. This will help align developments with the needs of each school.

The development of the Saltire Centre is aligned to the Learning and Teaching Strategy of the University. The development team are represented on the main groups planning learning and teaching approaches and resources.

It is the intention this year to produce a range of data at a teaching department level for support activities to discuss the development of practice in line with trends reported in national strategic documents and the University learning and teaching strategy. The location, interior design (Figure 5.7 a–c), café and architecture create an exciting modern environment supporting a sense of place and encourages student to come to the hub of the campus and engage with support services, information sources and each other. The Saltire Centre is well on the way to meeting the high expectations of its developers reported by the leading commentators (JISC, 2006; Scottish Funding Council, 2006; Boone, 2003).

References and further reading

Beards, D. (2006) 'Spaces for Learning'. Keynote address, SFC Conference, Stirling, Scotland.

Boone, M.D. (2003) 'Monastery to marketplace', *Library Hi Tech*, 21(3): 358–67.

Howden, J. (2003) 'Real@Caledonian: the Learning Café', *Serial*, 17(1): 15–18.

Howden, J. (2007) 'The Saltire Centre' *New Review of Academic Librarianship*, 12(2): 127–133.

JISC (2006) *Designing Spaces for Effective Learning: A Guide to 21st Century Learning Space Design*. JISC e-Learning and Innovation Team, HECFC conference 2006.

JISC (2007) 'Planning and designing technology rich learning spaces'. Available at *http://www.jiscinfonet. ac.uk/infokits/learning-space-design* (accessed June 2007).

Logan, L. Starr, S. (2005) 'Library as place: results of a Delphi study', *Journal of the Medical Library Association*, 93(3): 315–326.

Scottish Funding Council (2006) *Spaces For Learning: A Review of Learning Spaces in Further and Higher Education*. London: SFC/AMA Alexi Marmot Associates.

Student Experience Project (2006) Report. Glasgow: Glasgow Caledonian University, internal document.

Watson, L. (2006) 'The Saltire Centre at Glasgow Caledonian University', *Sconul Focus*, 37(Spring): 4–11.

6

Transforming library space for student learning: the Learning Commons at Ohio University's Alden Library

Gary A. Hunt

The Learning Commons at Ohio University's Alden Library (for information, see *http://www.library.ohiou.edu/serv/ lc/index.html*) is a collaboration between the University Libraries, Computer Services, Dining Services and University College. Its mission is to provide a modern learning environment that merges information resources with state of the art technologies in a central service point dedicated to the enhancement of teaching and learning for the entire academic community. Opened in the autumn quarter of 2004 (with a second phase added in autumn 2005), the Learning Commons occupies 28,000 sq. ft of renovated space on the second floor of the main library.

Alden Library's Learning Commons is widely regarded on our campus as one of the most successful renovation projects undertaken in recent years. It has had a transformative impact on the library in terms of increased user traffic, positive publicity, greater visibility, enhanced credibility and perceived contribution to student learning. Many of the lessons learned from building and operating the Learning Commons have influenced planning for a comprehensive $20 million renovation of Alden Library over the next 6 years. As the highly successful product of a campus partnership between several different organisational units, the Learning Commons has led to new thinking about how the library can best position itself strategically to serve the university's mission and compete for increasingly scarce resources.

In this case study I will: (1) provide some background information about the project, including its origins, conceptual framework, major components and anticipated benefits; (2) describe the planning process, which involved a unique collaboration between the library and several external units with little prior history of intensive cooperation; (3) discuss the outcomes of the project in terms of what has worked well, what needs improvement, and the results of formal assessment efforts; (4) describe plans for a 'Faculty Commons' modeled on the successes of the Learning Commons; and (5) discuss how both experiences have shaped our thinking about the future use of library facilities.

Project background and conceptual framework

Ohio University is a comprehensive, state-assisted institution of higher learning classified by the Carnegie Foundation as 'Doctoral/Research University Extensive' with over 19,500 students on its main campus in Athens, Ohio and 7,500 on five regional campuses. The University's main library, the Vernon R. Alden Library, is located in the centre of the Athens campus. More than a million visitors a year use the library to access its 2.5 million books and rich array of electronic resources. The University Libraries, which include two other facilities in Athens and five libraries on the University's regional campuses, hold membership in the Association of Research Libraries.

When planning for the Learning Commons began in early 2003, Alden Library was already the home of several physically and administratively separate services, each of which provided support for student learning. The Reference and Instruction Department (located on the fourth floor) was dedicated to helping students gather information from a variety of resources, both print and electronic, for use in their research, writing and other coursework. Reporting to Computer Services, the Instructional Support Lab (located on the second floor) was the largest and most heavily used open access computer lab on campus. University College's Academic Advancement Center (located on the first floor) offered academic support services (including tutoring, computer skills development and academic guidance) to all undergraduates. Also affiliated with University College, the Student Writing Center (whose director was located on the first floor but with operations dispersed throughout the building) provided writing assistance to both undergraduates and graduate students through one-on-one tutoring and by means of computer-based tools for improving writing skills.

The central concept of the Learning Commons was to physically combine all of these offerings into one integrated but multifaceted teaching and learning facility. Yet it took some time for this concept to come into clear focus.

For several years the library had been accumulating funds to renovate the second floor of Alden Library, which by 2003 was one of the last major areas not to have been substantially updated since the building opened in 1968. It is one of two entrance-level floors in a seven storey, 285,000 sq. ft facility, and our gate counts showed that traffic was about evenly divided between the two entrances on floors 2 and 4. So from a programmatic standpoint it was important to locate popular, heavily used services and resources in this space...but which ones, exactly?

In January 2003, the Dean of Libraries convened a task force (called the 'Core Team') to answer this question and develop a general plan for renovating the floor. Once the key components were identified, architects would be hired to refine the program and design the new area. From the beginning the dean stressed the need for the Core Team to approach its work with an open mind: to consider all of the options with an aim to achieve the 'highest and best' use of the space, without regard for territoriality, even if it meant major relocations of existing departments and personnel. With this in mind the Core Team soon faced an awkward reality: the most popular service already located on the second floor did not 'belong' to the library but instead consisted of the open access computer lab operated by campus IT. Even from a purely aesthetic perspective, it made no sense to spend more than $2 million renovating the rest of the floor while leaving this piece unaddressed.

The best solution was not simply to renovate the computer lab *in situ* but rather to make it an integral part of what came to be called the 'Learning Commons'. Accomplishing this merger presented many challenges, as will be described in the discussion below about the planning process. But once we became open to the idea that certain 'non-library' functions might be logical partners in creating a destination space for student learning, the path began to come into view. As mentioned above the university's Academic Advancement Center was also housed in the library, but in an out-of-the-way space on a subterranean floor. In addition to providing tutoring in mathematics, writing and study skills, the AAC operated the university's only open access multimedia lab. Although it was a popular service supported by a talented part-time manager, the lab was open for limited hours that did not include evenings or weekends.

In the end, there was not enough space to accommodate the entire Advancement Center on the second floor of Alden, so we elected to relocate only the Student Writing Center while creating a new multimedia lab with input from the ACC lab manager. (A full unification is slated to occur as the building master plan is implemented over the next several years.)

As the general plan for the Learning Commons began to take shape, the Core Team sought additional input from students, faculty and library staff through the use of focus groups, standing advisory committees and a series of 'town meetings'. When students were given a list of potential resources and services that might be located in the new space, the highest ranked item was access to computers and other technology, followed by reference librarians and group studies.

Program components

Eventually a consensus emerged that the Learning Commons would include 14 major components, each of which is depicted in the schematic drawing shown in Appendix A.

Reference and instruction department

Anchoring the information resources component of the Learning Commons is the Library's Reference and Instruction Department. All 10 reference librarians were relocated to the second floor along with a scaled down reference collection of about 15,000 volumes. (About 33 per cent of the original collection was either transferred to the general stacks in Alden or placed in remote storage.) We viewed reference service as essential to support the kind of learning, teaching and collaborative activity envisioned for the facility. It is here that students can receive direct assistance with finding information appropriate to their needs while at the same time becoming knowledgeable users of research databases and other online information resources. Reference librarians would be able to work collaboratively with Writing Center staff to assist students at all stages of the research and writing process, either one-on-one or in small group sessions.

Computer concourse

As the major IT partner in the Learning Commons, what was formerly the open access computer lab occupies a large area adjacent to the Reference and Instruction Department. All 70 workstations in this area, along with 24 others located throughout the floor, have been configured with oversized desktops so they can be easily used by two or more patrons at a time – a situation that is actually quite common. Along with the standard five-caster office chairs placed at each workstation, there are 40 smaller folding chairs with matching upholstery located throughout the floor, allowing students to adapt the workspace for their own needs In addition to the wide array of licensed software and productivity tools, computers in the lab offer the same information resources accessible from library workstations. Self-service zone printing is available from six release stations in the Learning Commons and 14 others located throughout the building. Scanning is offered here as well as in the Multimedia Center (see below).

| **Figure 6.1** | Computer concourse |

Central service desk

A central service desk is staffed jointly by Library and IT personnel. It has been designed to accommodate interaction between reference librarians and patrons as well as to provide software assistance and technical support for computer users. While the staff are separately responsible to the Library and campus IT, each working from their own section of the service desk, they have been cross-trained to deal with a range of issues. Thirty-two laptops are available for check-out from the Service Desk for use anywhere in the building, which has been equipped with a wireless network. IT personnel can also configure student owned laptops to access the wireless network.

Library workstations

Twenty-four library workstations are located in five clusters near the Park Place entrance, the central service desk, the

Figure 6.2 The central service desk

reference reading area, and the Student Writing Center. Just as the Computer Concourse workstations provide access to library information resources, the Library Workstations are configured with most of the popular applications software covered by campus-wide licensing agreements. From the user's perspective there is no longer a distinction between various public workstations in the library. Instead, there is a 'universal image' across all 300 workstations in Alden Library creating a common experience of information and capabilities throughout the building. More than anything else this has contributed to a large increase in our gate counts since the Learning Commons opened in autumn 2004.

User seating and study space

An array of seating options for users are available throughout the floor, including 29 four-seat study tables and 38 lounge

Figure 6.3 User seating and study space

seats accommodating up to 154 patrons. Separate zones have been created to accommodate different user preferences (e.g. teamwork and social interactivity vs privacy and quiet study) in ways that do not conflict with one another. Counting all available seats (including those at workstations, group studies, the instruction lab, and the cafe) the Learning Commons has a capacity for almost 400 patrons.

Public printing

The Library and campus IT collaborated to develop a uniform policy and technical solution that supports self-service zone printing from all workstations in Alden Library as well as those in several open access computer labs located elsewhere on campus. It is managed by 'P-Counter', one of several available enterprise print management systems, which had already been selected by campus IT at the time the Learning Commons project began. The system is configured to allow a quota of 50 free prints every month, after which a charge of 5 cents is made for each additional print. Charges are recorded in the Registrar's Office and billed to each student on a monthly basis, with the resulting revenues distributed to the unit where the printing occurred to offset costs for consumable supplies. There are six print release stations in the Learning Commons, with 14 additional sites located elsewhere in Alden Library. More than 80 per cent of all printing using the P-Counter system occurs in the library, with most of that amount generated in the Learning Commons.

Student writing center

The Student Writing Center was moved to a prominent location near the Park Place entrance, providing the organisational hub for students to meet with tutors. Two clusters with a total of 10 Library Workstations are located in the immediate vicinity, and office space has been provided for the Coordinator of Writing Tutoring.

Park Place entrance

A key goal of the renovation was to provide a more open, logical and inviting orientation for users entering Alden Library from Park Place. Large plasma screens controlled from the Reference Department display information about library resources and events, instructional sessions, room availability, etc. The entrance design incorporates a new handicap access ramp constructed as a separate project by the University's Facilities Management Department.

Presentation room

The J. Leslie Rollins Conference Room for Student Leadership is designed for groups of up to 12 students to practice group presentations and conduct meetings using technology typically available in corporate settings. In addition to the technology installed in each of the smaller group studies (see below) this room is equipped with an interactive whiteboard, DVD/VCR player, document camera, adjustable lighting system and a drop down screen. Furnishings are more upscale, with natural wood finishes and high back upholstered chairs.

Library instruction lab

A 30-seat Library Instruction Lab allows reference librarians and subject bibliographers to teach information competency skills either tailored for specific courses or as stand alone sessions advertised through campus media outlets. Equipped

Figure 6.4 The library instruction lab

with 30 workstations, two ceiling projectors, a document camera and pull-down screens, the lab has been designed with tiered seating to allow good visibility from all locations. It has also been designed with glass walls so that the teaching activities are showcased to the public in almost a theatrical, marquee-like setting. In this way we emphasise the important message that librarians are a vital part of the teaching and learning process. When the lab is not being used for instruction it is open to the public, thereby increasing the number of available workstations on the floor.

Adaptive technology room

The Lynn Shostack Adaptive Technology Room (which was already present on the floor) was renovated and upgraded for use by students with disabilities, particularly the vision impaired. It features state of the art technology for enlarged screen viewing, voice output readers and Braille printing.

Group study rooms

The Learning Commons includes eight group study rooms where students can collaborate on group projects, consult with librarians and tutors, and practice their presentations. These rooms can accommodate up to 10 people and are all equipped with a table, chairs, marker boards, A/C power outlets, network connectivity and an installed ceiling projector. Students using their own laptop or one that has been checked out from the service desk can give PowerPoint presentations, access the web or use standard productivity software to share documents, images or other content in a group setting.

Figure 6.5 A group study room

Figure 6.6 The multimedia lab

Multimedia center

An open access multimedia lab is available for use by students in any discipline while also being available for instructional use by both tutorial and library staff. Equipped with 12 state of the art workstations (both Mac and PC platforms) connected to various multimedia devices, the centre is supervised by a half-time graduate assistant with the help of several highly trained student employees. Students are able to import analogue video, convert it to digital video for manipulation on the computer and export it to a storage medium (CD, DVD, VCR) or as a video file for use in such products as web pages, E-portfolios, and PowerPoint presentations. A ceiling mounted projector enables users to display their work on a large screen from any workstation. Not only does this allow them to view and critique their work on the large screen, it also serves as a kind of 'advertising' for other students in the Learning Commons who may have never attempted to use multimedia. Examples from student work are also captured (with their permission) to create large format posters that are mounted throughout the area.

Café BiblioTech

What had been an unappealing vending machine area was replaced by a tastefully appointed café offering a well-selected line of hot and cold beverages and light food items. It is operated by the university Dining Services under a revenue-sharing agreement with the library. The name 'Café BiblioTech' was selected in a student contest that attracted more than 300 entries. Like all public areas in Alden Library, the café is served by a wireless network. It is common to find students eating in the café while using their own laptops or one borrowed at the Learning Commons service desk.

Figure 6.7 Café BiblioTech

Anticipated educational benefits

Libraries have always played an important role in supporting learning outside the classroom, but the Alden Library Learning Commons has taken that to a new level by adapting a major facility at the heart of campus to match today's learning and working environment.

Following are some of the most important anticipated educational benefits we hoped to achieve.

- **Concentrate technology resources where they can be widely shared.** There is a broad sense of ownership in the library. As its name implies, the Learning *Commons* is accessible to all members of the academic community rather than being limited to one group or discipline. It offers students a large concentration of computers on which to undertake research, writing and project production. Investing in this kind of facility helps to counteract the fragmentation of technology resources on our campus that had too often impeded learning in the past.

- **Create a holistic service environment for students.** The Learning Commons offers more seamless and efficient service for students, who are able to consult with librarians, work with tutors, and receive skilled assistance with their computing needs in a single convenient location. We anticipated there would be unique synergies to be found when librarians work collaboratively with technology specialists, instructors, and other learning professionals in the same physical space.

- **Support group work and project-based learning activities.** Traditionally libraries and computer labs have both been oriented toward the individual user. However the Learning Commons provides several well-equipped collaborative study areas of different sizes, a presentation room and a multimedia centre. All workstations on the floor are oversised to easily accommodate two or even three users at a time. In fact the entire area has been designed for group work in an atmosphere that promotes purposeful interaction between students, librarians, instructors and technology specialists.

- **Increase students' ability to develop their presentation skills and produce technology enhanced projects.** Although several academic departments at the university had well-equipped multimedia labs restricted for use by their own students, there was a need for a public access multimedia lab where students from all disciplines can work on technology enhanced projects with assistance from trained staff.

- **Permit extended hours of service.** The renovation has made it possible for the second floor of Alden to be operated in a cost effective manner when the rest of the building is closed. By concentrating most of the resources needed by students (especially undergraduates) in one location, they are able to work productively following their own schedules, which increasingly extend beyond the traditional library hours.

Planning process: a journey from mutual suspicion to successful collaboration

As mentioned earlier, all of the elements that were eventually combined into the Learning Commons had been physically housed in the library building for many years. But because they belonged to different organisational entities, each with their own reporting lines, budgets and personnel, there had been little active collaboration let alone any history of major joint undertakings. In many ways they found themselves working at cross purposes, with less than optimum results in terms of service quality.

For example networking support was provided by campus IT, which also managed the library's central server. But the library had long since found it necessary to develop its own systems department, which was responsible for the local area network, servers, about 200 public workstations plus all staff computing needs. The 100 workstations in the open access computer lab, by contrast, were separately managed, configured with their own image and providing different software than those in the rest of the library. Perhaps the most confusing aspect from the user's point of view was the different policies on public printing. It was available on library workstations at a cost of 7 cents per page. But the computer lab offered unlimited free printing to students. Not surprisingly this led to a great deal of wasteful printing and unsustainable costs for Computer Services, which prior to the opening of the Learning Commons was spending more than $80,000 a year on paper and toner alone. Students quickly learned to do their research on library workstations, download the results or save them to their account on a university server, then physically move to the computer lab in order to print them out.

In retrospect, there was a remarkable sense of disengagement from many students who were present in the building. From the perspective of some librarians and library administrators, services such as the Academic Advancement and Student Writing Centers were regarded as interlopers in 'our' space. It's true that they attracted students, but unless those students were entering the building to use 'our' resources there was little attempt to engage them. On the contrary they were apt to be seen as a nuisance, creating too much noise and interfering with more 'serious' library users.

On a larger campus these issues might have been addressed by creating a separate undergraduate library or even an integrated student learning centre of the kind found at the University of Arizona or the University of Georgia. That was not an option in our case, and so forced to continue cohabiting the same building we chose to collaborate with our non-library partners to create a new kind of learning environment for students.

In spring 2003, the Dean of Libraries created a 'core team' to oversee planning for the Learning Commons. Chaired by the Associate Dean of Libraries, this group included representatives from all three major partners in the venture (the University Libraries, Computer Services and University College) together with a project manager from Facilities

Planning. The Core Team was given two overarching responsibilities: to work with architects to create a program and physical design for the Learning Commons, and to develop an operating plan to determine how the facility would function once it had opened to the public (see Appendix B: Planning process). The Core Team functioned as the guiding force in the enterprise, making sure the timelines were being met, resolving key issues that needed to be addressed, identifying the necessary resources, preparing budgets, seeking financial support and serving as liaison to the three executive sponsors. The Core Team met at least once every week during the planning phase from April 2003 to September 2004 and for the first few months of actual operation in the autumn quarter of 2004. Other meetings were held as needed to handle specific tasks, such as the selection of architects. (Although its composition has changed, the group still meets on a monthly basis to address various operational issues as they arise.)

Reporting to the Core Team were three 'functional teams' for technology, services and communications (see Appendix B). Many of the functional team members were also part of the Core Team, but others were drawn from the three partnering organisations as well as from University Communications and Marketing. The Technology Team focused on hardware and software selection, networking requirements, image management, print management, authentication, metering and maintenance. The Services Team worked on developing an operating plan that would address such matters as service desk functions, staffing, training, and hours of opening. As planning went forward a Communications Team was established to keep staff informed about the Learning Commons, provide construction updates, develop publicity for the autumn 2004 opening, and design its web presence.

Throughout the planning process we sought input from several other sources in addition to the original partners. A few examples are cited below.

- We created a **Learning Commons Advisory Committee** consisting of campus IT leaders and faculty members involved in technology enhanced teaching and learning initiatives. Input from this latter group of 'early adopters' was especially helpful in planning the Multimedia Center, which has become an important part of the Learning Commons.

- Knowing that students would resist moving from unlimited free printing to a fee-based system, we negotiated the specific quotas and charges with the **Student Senate.** (It helped that one of the student members of the University Library Committee was also a member of the Student Senate and an enthusiastic supporter of the Learning Commons.) This allowed us to educate student opinion leaders in advance on the reasons for the new printing charges; and giving them a voice in deciding what the actual charges would be helped to blunt criticism when they were implemented in autumn 2004.

- We worked with the student dominated **Dining Services Development Committee** to plan the layout, menu offerings and other amenities for the Café Bibliotech (which was completed in phase 2 and opened in autumn 2005).

Obstacles to cooperation

Throughout the planning process I sometimes needed to remind participants that 'collaboration is never easy'. Not only had there been little experience working together, but at some point it almost seemed that we spoke different 'languages'. Both the librarians and the IT professionals were committed to providing good service, but their ideas about what constituted good service were in some ways poles apart. There was also an initial lack of trust that needed to be overcome before real progress could be made.

In terms of what might be called their 'service philosophy', the computer lab staff, their managers and those who provided technical support were mainly concerned about the dependability of the hardware and systems for which they were responsible. Were there enough functioning computers, printers and other pieces of equipment to meet the demand? Could they be counted on to perform properly, without interruptions or slow downs? Could technical failures be quickly diagnosed and effectively handled when they did occur? Were there adequate security measures in place to prevent users from damaging equipment or compromising the systems? In other words the IT partners were primarily focused on the *reliability of service,* defined for the most part in technical terms.

Professional librarians, however, view themselves as educators with a service philosophy based on meeting the needs of the individual user. Those of us coming from a public services background were accustomed to monitoring the satisfaction of our users and trying to determine (through surveys and focus groups for example) what we could be doing to improve service offerings. From our point of view the IT professionals seemed reluctant to take on new roles or try new approaches, especially when doing so might distract from their primary duty, which was to keep the system running smoothly. From their perspective, librarians were naïve or uninformed about the demands this entailed.

There were three key issues that initially divided the library and IT partners. First was the 'check on' practice employed by the computer lab, which required students to identify themselves at the entrance and be assigned to a specific workstation. This served several purposes, including security and software license monitoring, but the main reasons for the policy were to limit access to enrolled students and control the time each was able to spend on a machine during periods of peak demand. In fact there were times when demand for computers did exceed the supply and students had to wait their turn at the lab entrance. As software productivity tools and free printing were available only in the lab, it was common for it to be crowded when workstations elsewhere in the building were relatively underutilised.

From the library's point of view, the best solution was to configure all public workstations in the same way – with the same resources, software tools and printing capabilities – not just in the new Learning Commons but throughout the entire building. We argued there should be a single 'image' appearing on every machine, controlled by the library's Systems Department. This would increase the overall number of available machines from around 100 in the old computer lab to more than 300, eliminating the need to cordon off the lab and ration access to computers by a check-on system. It would also promote what has been called a 'universal experience of information'. Patrons would no longer need to move from one computer to another in order to perform different tasks, which was confusing and inconvenient. For this integrated approach to work well it would be best for all public workstations to consist of the same hardware with the same specifications and on the same replacement schedule. Finally, the library systems staff felt strongly that under these circumstances they should be given responsibility for maintaining all machines in the building. Accustomed to supporting the old computer lab, IT personnel were reluctant to cede that job to the library when it had been incorporated into the Learning Commons.

Factors promoting cooperation

Several important factors eventually helped us overcome these divisions and move toward a shared vision of how the Learning Commons should operate. One was simply dissatisfaction with the status quo, especially the crisis over public printing and the financial drain it represented to Computer Services. The old computer lab was a crowded, unattractive facility with ageing technology that need to be replaced. If solving these problems required cooperation with the library, it was worth the effort to find common ground.

Another positive influence was what might be called the 'rhetoric of cooperation' that prevailed on our campus, where the atmosphere was filled with appeals from higher administration to break down organisational 'silos' and work together to achieve university-wide strategic priorities. All of us involved in the project knew we stood to benefit from a successful collaboration in terms of both political and financial support. In the end this perception turned out to be accurate, and it encouraged us to keep working together despite the difficulties.

The executive sponsors (see Appendix B) were asked to intervene on several occasions when members of the Core Team were unable to reach consensus. Their involvement was critical in resolving such issues as print management, control of the image and technical support. In particular, the Director of Computer Services drafted a so-called 'service level agreement' between CS and the Library that clarified these and other points in ways that allowed us to move forward.

I cannot emphasise enough the positive influence of conducting site visits to other libraries that had completed similar projects in the recent past. We made it a point to invite representatives from all the partners on these trips, which were paid for by the Library and generally involved using the university airplane to cover as much ground as possible in a single day. In all we visited six institutions in the course of planning for the Learning Commons, including: Georgia Tech, Emory, Indiana University, UNC Charlotte, Wayne State and Eastern Michigan. All of these visits helped to overcome resistance by encouraging people to think outside the box and focus more on the impressive results that could be achieved through cooperation and less on the potential threats that it posed.

It also helped matters that the Library had both money and space to devote to the project. For several years we had been accumulating funds through private gifts, endowment income, operating surpluses, internal loans and other sources for the purpose of renovating the second floor of Alden Library. For their part the non-library partners knew they would benefit from occupying a beautifully renovated area in a better location equipped with new furniture and state of the art technology – all of which was being provided at little or no cost to them. Needless to say, this was a powerful inducement for them to cooperate with the library and accept its terms.

But probably the most important dynamic promoting cooperation was the influence of the Provost, who serves as the chief academic officer on our campus, overseeing the 10 colleges as well as both the library and central IT. From the beginning the library knew that the Learning Commons project was closely aligned with the Provost's own priorities, foremost of which was harnessing the power of technology to improve teaching and learning. At the end of the day the

Provost let it be known that he expected others to follow the library's lead.

Outcomes

Prior to the opening of the Learning Commons, Alden Library was experiencing gradually declining levels of use as measured by such indicators as gate counts, circulation of print materials and reference transactions. Those familiar with the annual statistics published by the Association of Research Libraries (ARL) will know that these are well-established national trends going back to the early 1990s. Like many academic libraries we had placed much emphasis on making our resources available over the web with the result that there were fewer reasons for patrons to visit the library itself. Students (especially undergraduates) who did come to Alden Library were often overwhelmed by its size and complexity. Many found the atmosphere formal and off-putting, especially compared to the more physically appealing suburban public libraries with which they were familiar. As one student said in a focus group conducted several years ago, 'I only go the library when I have to, and then I try to get in and out as soon as possible'.

The Learning Commons has transformed Alden Library into a popular destination place for students, who are visiting the building in much greater numbers and staying longer. Since the facility opened in September 2004 our gate counts have increased by approximately 60 per cent on an annual basis. Although we are not able to document the length of time patrons spend on average in the building, occupancy rates for both public workstations and group study rooms are very high, suggesting that they are being used for protracted periods in many cases. In short the library is much busier than ever before, not just on the second floor where the Learning Commons is located, but throughout the building. There is a palpable sense of energy and excitement that is a dramatic departure from the past.

The Learning Commons has generated terrific press coverage for the library, which enjoys a higher profile on campus while earning a reputation for innovation and openness to change. It has attracted visiting teams from more than 20 other academic libraries, not just in Ohio and surrounding states but from as far away as Georgia, Florida and California. Finally, the mere fact the library was able to forge productive partnerships across organisational boundaries must itself be counted as a positive outcome – one that has in turn led to increased credibility with campus decision makers. Despite the fact that it took longer to negotiate, required occasional intervention and probably cost more (at least in staff time), the collaboration has proven to be well worth the effort. It gained the library broader political support and generated more energy than would have resulted from a standalone project. Most significantly, the final product is clearly better for our students and other library users.

Assessment efforts

Several assessment tools have been used to measure the impact of the Learning Commons on user satisfaction and academic performance, as well as to solicit opinions on how it might be improved.

For example the Ohio University Libraries have participated in the LibQUAL survey developed and administered by the Association of Research Libraries on three occasions in 2001, 2002 and 2005. Results from the last two surveys provide indicators of perceived service quality before and after the Learning Commons opened in the autumn of 2004. In both years the library's highest score was on the 'Library as Place' dimension of perceived service quality, with an 'adequacy mean' score of 0.75 in 2002 vs 0.85 in 2005. Moreover, this dimension was the only one to demonstrate improvement between these two iterations of the survey. Of the five specific items included in the Library as Place dimension our score on the 2005 survey was especially high for 'Community space for group learning and group study' (with an adequacy mean of 1.31) and 'A comfortable and inviting location' (with an adequacy mean of 0.93). In fact these were the highest scores among all 22 recorded on the survey, a clear indication that the Learning Commons was meeting users' expectations in at least two areas.

Interestingly, when LibQUAL survey participants were asked to rate the library on how well it was providing 'Quiet space for individual activities' the response, while positive with an adequacy mean of 0.50, was significantly lower than for any of the other five items under the Library as Place dimension. These results suggest that while the Learning Commons seems to be satisfying the need for group learning, the library should do more to offer different kinds of spaces more conducive to individual study.

Since the Learning Commons opened we have administered one paper-based questionnaire as well as several web-based surveys designed to be completed in 60 seconds or less. Some have been quite general, asking respondents simply to tell us what they like and dislike about the facility. Others have sought input on specific topics, such as public printing, instant messaging services, and future expansion of the Multimedia Center. We have also conducted focus groups populated largely by students who also work part-time in the Learning Commons and can thus offer the perspective of well-informed users. Results from these assessment efforts have been informative, helping us to better understand what has worked well and what needs improvement in the Learning Commons. More will be said about the latter topic in the section below.

Impact of the Learning Commons on student academic success

In January 2006 the Provost asked the Dean of Libraries for data showing the impact of the Learning Commons on student engagement and academic success, with a particular focus on first-year students. While earlier surveys had been informative, the number of replies was too small to draw statistically valid conclusions. And as these surveys were all conducted anonymously there was no way to correlate the results with any extrinsic factors, including measures of student academic success (e.g. GPA and retention).

The most comprehensive single source of data on users of the Learning Commons comes from the print management system. When students print using P-Counter they are asked to enter their unique ID so the system can decrement their quota of 50 pages per month and then charge them for any printing that exceeds the quota. There are some obvious limitations to this data. It tells us who printed, where they printed and how much they printed, but nothing else about their use of Learning Commons resources: e.g. reference services, group studies or the writing centre.

It is also likely that the P-Counter data understates actual use of the Learning Commons, as some students presumably visit the facility without availing themselves of public printing. But the P-Counter data does provide the best available empirically valid proxy for the student population using the Learning Commons in a format that can be readily correlated with other factors.

In February 2006, the Library pulled all data on student printing from the 2005 autumn quarter, organising it according to where the printing had occurred: (1) the Learning Commons, (2) Alden Library locations other than the Learning Commons, (3) Computer Services Center, and (4) McCracken Hall. This user data was provided to Institutional Research to be correlated with such factors as gender, class rank, college, major, race/ethnicity, ACT scores, GPA and retention. Following are some highlights from their analysis.

A total of 9,237 students printed in the Learning Commons or about 47 per cent of the autumn 2005 Athens campus enrolled student population of 19,594. Given that the data almost certainly undercounts the number of students actually using the Learning Commons, we can safely conclude that more than half of the entire student body used the facility on one or more occasions during the quarter. Among undergraduates freshmen were the least likely to print in the Learning Commons, with utilisation rates increasing as students advance in class rank (Table 6.1).

Table 6.1   Learning Commons use by class rank (autumn 2005)

Class rank	No. of users	Percentage of total users	Enrollment	Percentage of Enrollment
Freshman	1,594	17.26%	4,367	36.50%
Sophomore	1,614	17.47%	3,612	44.68%
Junior	1,973	21.36%	3,346	58.97%
Senior	3,077	33.31%	5,293	58.13%
Masters	710	7.69%	1,823	38.95%
PHD	227	2.46%	724	31.35%
MED	42	0.45%	429	9.79%
Total	9,237	100.00%	19,594	47.14%

These utilisation rates may confirm the hypothesis that underclassmen (especially freshmen) are less engaged and less challenged academically than juniors and seniors. The difference becomes very noticeable between the sophomore and junior years. Another explanation for the lower use by freshmen and sophomores could be their greater access to computers in the residence halls. It is still noteworthy that more than 36 per cent of enrolled freshmen did print in the Learning Commons, even though they are the least represented group among undergraduates. Based on these results, the Library is exploring ways to promote greater use of the Learning Commons by freshmen and sophomores, including the creation of a full-time position for a 'First Year Experience Librarian'.

Analysis by race/ethnicity shows that among students of all ranks international students and Blacks were the most likely to use P-Counter in the Learning Commons, followed by Hispanics and Caucasians in that order. Asians and American Indians were least likely to participate (Table 6.2).

Table 6.2   Learning Commons use by race/ethnicity – all class ranks

Race/ethnicity	No. of users	Percentage of total users	Enroll-ment	Percentage of students	Percentage participation
American Indian	19	0.21%	50	0.26%	38.00%
Black	374	4.05%	728	3.72%	51.37%
Asian	84	0.91%	204	1.04%	41.18%
Hispanic	138	1.49%	282	1.44%	48.94%
Caucasian	8,107	87.77%	17,400	88.80%	46.59%
International	515	5.58%	930	4.75%	55.38%
Total	9,237	100.00%	19,594	100.00%	

The GPAs of all undergraduates using the Learning Commons are significantly higher than undergraduate students who did not use any of the facilities where P-Counter is available (Alden, CSC and Education). Interestingly the ACT scores for all groups are roughly the same; it is the academic performance that differs. In other words their *measured academic potential* is similar, but users of the Learning Commons are more likely to fulfil their potential (Table 6.3).

For freshmen there is an even larger difference in the mean GPAs of those using the Learning Commons and those who do not: 2.87 vs 2.71 (Table 6.4).

Table 6.3 Undergraduate ACT Scores and GPAs of Learning Commons users – all students (autumn 2005)

Location	No. observed	ACTC	Autumn 2005 GPA	Age
Learning Commons	8,258	23.47	3.02	20.64
Alden Library	6,522	23.29	3.02	20.66
Computer Center	1,632	23.27	2.99	21.60
McCracken	809	22.81	3.29	21.65
None (did not use P-Counter)	6021	23.50	2.89	20.47

Table 6.4 ACT Scores and GPAs of Learning Commons users – freshmen only (autumn 2005)

Location	No. observed	ACTC	Autumn 2005 GPA	Age
Learning Commons	1597	22.89	2.87	18.66
Alden Library	1194	22.56	2.84	18.69
Computer Center	127	22.57	2.74	18.92
McCracken	22	22.31	2.89	19.91
None (did not use P-Counter)	2243	23.20	2.71	18.79

Table 6.5 Freshman retention: Learning Commons users vs other groups (autumn 2005–winter 2006)

Location	No. observed	Retention rate
Learning Commons	1,441	94.99
Alden Library	1,080	95.58
Computer Center	117	92.13
McCracken	16	94.12
None (did not use P-Counter)	1,974	93.07

Retention rates for freshmen who used either the Learning Commons or Alden Library are significantly higher than students who did not use any of the facilities where P-Counter is available (Table 6.5).

From this data it is impossible to deduce a causal relationship between use of the Learning Commons and improved academic performance. It may simply be a matter of self-selection in which the better, more serious students choose to come to the Learning Commons in the first place. What we can say is that there is a positive correlation between use of the Learning Commons and academic performance. It offers a place for good students to work by themselves or with others in an atmosphere that makes learning look exciting and even fun. In a campus environment offering many ways (and places) for students to distract themselves, engaging them in activities that are related to success is a good thing in itself. As one younger reference librarian has said, 'The Learning Commons has made it look 'cool' for students to work hard'.

What works well?

Two and a half years after the Learning Commons opened its doors to the public, it is possible to draw some conclusions about what works well, what should have been done differently, and what still needs improvement. One of the outstanding features of the space is its attractive contemporary design, including the vibrant colours, dramatic use of light and a sweeping, uncluttered look. During the design development phase we asked the architect to create an area that would be appealing to today's undergraduates. The result is a radical departure from anything else seen in Alden Library, but one that the students love. At the time some of the staff members who were to inhabit the Learning Commons found the proposed colour palette a little extreme, but in retrospect it was very important to keep the focus on its primary users. My best advice to librarians who become involved in similar projects is to hire talented designers, provide them with general guidance on the ambience you want to create, and then trust their professional judgment!

Other design features that have proven to be especially successful include the oversized workstation seating, the extensive use of glass walls throughout the space, and the integrated central service desk. As mentioned earlier the workstation furniture was custom built to accommodate two or even three users at a time. In addition, we supplemented the five-caster seating with half again as many light weight, collapsible four-caster chairs stacked in various places throughout the floor where they can be easily moved into place when needed for this purpose. As a result of these design choices it is very common to find two or more students working collaboratively at the same computer.

Although glass walls are more expensive than standard drywall construction, the results have been well worth the investment. Not only does the glass present a clean, modern look; it allows even the most casual visitor to see at a glance all the activity occurring in the group studies, the instruction lab and the student writing centre. It also serves an important purpose by making learning visible while at the same time advertising our contributions to learning. For many years librarians had been appearing before classes or giving workshops on information seeking skills. But until now, most of this high value-added work was occurring behind closed doors, visible only to the participants themselves. The instructional lab in the Learning Commons, by contrast, has been designed to showcase our librarians teaching in an almost theatrical, marquee-like setting.

The configuration of the central service desk has increased the visibility of reference services, which are now the very first thing patrons see when entering the building. This layout together with all the other attractions located on the floor has helped to maintain our reference statistics at a steady level in contrast to the declines experienced at most other large academic libraries. The 'one-stop shopping' concept embodied in the Learning Commons has been very successful – almost too successful at times when the facility becomes too crowded!

Another major reason for the success of the Learning Commons is that from day 1 it was equipped with state of the art technology – probably the best available to students anywhere on campus outside of a few restricted access departmental labs. Theoretically this could have been achieved without the Learning Commons, but realistically the political support it generated was essential in obtaining the funding needed for technology investment. In any case, feedback from surveys and focus groups indicate that users are very pleased by the quality of the hardware and wide range of software tools available not just in the Learning Commons but throughout the building.

Our determination to promote a universal image across all public workstations in the library has also been amply rewarded. It has been a major factor behind the 60 per cent increase in our gate count; and because users have access to the same resources anywhere in the building (including networked printing) it has helped alleviate overcrowding the Learning Commons itself. Some library public service staff members were apprehensive at the thought of having to be 'experts' on all the software, but these fears have proved largely unfounded. They have been trained to provide basic assistance with the most common applications, but for in-depth support users are directed to the Learning Commons.

Finally, the extended hours of the Learning Commons, which is open a total of 134 hours a week when classes are in session, must be counted as a success. From midnight until 3 a.m. there are rarely fewer than 100 students using the facility. During final exam periods it is often filled to capacity.

What needs improvement?

Although the Learning Commons has been extremely successful over all, there were some unanticipated situations that needed to be addressed as well as some ongoing challenges that will take time and additional resources to resolve. For example, security problems began to emerge as soon as the facility moved into 24/5 operating mode in October 2004. Although Ohio University is located in a small university town in rural southeast Ohio, there is a small population of homeless people, some of whom began showing up in the Learning Commons after the usual midnight closing hour for the rest of the building. In a few cases they were becoming disturbing to other patrons. This is a familiar problem for public libraries located in urban areas, but it was new to us and required an immediate response. We were reluctant to restrict access to members of the Ohio University community, both because the logistics of enforcing such a policy would be difficult and because we are committed to a century old tradition of allowing the general public to use the library. In the end we opted for a new policy on 'disruptive behaviour' prohibiting such conduct as extended sleeping, vagrancy, emitting offensive odors, violating personal space, or obscene activities. The policy also stipulates that the library is reserved for use by university students, staff and faculty between midnight and 7 a.m. and that affiliation status is established by possession of a valid ID. While the lack of an ID does not in itself prohibit use of the Learning Commons during extended hours, disruptive behaviour may be cause to request an ID, and in such instances failure to produce one will result in exclusion.

To help enforce this policy we arranged for the university police department to make regular patrols of the Learning Commons after midnight and also to respond immediately to any calls for assistance from the evening supervisors, who were equipped with cellphones that could be used for this purpose from anywhere on the floor. In several cases people have been removed from the library for violating the ban on sleeping or other provisions of the disruptive behaviour policy. Apparently the message has gone out to the community, because problems of the sort that emerged in the first year of the Learning Commons have now decreased substantially.

Another unanticipated problem has been the increased workload for custodians, which became especially noticeable after the café opened in autumn 2005. Although food is not allowed outside the café and drinks are supposed to be in closed containers, enforcement of these rules has been virtually non-existent. These circumstances along with the huge volume of traffic in the Learning Commons and extended hours of operation have combined to overload the custodial crew. The situation has been addressed as well as possible by adjusting shifts so that the most effective workers are now assigned to the Learning Commons.

Although the library obtained funding from the Provost for a new position in the Systems Department in response to the increased workload imposed by the technology in the Learning Commons, there is a need for greater support, particularly during evenings and weekends when Systems staff members are not physically present in the building. Learning Commons employees have been trained to troubleshoot technical problems, and there is always a designated 'duty officer' in Systems who can be paged at home during evening and weekend hours when necessary. But the scope of the installed technology infrastructure throughout the library is sufficient to require the presence of a highly qualified technician on evenings and weekends.

The increased traffic on the floor and the installation of so many computers, monitors, printers and other equipment has also overloaded the HVAC system, leading to intolerable temperatures on some days during the summer months. Critical parts of the HVAC infrastructure in Alden Library are more than 20 years old and well beyond their useful life. Increasing the load on the system has made a bad situation worse. We knew this could be a problem but simply did not have the funding in our renovation budget to address it at the time. The necessary upgrades are scheduled to occur as part of a $20 million comprehensive renovation of Alden Library over the next 6 years.

The library's master plan also calls for the Learning Commons to be expanded so it can finally accommodate the entire Academic Advancement Center (including tutoring services, study skill development and academic guidance), thereby fulfilling our vision of bringing all the services dedicated to the enhancement of student learning together in one place. This expansion will also eliminate the redundancy of having two multimedia labs (one on the first floor and another on the second) by consolidating them in the Learning Commons.

One of the other original goals of the Learning Commons was to create a space where faculty would be able to work alongside students either as teachers and mentors (e.g. collaborating on technology enhanced projects) or as researchers (e.g. investigating student learning styles.) For various reasons, this dream has not yet been realised. The Learning Commons has evolved into an overwhelmingly student-centred environment, filled with energy and immensely appealing to younger adults, but less so to faculty.

Next steps: creating a Faculty Commons

Based on the success of the Learning Commons we have concluded that the next logical step is to create a similar destination space for faculty. This project will also involve a cross-organisational partnership, in this case between the University Libraries, Academic Technology, and the centres for Teaching Excellence and Writing Excellence.

Like most large institutions of higher learning, Ohio University provides a number of faculty development programs aimed at supporting faculty in their teaching, learning and research. **Academic Technology** promotes the use of information and communications technologies for teaching, learning and scholarship. It operates the **Academic Design Studio,** a resource for faculty, instructors and graduate teaching assistants interested in using technology to enhance teaching and learning. The **Center for Teaching Excellence** enhances the connection between teaching and learning through programs, workshops, discussion groups, dissemination of resource materials, and individual consultations. The **Center for Writing Excellence** collaborates with other faculty development units and is dedicated to enriching student learning and faculty teaching through writing. It offers faculty workshops and individual consultations in teaching development that enable faculty to re-imagine the way they include writing in their courses.

The University Libraries also provide a range of services that focus primarily on faculty members. For example the **Graphics, Photography and Multimedia** department assists faculty to enliven course content and research presentations by incorporating imagery, sound and video. Depending on need and customer preference, it offers training sessions, one-on-one assistance and full production services. In addition, librarians consult with faculty to assist them with research, work on grant proposals, provide classroom-based library instruction and develop collections in support of academic programs.

The Alden Library Faculty Commons will combine all of these offerings into one comprehensive faculty development centre. Following the same planning process used for the Learning Commons, a cross-organisational team has been assembled to work with architects and University planners to design the facility and develop a technology plan. As of this writing construction documents have been completed and put out to bid, with work scheduled to begin in time for the Faculty Commons to open at the start of the 2007 autumn quarter.

Program components

The Faculty Commons will include 12 major components, each of which is depicted in the schematic drawing shown in Appendix C.

Reception area (room 305)

As users enter the Faculty Commons they will be met by a Receptionist, who will guide them to the services and resources they need. The Receptionist will also schedule conference rooms, make appointments and provide clerical support. This position will be staffed by a half-time classified employee supplemented by student assistants.

Open area/lounge seating

Moving past the reception area visitors will enter a large, open space surrounded at the periphery by several conference rooms and offices for the professional staff associated with the Faculty Commons. These rooms have been designed to allow natural light to pass through into the open area, which will be filled with attractive clusters of soft seating, flexible work surfaces, technology resources and a 'coffee kiosk' with light refreshments. In several focus group sessions conducted during the planning stages participants made the point that there were few places on campus for faculty to gather, at least not central places easily accessible to faculty from different departments. We have designed the Faculty Commons to be a 'destination space' for faculty. Not only will they come to use the specific services and resources provided there; but they will also be able to meet together to share experiences, collaborate on projects, learn from their colleagues or just socialise in an inviting, comfortable place intended exclusively for their use.

Staff offices (rooms 308, 308a, 309, 310, 311, 312, 313, 314, 316, 317 and 318)

The Faculty Commons will be home to approximately 14 professionals from Academic Technology, the centres for

Teaching Excellence and Writing Excellence, Graphics and Multimedia Services, and Collection Development. Not only will these programs enjoy a more visible presence on campus; but they will also be able to collaborate and achieve a level of synergy that is not possible in their separate locations.

Coffee kiosk (room 329)

Food and drink are important ingredients for creating the kind of informal social atmosphere we are seeking in the Faculty Commons. Consisting of a moveable countertop surrounded by four to six stool seats, the Coffee Kiosk will feature several coffees and light refreshments supplied each day from the Café BiblioTech on the second floor of Alden Library. We envision faculty using the Coffee Kiosk before and after attending scheduled events or simply gravitating to it while working with each other or with staff in the Faculty Commons.

Large conference room (room 307)

The Faculty Commons will contain three rooms that can be used for group meetings of various kinds, including brainstorming, project collaboration, videoconferencing, and training sessions. The largest of these will be a 20-seat conference room furnished with moveable tables and chairs that can be configured in various ways depending on the type of meeting and number of attendees. To enhance the meeting experience the space will be equipped with interactive whiteboards and a teleconferencing system, enabling faculty to collaborate at a distance with persons at other universities, government organisations, business partners, and funding agencies. For example a cross-disciplinary faculty team at Ohio University might collaborate with their counterparts at another higher education institution and an industrial partner to develop a grant proposal.

Small meeting rooms (rooms 319 and 320)

Two smaller 8-seat meeting rooms will be available for use by faculty groups, advisory boards, and working committees. One of these rooms (320) will be an informal space designed for brainstorming and collaborative group work. It can be reserved in advance or simply used 'on the fly'. The other (319) will be a more formal meeting room intended for presentations and training sessions offered by the Faculty Commons. Both will be equipped with interactive whiteboards to facilitate 'information emersion' and allow results to be easily saved and distributed.

Faculty showcase (room 330)

An important goal of the Faculty Commons is to recognise and celebrate excellence in teaching, learning, research and creative activity. Prominently located near the entrance will be a Faculty Showcase with two main components: a 'drama wall' displaying still images (e.g. photographs and posters) that portray faculty achievement and a 'video tree' featuring clips of faculty employing best practices in the classroom, making innovative uses of technology or engaging in public performances of their work. Content will be harvested from activities in the Faculty Commons itself (e.g. research posters, web pages and PowerPoint presentations produced by Graphics, Photography and Multimedia) as well as from external sources such as University Communications and Marketing. The plasma screens will also be used to advertise upcoming events.

Teaching and learning space (room 302)

With seating for up to 80 people, the Teaching and Learning space will serve as a training and demonstration site for new learning technologies, innovative teaching methods and the latest research resources. Staff from both the Faculty Commons and the Library will collaborate to offer a variety of workshops, demonstrations and hands-on training sessions. Guest speakers will be invited to discuss the scholarship of teaching and demonstrate innovative pedagogical practices. Librarians will offer sessions on bibliographic instruction, information literacy or the use of advanced research databases. A video recording system will allow these sessions to be recorded for future use or to enable faculty members to record their own teaching for evaluation and feedback.

The diffusion of new technologies is greatly enhanced when faculty can experience them in a realistic classroom setting, but without the pressure of an actual instructional session. The Teaching and Learning space will be equipped as a standard 'smart classroom' with interactive whiteboards, a multimedia podium, portable laptops, and associated peripheral devices (e.g. 'clickers' for demonstrating audience response systems.) To maximise flexibility portable laptops will be used instead of installed computer workstations. Combined with moveable tables and chairs, this will allow the space to be easily reconfigured for audience seating, small group work or other applications. The Teaching and Learning space will be located immediately outside the Faculty Commons so it can be used by both Faculty Commons and Library staff at any time the building is open.

Graphics services (rooms 331, 332 and 333)

Professionals in the Graphics, Photography and Multimedia department sometimes say that their mission is 'to help faculty look good' by effectively using imagery, sound and video in their classroom teaching, conference presentations and publications. The Graphics Services unit concentrates on print media such as research posters, booklets and handouts. Customers will drop off and pick up work near the entrance to the Faculty Commons (333), and production will take place in the workroom (332) and the printing/copying room (332). In addition faculty will be able to borrow a digital camera to photograph experiments, student projects, field research and similar subjects for use in research posters or web pages. Products generated by Graphics Services will be displayed on the 'drama wall' both to advertise its capabilities and showcase the underlying faculty work.

Multimedia services (rooms 321, 322, 323, 324 and 326)

Staff members in this unit work with faculty to incorporate multimedia in their teaching, public presentations and research publications. They offer a full range of services, from generating original audio and video, through design, editing, format conversion, and final production. Using advanced illustration software, they can create professional looking graphics (maps, table, charts, photographs, etc.) for print publication or posting on the web. A growing service is assisting faculty to record their lectures for distribution on Blackboard and/or via Podcasting. For faculty members who want to become self-sufficient, Graphics staff provide training sessions and one-on-one assistance in using multimedia tools. Faculty members can begin work in the private staff offices and migrate to the public Multimedia Lab (see below) as they become more self-sufficient.

Multimedia Lab (room 325)

As mentioned above, the Multimedia Lab will be used by faculty working independently (with occasional assistance as needed) to design, edit and produce multimedia objects for use in their teaching and research. Some faculty members have a good deal of expertise and require only the hardware and software resources to accomplish what they need. Others may begin working on a project with one-on-one support from staff in Multimedia Services and then transition to the open lab when they are comfortable with the technology. In either case they will be able to use three state of the art multimedia equipped workstations (for both Mac and PC platforms) running the latest software.

Faculty 'Sandbox'

The 'Sandbox' will consist of a cluster of high-end workstations available for faculty use under the supervision of the Academic Design Studio. Here instructional design specialists, assisted by highly trained student employees, will work with faculty on creating or improving their web pages, incorporating multimedia in the classroom, using desktop videoconferencing, using PowerPoint in more interactive ways and other applications.

Conclusion

Some observers have said that the migration from print-based to electronic information resources, the emergence of virtual reference services and similar developments will reduce or perhaps even eliminate the importance of the library as a physical place. However, our experience with the Learning Commons has taught us that this need not be the case. An alternative future for library facilities can be envisioned in which they become the acknowledged hub of the academic experience – popular destination spaces cultivating both student and faculty success. But seizing this opportunity will require us to make our buildings more people-centred, with less space devoted to legacy print collections. It will mean creating environments that provide greater support for student learning, but also for faculty to conduct research, receive assistance with grant writing, practice incorporating new technologies and collaborate with each other in the presence of librarians, technology specialists, teaching experts and other professionals. Making the 'highest and best use' of expensive library facilities located on prime real estate at the heart of campus requires us to think carefully about what activities and resources should occur in those spaces vs those that can be located elsewhere. Unless librarians develop their own vision based on logical partnerships consistent with the library's mission, there are others who will advance their own agendas.

Appendix A

Floor plan of the Learning Commons (these plans are also available online at *http://www.library.ohiou.edu/serv/lc/index.html*).

Ohio University
Alden Library Learning Commons
Floor Plan

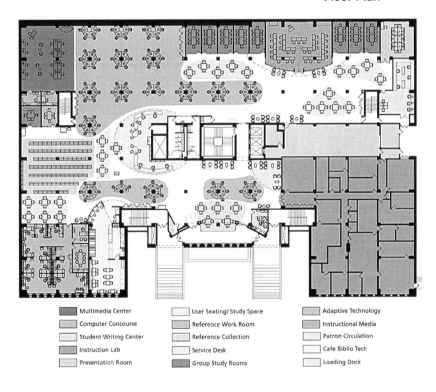

▓	Multimedia Center	▢	User Seating/ Study Space	▓	Adaptive Technology
▓	Computer Concourse	▓	Reference Work Room	▓	Instructional Media
▢	Student Writing Center	▓	Reference Collection	▢	Patron Circulation
▓	Instruction Lab	▢	Service Desk	▢	Cafe Biblio Tech
▢	Presentation Room	▓	Group Study Rooms	▢	Loading Dock

Appendix B

Planning process.

Ohio University
Alden Library Learning Commons
Planning Process

Vision

Mission

Goals

Advisory Committee

Sponsors / Executive Oversight

Libraries (L)
Dean of L

Information Technology (IT)
Computer Services (CS)
Director of CS

University College (UC)
Academic Advancement Center (AAC)
Dean of UC

Core Team

Libraries (L)
Associate Dean
Assistant Dean Public Services
Head of Reference & Instruction
Head Library Systems

Timeline

Computer Services (CS)
Assistant Director CS
Computer Lab Manager

Facilities Planning
Project Manager

Issue Resolution
Resources & Budget

University College (UC)
Director AAC
Coordinator Student Writing

Liaison with Sponsors

Facility Design

Operating Plan

Technology Team
Head of Library Systems (L)
Network Administrator (CS)
Academic Skills Instructor (AAC)
Technical Support Analyst (L)
Network Administrator (CS)
Reference Librarian (L)
Head of Reference & Instruction (L)

Services Team
Head of Reference & Instruction (L)
Computer Lab Manager (CS)
Tutor Coordinator (AAC)
Coordinator Student Writing (AAC)

Communications Team
Reference Librarian (L)
Assistant Dean of Development
Manager of Training & Central Lab Support (CS)
Coordinator College Print & Electronic Communications (UC)
Administrator (L)
University Communications Media Specialist

Potential Issues
Hardware needs
Image management
Printing & payment
Authentication
Metering
Troubleshooting & maintenance

Potential Issues
Service desk functions
Staffing (regular & student)
Core competencies
Training
Service hours

Potential Issues
Publicity
Web presence
Internal communication
Construction updates

275

Appendix C

Floor plan of the Faculty Commons (these plans are also available online at *http://www.library.ohiou.edu/fc/*).

Ohio University
Alden Library Faculty Commons
Floor Plan

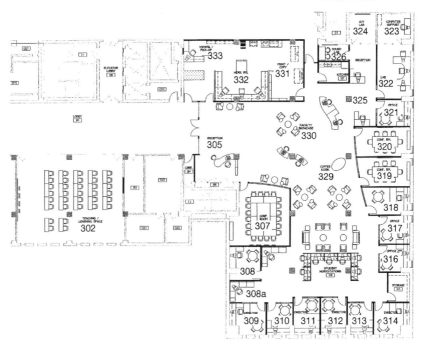

7

Supporting the Learning Commons concept in 'real life'
Jennifer Stringer

If you build it, they will come. *Field of Dreams* (1989)

Introduction

If only it were as easy as in the movie 'Field of Dreams', where a farmer builds a baseball field in the middle of an Iowa cornfield and all of his dead baseball heroes show up to play ball. If only we could build technology enhanced learning spaces – Learning Commons – and have faculty just show up ready, willing, and able to 'hit a home run' on our playing field. Unfortunately, it doesn't usually work that way. It takes careful planning, resources, and a well thought out support structure to enable faculty to be comfortable to experiment with new technologies that support innovative methods of teaching and learning and for students to take advantage of the flexibility that these kinds of spaces encourage.

This chapter stretches the definition of what a Learning Commons is by discussing more formalised learning spaces, their technologies, and support. It covers support structures, technology adoption and faculty development and then tells several 'Learning Commons stories' that illustrate the process of how to introduce and support different technologies that encompass this broader idea of a Learning Commons.

'Spaces designed in 1956 are not likely to fit perfectly with students in 2006' (Oblinger, 2006). We are living proof of EDUCAUSE Vice President, Diana Oblinger's words. Stanford University School of Medicine moved into their current learning facilities in 1959. Although they served the school well over the years, they did not support faculty in exploring curricular innovation. When the school began planning for a new education building that will open in 2010 we were given the opportunity to develop, pilot, and implement new classroom technologies and renovate several teaching spaces. The goal was to allow faculty to become comfortable with new classroom technologies, experiment with new teaching methods supported by more flexible spaces, and then enable the school to explore sustainable support models to ensure that our spaces remain vibrant, up-to-date, and well managed.

Educational technology: the birth of a new support organisation

At Stanford University the Schools (Law, Medicine, and Business) have control over their own spaces and provide their own support. The School of Medicine had supported the same spaces with the same disjointed organisational structure for many years. The support was fractured and there was no clear leadership in providing coordinated service and no one group had the authority or the resources to support change. The Senior Associate Dean for Information

Resources and Technology determined that with the plans to build a new library and education building a new organisation was needed to support the decision and allow a successful transition.

The Educational Technology Services group was formed by combining services and personnel from three different organisations reporting to three different areas of Information Resources and Technology (IRT) in the School of Medicine:

- Learning Technologies – Course management system, teaching with technology, and software development.
- Video Services – Course videotaping and AV support of learning spaces.
- Instructional Facilities – Room scheduling, learning spaces support, and computing classrooms and student computing.

These services merged together to form an organisation whose goal is to provide a streamlined, comprehensive, single point of service to provide for the technology and spaces that support teaching and learning in the institution. In this support model, when a learning space is booked all of the accompanying services are reserved at the same time including the layout of the room, video capture and streaming of the session, laptops for teaching and small group activities, audience response system and key pads, special support for large events, and requests for training on technologies. The request is automated through an enterprise room and resource reservation system that is used by almost all spaces on campus. The system supports workflow including email notification for staff and the room requestor. It tracks all of our room and technology utilisation so that we can continue to plan for changes and upgrades to our spaces.

The EdTech organisation has continued to develop and partner with appropriate groups with IRT and across the campus, as support needs grow and change. EdTech was originally within the Medical Library and Knowledge Management organisational structure. This provided an opportunity for educational technologists and librarians to develop a model for integrating current activities supporting education with the emerging model of knowledge-based learning.

As IRT began to solidify its own structure a new IT Services group was created. It brought together a number of areas including Public Web Services, Data Center, Administrative Computing, and Desktop Support. EdTech was realigned and placed under this larger IT Services group reporting to the Associate CIO of Information Technology Services. EdTech is still housed physically in the Library. However, the change has allowed for greater linkage between EdTech and the IT service providers. It has resulted in the creation of a new walk-up computer support service that will be launched in the autumn of 2007. EdTech has continued to partner with the Library to jointly support public computing spaces and provide online curricular resources to the students.

Learning Commons stories

The following stories illustrate a number of different projects that fall under this broader definition of 'Learning Commons'. We have learned different lessons from each project and tried to build upon our successes.

New presentation technologies: supporting traditional learning environments with new technologies

In January of 2004, our 1950s classrooms underwent their first major overhaul since they were built. We installed new presentation technologies in our two largest lecture halls to meet our faculty members' growing collection of digital media and to make it easier to create dynamic learning interactions. We installed higher resolution projectors to display high quality images, document cameras for live display of 3D objects, tablet computers that allowed for the annotation of PowerPoint slides, purchased an audience response system, and developed an intuitive way to manage the display of multiple media sources.

Perhaps the most controversial change was the decision to remove the 35 mm projectors from the spaces. The teaching of medicine is heavily dependent on all kinds of images, pathology, histology, anatomy, etc. Most of our faculty members were still teaching from slide carousels that they had created years ago. They would pull them out for the one or two lectures they taught every year and then put them away to gather dust until the next year. Students only saw the images during the lecture and they had no ability to use them for study. Faculty had previously argued that our projectors were not high enough resolution to show the slides in great detail and so we had kept the slide projectors going. However, with our renovations we were able to put in higher resolution projectors. Now we had to help faculty make the transition. We created an initiative called 'Go Digital!' where we set aside funds to take faculty members 35 mm slides and send them out to be digitised. Faculty could apply for the funds to digitise their teaching slide

283

Figure 7.1 New equipment installation

collections. We also personally contacted faculty who we had identified as heavy 35 mm slide users and encouraged them to participate in the program.

We also created a faculty development program and comprehensive support to encourage widespread adoption of the other interactive teaching technologies that were being installed in the classrooms. The technologies were brought in for faculty to try them out and give us feedback before they were installed in the spaces. We made individual contacts with every faculty who had lectured in the core curriculum in the previous year and offered training sessions and we worked within departments to train faculty together.

Results

In the first quarter alone, we digitised hundreds of slides through the 'Go Digital!' initiative. Over 50 per cent of the faculty used 'digital ink', the tablet computer to annotate their slides, and 9 per cent used the document camera. The use of the audience response system has grown considerably. Many faculty and TAs use it for in-class review sessions and we receive support requests for its use at numerous special courses and presentations including new student orientations and information literacy classes.

Anatomy's story of adoption: digital ink

The Anatomy course is one of the first classes that the students take in medical school. The course has been traditionally taught at Stanford with lectures preceding dissection labs. The lectures often included very elaborate multi-coloured chalk drawings of the specific areas of the body that the students were going to dissect. Students took copious notes and tried to recreate the drawings and, of course, the drawings would be erased at the start of the next lecture. What better way to utilise our digital ink technology than to allow the faculty to draw their structures electronically and then save them to the server so that students would have a copy available to study.

Understanding the first two steps in the innovation decision process are knowledge and persuasion, we wanted to introduce the technology to our faculty in a positive way (Rogers, 2003). We knew that we had to introduce the technology in a low stakes environment to give our faculty knowledge of the innovation and allow them to try it out in a safe environment where questions, feedback and even mistakes were encouraged. We set the tablet display and computer up in a room before it was ever installed in the classrooms. The fact that we let them explore the technology before it was installed also allowed them to have a sense of ownership over the decision. We encouraged the anatomy faculty to come and try out digital ink to get a sense of its usefulness.

We recognised that a key to adoption for the entire faculty in Anatomy would be gaining the support of a key stakeholder, the course director. Not only was he the director of Anatomy, but he also was a very busy practicing clinician who spent many hours taking care of sick babies in the neonatal intensive care unit. His time was very valuable and we had to contact him more than once before being able to set up a training session, but once we did he readily recognised the benefits of using digital ink to both annotate lecture slides and to draw anatomic structures freehand. Once we had the support of the course director we set up several training sessions for the full anatomy faculty to become familiar with the technology. To our surprise, the anatomy faculty began to train each other in the use of the technology and to suggest possible uses beyond our initial suggestions and the Anatomy faculty successfully made the transition from chalk to digital ink in one quarter.

Lessons learned

- Keep contacting faculty – Personal contacts make all of the difference. Our most successful faculty member was

Figure 7.2 Chalk and digital ink comparison

contacted four times before we signed him up for a training session.

- Create a safe environment – Create a place where faculty can try new things out in a low stakes environment. No one wants to look technically challenged in front of their colleagues or their students!

- Let them train each other – We look for a technology champion among faculty who will then help us train the rest. They can provide a first-hand account for other faculty of what works well and what they find more challenging about various presentation technologies.

- Just in time refresher training – When faculty call to request a room, they are asked if they need training on any of the technology in the space. We often have faculty request that someone meet them in the room a few minutes before their lecture to give them a quick refresher on how to use the technology.

- Provide point of service support – We hire a student to be in the room to help faculty with technology enhanced presentations (sort of like the kid who used to run the projectors in high school).

TECH Desk pilot: technology expert consulting hours

The TECH Desk was a pilot project that ran for 6 months in the early winter and spring quarters of 2004. The goal was to gauge the need for a more substantial long-term technology support service. It was a joint effort between three different groups within our organisation: Lane Library, Learning Technologies, and IRT Operations. The desk was physically located at the Reference Desk in the medical library and was open 9 hours each week: Monday, Wednesday and Thursday, noon to 1 p.m. and 4 p.m. to 6 p.m. Two people were assigned to each hour for a total of 18 person hours a week and because staffing levels were limited, no telephone or email support was offered.

People from each of the service organisations were identified to staff the TECH Desk. Their skills were analysed and they were divided into two general groups, Applications and Hardware/Networking. An attempt was made to assign people to work together, one from each group, who complemented each other's skill set. We provided everyone assigned to the desk with basic in-person customer support training and cross-training in basic networking issues. Early in the project it became obvious that many questions brought to the desk involved networking, specifically setting up wireless access. Therefore, we made sure that someone was always at the desk that had the appropriate skills and network access to provide immediate wireless set-up for users.

The TECH Desk marketing strategy employed a variety of techniques, including use of email listservs, newsletters and other University and school news publications, posters, buttons and fliers. Somewhat surprisingly, when users were asked how they had heard about the service, many identified the two TECH Desk posters that we had placed on easels in front of the library and the hospital. After the initial marketing blitz, the TECH Desk posters were virtually the only form of ongoing publicity.

Results

The TECH Desk clientele came from various Medical School groups, with faculty (30 per cent) and medical students (24 per cent) best represented. Many of the other users came from the clinical setting and included nurses and residents.

The TECH Desk was very busy, but never overwhelmed. The questions answered covered a broad spectrum of technical and application issues. The category with by far the most questions (39 per cent) was wireless networking. The next most active category, with 10 per cent of all questions, was application support, which included software other than Endnote, PowerPoint and security. All other categories of questions each accounted for 7 per cent or fewer of the total. Although the average time spent on each question was 17 minutes, many of the questions took over an hour to answer.

The goal of the TECH Desk was to provide general purpose walk-in consulting and troubleshooting to support the SUMC faculty, students and staff. However, the usage data suggested that the service was perceived primarily as a highly technical laptop, wireless and PDA 'fix-it' service, and less as a software application consulting resource. According to comments from some of the members of the library's strategic planning focus groups, one reason for this may be that the name 'TECH Desk' seemed to imply the more 'nuts and bolts' technical type of service. However, when software application oriented questions did come up, the availability of complementary skill sets was quite valuable. The central location of the library seemed to enhance the use of the TECH Desk service.

The location of the TECH Desk next to the library's Information Desk led to interesting synergies with TECH questions occasionally leading to reference questions and vice versa. Unfortunately, the TECH Desk user interactions sometimes conflicted with Information/Reference Desk interactions, mainly due to crowding and noise.

The limited hours, as well as the absence of phone and email support, definitely impacted the usefulness of the service. Several members of the library's advisory group stated a preference, not surprisingly, for '24/7' technical support.

Although we ended the TECH Desk pilot in 2004, the recommendations for a more comprehensive support service remained on our radar. As with many organisations, we had multiple priorities competing for limited resources and the time just wasn't right to develop an entirely new service. In 2007 we had the opportunity to invest energy and resources into reviving the TECH Desk concept. The desktop support staff was being moved in closer proximity to the classroom and public computing staff in EdTech. With an increased number of computing support staff in the same space, the ability to staff another service point became a reality. The new TECH Desk is planned to open in the autumn of 2007 and will implement the recommendations that came from the pilot, including more comprehensive hours, phone and email support, and a greater focus on hardware and operating system support.

Lessons learned

- Simple marketing works – The team recommended a more sustained marketing approach, but noted that just a couple of well placed signs generated a tremendous amount of business.

- Customer support training is key – Although all of the people who staffed the TECH Desk provided technical or desktop support, most of them had never been on a 'service desk' before this pilot. We provided everyone with the training and used good old library 'reference interview' techniques as a starting point to train our staff.

- Don't give up hope – We thought that our original pilot would naturally develop into a service that filled a clear need in our school. However, it took several years and the right timing for that to become a reality.

Technology for team-based learning: supporting transformational change in an innovative space

The school of medicine underwent a major curriculum reform in 2003. The goals were to better integrate the basic science and clinical curriculum, introduce clinical medicine earlier, and reduce the number of hours that students spent in lecture. Practice of Medicine was one of the courses that came from this effort. It currently occupies about 30 per cent of the preclinical course time. Much of the course is taught in small groups, but the faculty were interested in using a team-based learning (TBL) approach to replace some of the lecture time (Michaelsen, 2004). This approach allows a single faculty member to lead teams of students through a series of activities to solve a particular problem in one large space.

We didn't have a space that could support this kind of teaching. All of our spaces were traditional lecture halls with raked floors and theatre style seating. We needed to create a large flat-floored space that allowed for flexible table and chair configurations and had the appropriate presentation technologies to enable students to present their work. However, before we invested in redesigning an existing classroom we wanted to visit other spaces and then develop pilots to understand what we actually needed in our space. We made site visits to Wallenberg Hall on the Stanford campus and the TEAL classroom at MIT to understand how they were using technology to enable interactive teaching (Hagström, 2004; TEAL, 2007).

After spending time understanding what others were doing we designed several pilots to test out different space configurations and technologies. We utilised our smaller flat-floored spaces that were being used for small group and

Figure 7.3 Using our multidisciplinary labs as test space for our Team Learning classroom

| Figure 7.4 | TLC room layout |

| Team Learning (54) | Small Group (60) | Case Style (66) | Lecture (80) |

microscope teaching and reconfigured them to approximate several different TBL and other small group learning formats. We worked with two faculty members to adopt some of their course sessions to utilise a TBL or small group format. Based on their feedback and recommendations we designed a flexible classroom.

In late 2005 we opened the Team Learning classroom, the 'TLC' to begin to support the new curriculum and its emphasis on team-based sessions and interactive lectures. The room is outfitted with dual screen projection, video capture, 40 laptops, a mobile podium with 'digital ink', and a dedicated audience response system. The room can be configured to support TBL, small group, interactive case-style lecture, and large lecture teaching.

Results

The TLC is the favourite classroom of faculty and students. The room is the most heavily booked space in our classroom inventory. We reconfigure the space, changing it from case style to team learning format, an average of once per day. The usage break down of the different configurations is as follows:

- 63 per cent team learning and small group;
- 33 per cent case style;
- 2 per cent lecture.

Faculty members also take advantage of the other technologies in the room. Laptops are used in 18 per cent of the sessions and audience response systems are used in 13 per cent of the booked activities.

We also work closely with the Division of Evaluation in the Office of Medical Education. They conduct focus groups on the curriculum quarterly where they gather feedback from faculty and students. Below are representative comments from their reports regarding the TLC:

Students:

'More intimate and less intimidating.'
'Appreciate tables for laptops.'

Faculty:

'Team learning as we'd envisioned.'
'Livens up the learning climate.'
'More intimate.'

Lessons learned

- Technology does not make a 'bad' teacher a 'good' teacher – This seems so simple, but it is important to develop a comprehensive faulty development program that goes beyond technology and spaces to support pedagogic change.

- Tables and chairs matter – Lightweight sturdy furnishings on wheels are key. We developed our most popular room configurations by working with faculty and just moving things around until they 'felt right'.

- You can never have enough power and data – Even though our room is wireless, many of the activities still require a higher bandwidth connection and when you put

30 laptops in a room you need a lot of bandwidth. Put power everywhere; power on the walls and power on the floors. Make sure you have enough as it always costs more to put in later.

- Plan for the future – We wanted our space to be flexible to grow with changes in educational pedagogy and projector positions! We utilised open cable trays for our networking and AV cabling and we used a unistrut grid work for the ceiling so that our staff could move and add projectors, lights, and microphones to accommodate changes in technology.

Looking to the future

Stanford School of Medicine will break ground on our new Learning and Knowledge Center the 'LKC' in late 2007 (*http://lkc.stanford.edu*). We will use the data and experiences that we have from our pilots to help shape the directions of the learning spaces in this building. We will continue to support pedagogic change within the School of Medicine curriculum and work toward enabling faculty and students to create a seamless environment between formal and informal learning.

We believe that the blending of formal and informal learning spaces will only increase and we are working in conjunction with the library to redesign student computer and other informal learning spaces to create flexible Learning Commons for a new generation of students.

References

Hagström, S. et al. (2006) *Blurring Boundaries: A Description and Assessment of the High Performance Learning*

Spaces in Wallenberg Hall, Stanford University. Stanford, CA: Stanford University. Available at *http://wallenberg.stanford.edu/teachresources/findings/HPLS/*.

Michaelsen, L.K., Knight, A.B. and Fink, L.D. (eds) (2004) *Team-Based Learning: A Transformative Use of Small Groups in College Teaching*. Sterling, VA: Stylus.

Oblinger, D.G. (ed) (2006) *Learning Spaces*. Washington, D.C.: EDUCAUSE.

Rogers, E.M. (2003) *Diffusion of Innovations*, 5th edn. New York: Free Press.

TEAL: Technology-Enhanced Learning Active Learning (2007). Cambridge, MA: Massachusetts Institute of Technology. Available at *http://web.mit.edu/edtech/casestudies/teal.html*.

8

Putting learners at the centre: the Learning Commons journey at Victoria University

Shay Keating, Philip G Kent and Belinda McLennan

Introduction

Victoria University (VU) implemented an Information Commons in each of its 11 campus libraries in 2005. Since then, VU has begun planning and development to redefine these spaces according to a 'Learning Commons' model. The initiative has been based on the collaboration of three areas of the university: Library, Teaching and Learning Support and Information Technology Services.

The implementation of each Learning Commons has been staggered with the first of the new facilities opening in November 2006 at VU's City Flinders Street campus in Melbourne's Central Business District. Planning is underway for another four facilities. The most significant development will be at VU's largest campus situated in the western suburbs of Melbourne planned for 2009. Transforming the existing Information Commons to a Learning Commons, this facility will be linked to a student pedestrian and retail precinct and will be the most comprehensive expression of this concept.

The evolution from an Information Commons to a Learning Commons model at VU has occurred within the context of larger scale strategic shift in the university's focus from a largely teacher-centred to a learner-centred university. This chapter explores the planning processes to develop a 'shared' understanding of how a Learning Commons with a learner-centred focus could support and engage students given that VU has multiple campuses and a highly diverse student population. While this is still a work in progress, some important lessons have been learnt.

The Victoria University context

Students

While increased diversity in student populations is now universal, this is particularly true at VU. As one of only five Australian dual-sector universities that incorporates both higher education and TAFE (post-secondary technical and further education),[1] VU provides education to students from the full range of qualifications – entry level to post-Doctoral – within the Australian Qualifications Framework.

VU's circumstances are also somewhat unusual among Australian universities because of the fact that it has a specific, legislated responsibility for the western region of Melbourne in the state of Victoria. VU has 11 campuses of varying sizes around the inner and outer western suburbs of Melbourne. This region is characterised by both a high concentration of industry and the cultural and linguistic diversity of its residents. It is home to numerous waves of migrants to Australia. In describing the West, Sheehan states:

> Generally speaking, the West remains a region with a strong migrant focus, with 33 per cent of the region's

population being born overseas, by comparison with a Victorian (state) share of 24 per cent...In 35 per cent of households in the western region a language other than English is spoken, by comparison with a Victorian average of 20 per cent. (Sheehan and Wiseman, 2004; p. 18)

However, there are strong variations within the West. For example in Brimbank one of the local municipalities close to VU a much higher proportion (53 per cent) of the residents speak a language other than English at home (Sheehan and Wiseman, 2004).

Generally the West is an 'area characterised by higher than average unemployment rates, lower than average income levels and under-resourced social capital' (Equity and Social Justice Branch, 2003; 2). For instance, the proportion of persons in the west employed in advanced knowledge service activities – managers and administrators, professionals and associate professionals is lower (32.1 per cent of employees) than for Victoria as a whole (40.1 per cent) (Sheehan and Wiseman, 2004; p. 20). In addition, a comparison of educational qualifications reveals that the proportion of the population of the western region who have a Bachelor's degree is substantially lower than for Victoria as a whole, and in some municipalities in the West the proportion is only about half the Victorian average. (Sheehan and Wiseman, 2004: p. 20).

VU's student population mirrors this diversity, drawing approximately half of its student population from the western region. Of all Australian universities, VU has the highest proportion of culturally and linguistically diverse (CALD) students. In comparison to other Australian universities, VU also has high proportions of low socio-economic status (SES) students, part-time students, first in the family university students and students who work in paid employment above 15 hours a week.[2] These characteristics are all associated with lower progress rates and higher attrition rates.

The challenge for VU is to embrace the diversity of its student cohorts. Supporting all students in their learning provides some challenges, as a one size fits all approach will not adequately support the diversity of students backgrounds and needs. VU manages diversity in a number of ways. For example, the approach taken to supporting TAFE and higher education students by the University's Student Learning Services department varies. TAFE students are provided with concurrent assistance (CA), which provides individualised and flexible academic support in language, literacy, learning, maths and technology for campus, industry-based and distance students across all campuses. Students can go to one of eight study labs where they work with an experienced CA staff member. This approach allows TAFE students to have ongoing focused and individualised support for their studies. In comparison, the higher education students have access to online resources, they can book an appointment to see a Student Learning Services staff member or they can attend scheduled workshops on academic skills. These varying approaches have had to be assimilated in the Learning Commons model.

Direction of the university

With a new Vice-Chancellor and President in 2003 came a renewed commitment to being the 'major education provider in, and *for* the western region'. The overarching mission of the University became 'to transform the lives of individuals and develop the capacities of industry and communities within the western Melbourne region and beyond through the power of vocational and higher education' (Victoria University, 2004a). The role of the University was therefore re-cast an enabler of the West. As Sheehan states, VU 'is firmly committed to a strong leadership role in supporting the actions needed to drive the western region towards a prosperous and sustainable knowledge economy' (Sheehan and Wiseman, 2004; p. 2).

The strategic plan that was developed in 2004 embodied the notion of learner-centred teaching. From 2004–2006 a key priority of the University has been to develop a teaching and learning policy framework that supports and facilitates this shift from teacher-centred to learner-centred practice. VU's overarching Learning and Teaching policy highlighted this approach through general policy principles that reflect the values and strategic objectives of the University. The first policy principle states that the University's foremost focus is on learning.

> The purpose of teaching is to enable learning. A central focus of the University is therefore the provision of environments that promote high quality learning. (Victoria University, 2004b).

Another principle states that the University is committed to accommodating the diverse backgrounds and learning needs of our student cohorts. In addition, the policy states that at VU the needs and aspirations of students should be the starting point for the design and delivery of any program or of any student learning support service, and that collaborative learning approaches are intrinsic to 'learner-centredness'.

Two key understandings of being 'learner centred' underpin the move towards aligning VU with learner-centred practice. Firstly, as Weimer eloquently states, 'Being learner centred focuses attention squarely on learning: what the student is learning, how the student is learning, the conditions under which the student is learning, whether the student is retaining and applying the learning, and how the current learning positions students for future learning' (Weimer, 2002; p. xvi). Student learning is therefore placed at the centre of what we do and what we plan to do. Secondly, learner-centred approaches are those that encourage active learning; that is, they engage students in their learning and require them 'to question, to speculate and to generate solutions' (Biggs, 2003).

> Active learning requires students to take responsibility for their learning in both collaborative and independent learning situations, and is dependant on students developing and employing generic skills and attributes. (McLennan and Keating, 2005; p. 5)

The ability for students to work collaboratively is now a requirement for all VU higher education and TAFE students in their courses and in future employment.[3] As the recent introduction of a problem-based learning (PBL) approach to first year Bachelor of Engineering has identified, being learner-centred generates the need for new types of learning spaces that cater and support collaborative groups working together for extended time on projects.

In this environment various areas of the University were starting to consider the implications of establishing a learner-centred culture at VU. It was recognised that this shift needed to involve not only teaching practices, but re-purposing of learning environments throughout the University to promote active and collaborative learning.

The planning process

The Information Commons

When the Learning Commons approach was first proposed, the Library had already begun a process of re-development. In late 2004 VU received an Australian government Higher Education Innovation Program (HEIP) grant to upgrade the library information technology facilities at all campuses to move towards an Information Commons approach. Consequently, libraries were equipped with a range of new computers, wireless facilities for laptop use, casual furniture and new desks suited to both individual and group study. Computers were enhanced with a range of information resources and software that ensured consistency with the University's standard operating environment (e.g. Microsoft Office suite) as well as discipline-based software (e.g. AUTOCAD) for specific campus applications.

In addition, Library staff members were trained in basic IT support. The training program was designed to ensure consistency of skills in client assistance roles at a single service point. As well as basic computer troubleshooting, reference and directional skills, library staff were trained to refer higher order problems to appropriate specialists. A formal evaluation of the program was conducted and positive outcomes and improved staff morale were reported.

New IT staff members were also employed at three of the busiest campus libraries to answer more complex student technology queries. The positions were funded by the Information Technology Services department during semester time, and the new staff members were drawn largely from a workplace training scheme for information technology undergraduates.

These developments were influenced by the notion of the Information Commons as a space where students have access to library resources, productivity software, areas to work individually or in groups, reference assistance and technical support to research and produce projects all in the one location (Church, 2005). It was immediately obvious that these enhanced facilities were popular with students and met their needs in ways that the existing library spaces did not. As a result the Library experienced a rise of 15 per cent in student attendance between 2005 and 2006.

At this point, VU was at the stage of what Beagle terms 'isolated change' (Beagle, 2004). It was still a library-centric model and to a great extent not integrated with other university initiatives. Importantly though the development of the Information Commons was a useful starting point in reconceptualising how the University's learning spaces could support student learning and a first step in the move to a Learning Commons model.

The move to a Learning Commons model

The idea to move from an Information Commons approach to a Learning Commons approach emerged out of a university-wide rethinking of how we support 'learners' and their learning both inside and outside of the classroom. Initially a high-level working group was formed to consider VU's strategy. It included the University Librarian, Deputy Vice Chancellor Education Services, Pro-Vice Chancellor Teaching and Learning Support, the Director of Information Technology and the Director of Marketing and Communications.

At this time, staff members from the Library and from Teaching and Learning Support began to explore the concept of a Learning Commons in more depth. A number of key staff from both areas undertook study tours to look at Information and Learning Commons at other universities in Australia and overseas including the University of Newcastle, University of Auckland, University of Guelph, Stanford University, University of California, University of Virginia, Cornell University, Columbia University, Sheffield Hallam University, University of Coventry, University of Hertfordshire, and Glasgow Caledonian University.

Staff from Teaching and Learning Support undertook a literature review to inform the strategy group's decision and ensure that there was a balance between operational and learning issues. This report (Keating and Gabb, 2005) explored how the Learning Commons concept could apply to a multi-campus, dual-sector University with a highly diverse student population. Drawing on Remy's depiction of the broad mission of a Learning Commons as 'not merely to integrate technology, reference...and services' as was typical with the Information Commons but to 'facilitate learning by whatever means works best' (Remy, 2004), the literature review explored both what sort of learning could be facilitated and how students could be best supported in these spaces. Different staffing models for collaborative service delivery were also explored.

Based on lessons learned from other universities, a number of general principles were extrapolated in the literature review and were used to guide the planning and development of VU's Learning Commons model. The principles that are outlined in Box 8.1 were agreed to by the strategy group.

In the literature review these principles were contextualised and applied to both the physical and virtual space of the Commons and the service model, which supports the operation of the Learning Commons. The notion that these

Box 8.1   **VU's principles for a learning commons**

Learning oriented

Facilitates active, independent and collaborative learning.

Learner centred

Focuses on student needs, preferences and work patterns.

University wide

Part of university-wide development of learner autonomy.

Flexible

Responsive to the changing needs of learners for resources and support.

Collaborative

Based on collaboration between different learning support areas in the University.

Community building

Provides a hub for physical and virtual interaction for staff and students.

Source: Keating and Gabb (2006); 16.

spaces should be learner-centred was key and became pivotal in the early planning of the Learning Commons at VU. This was articulated in the literature review as follows:

> **The physical space**
> The physical space is designed to accommodate student needs rather than those of the organisation. It

accommodates the social as well as an academic dimension of study and provides an environment that is welcoming, non-threatening and not dominated by staff. The place is highly visible, centrally located in the campus and close to other student services.

The virtual space
The virtual space allows students to access online materials and services such as learning support. Online resources range from those for specific units of study to those providing generic support for all students.

The staffing
Those staffing the Learning Commons are approachable, easily recognisable and provide a continuum of service including effective referral to other staff members. Student assistants are used not because they cost less but because they help to shape an environment that is welcoming and non-threatening for students and because they learn a great deal from the experience. Student feedback on the facilities and service is collected in a variety of ways and used to improve the service. (Keating and Gabb, 2005; 17–18)

The strategy group agreed that the Learning Commons concept complemented the University's strategic direction and was supported by teaching and learning policies that emphasised the shift occurring in education from 'institutions to learners and from teaching to learning' (Chappell, 2003). It was also decided that this should be conceptualised as an approach rather than just a building and be implemented in each of VU's 11 campuses. While they would all have to meet the general principles, it was acknowledged that each Learning Commons would necessarily be different in terms of its size, physical design including links to other facilities on campus, staffing mix and opening hours in response to the student cohorts and courses at each particular campus.

Cross-divisional task forces were set up to undertake planning for each of the campus Learning Commons. This work was initially overseen by a project manager seconded from Information Technology Services and included representatives from Library, Teaching and Learning Support, Information Technology Services and Facilities. These task forces developed a project brief for functional requirements for the implementation of the Learning Commons on each of the campuses.

The implementation of each Learning Commons has been staggered. In November 2006, the first of the new facilities opened at the City Flinders St Campus in Melbourne's central business district. Planning is underway for another four facilities. The most significant development will be at VU's main Footscray Park Campus planned for 2009.

The physical space

The physical space of the Learning Commons varies significantly from campus to campus although still remaining consistent with the principles adopted for VU Learning Commons. The planning process has had to accommodate very different space requirements, budgetary concerns and needs of student cohorts.

In each Learning Commons, the space has been designed to accommodate a variety of learning preferences and work patterns providing spaces where individuals and groups of students can work and develop autonomous learning habits and confidence along a continuum from supported to self-directed learning. For instance, in the City Flinders Campus there is a continuum of spaces for individuals, small groups, larger work groups and classroom spaces. At the Nicholson St Campus, which is a TAFE only campus, the master plan for the Learning Commons incorporates this range of spaces, however, it also includes a self access area and a study lab that were previously located in other areas of the campus. This acknowledges that while the resources are there for students to work autonomously, TAFE students also seek more structured learning support than their higher education counterparts in the self-access and study labs. These features are not currently planned for in the Learning Commons facilities at other campuses, but are a key aspect of adapting the model to suit the specific needs of the students that attend the campus.

The concept plan for the Nicholson St Campus Learning Commons highlights these features (Figure 8.1).

Another example of how the design of these spaces varies is at the St Albans Campus Learning Commons. In the St Albans Campus concept plan, an area has been created specifically for Careers Support. Within this space students will have access to online and paper-based resources and 'face-to-face' support in careers development.

The concept plans for the St Albans Campus Learning Commons highlights this inclusion of the Careers Support area as well as integrated work areas for rovers, IT, library and Teaching and Learning Support staff members. The plan also includes an integrated service desk.

As Bennet points out a library designed for active learning allows students to spend time on learning (Bennett, 2005). One of the ways a library can do this is by accommodating the social dimensions of study by allowing students to interact with one another. This is being dealt with in a number of ways. For example, comfortable, casual and

Figure 8.1 Nicholson St Campus Learning Commons concept plan

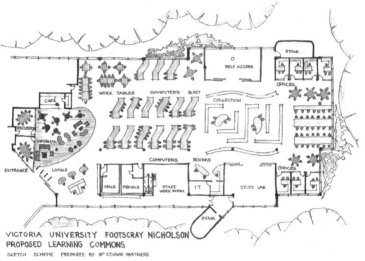

movable seating is a feature of each of the designs to encourage informal group discussion. The range of spaces and the flexibility of the spaces support the diverse ways that students learn and behave and accommodates students working individually or collaboratively.

Students enjoy working collaboratively at the City Flinders St Campus Learning Commons and utilise casual seating areas with wonderful views at this location (Figure 8.2a–c).

Food outlets are either co-located or within the space to encourage longer-term use of these spaces. Food outlets are becoming a standard feature of library design (Bennett, 2005). Bennett notes that conversations about class content (an indicator of active engagement) are more likely to occur in domesticated spaces such as cafeterias and refectories (Bennett, 2005). Again, exactly how food fits into the

Figure 8.2 City Flinders St Campus Learning Commons casual seating areas

(a)

(b)

Figure 8.2 *(Cont'd)*

(c)

Learning Commons varies from campus to campus. The City Flinders St Campus does not have a café as the campus is located in the heart of Melbourne's busy central business district, which has a multitude of food outlets. However, food and drink vending machines are available for easy access in the Commons. In comparison, the plans for the Footscray Park Campus physically link the Learning Commons to a student precinct with a variety of food outlets. Given that this campus is surrounded by a residential area, the provision of options for students to access food is important. The Footscray Nicholson St Campus plans has a small café within the Learning Commons building itself (see concept map; Figure 8.1).

Each of the Learning Commons is centrally located on the campus. In some cases these developments are being used to help create an obvious campus hub. For instance, the Footscray Park development will incorporate the transformation of the existing Information Commons to a Learning Commons, new faculty facilities and a student pedestrian and retail precinct physically linked to the Learning Commons. Within this precinct students will have access to resources, assistance, peers and sustenance. The plans for the Footscray Nicholson St Campus transform the existing library that was situated at the back of the campus but also incorporates additional space to link it to the front of the campus. This will ensure that the Learning Commons is easily accessible from the street entrance to the campus and is a visible and prominent part of the campus. Providing a student hub on campus is recognised as a key strategy for increasing the opportunities for students to integrate socially and has enormous potential to assist the University's strategic intent to better manage students' transition to University life. This is especially important for first year higher education students at VU where effective transition to University life is a significant determinant of retention.

Student feedback has indicated a desire for extended access to Commons facilities. VU has a goal of 24/7 access though the logistics and staffing model to support this have yet to be determined. Some campus facilities lend themselves to after hours swipe card access. Planning for new larger facilities includes the need to 'lock down' specific areas or floors of a building to provide flexible, safe and secure access through the various phases of the academic year.

The staffing model

The service model at VU is in the early stages of development and involves both collaborative working arrangements and co-location of Library staff with certain sections of Teaching and Learning Support and Information Technology Services in the physical space of the Commons. While the Library will act as the manager of the facility, the spaces will be jointly staffed by these three key educational service partners.

A three-tiered service model has been developed and will be refined in practice. The frontline or first tier will be provided by student rovers, which are discussed in detail later on in this chapter. Second and third tiers of support will be provided by experienced Library, Teaching and Learning Support and Information Technology Services staff. An example of second tier support offered by Teaching and Learning Support is regular study laboratories or 'drop in' sessions while third tier support involves face-to-face consultations between student and a learning support staff member in a private office. Other second tier support would include specialist facilities (e.g. laptop loan or IT recovery) while third tier support includes workshops and training sessions.

Second tier staff will operate from an integrated service point in the Commons with a differentiation of activities. As McKinstry and McCracken highlight, the preference for the one desk model is based on the notion that 'a student often does not know if he or she has a technical, productive or informational question' (McKinstry and McCracken, 2002). In addition, as Crockett et al. warn, staff members at separate desks tend to isolate themselves and this isolation may increase over time (Crockett et al., 2002). The intention is to pool expertise in order to develop new collaborative service patterns and systems that are oriented towards supporting both learning and learners. It is recognised though that the process of developing new service patterns will take time.

The services offered to students will be both physical and virtual. The virtual space supports the operation of the Commons but also provides flexible access to many of its services beyond the walls of the buildings. The virtual Learning Commons will be consistent with the principles adopted for VU Learning Commons and will support users who cannot always attend or who choose not to attend the physical space of the Learning Commons. It is particularly important for those VU students who do not spend a great deal of time outside classes on campus, or who are one of over 4,000 offshore located VU students. The virtual service will seek to integrate more closely with academic delivery. It will include course content material, existing library website services such as database searching, and Teaching and Learning Support services (including online bookings for staff consultations, which may also be virtual).

Student rovers

Early on in the planning process student assistants were identified as a desirable component of the Learning Commons. The rationale for using student assistants is based on the idea that many students 'find it easier to approach Student Rovers first for guidance or assistance, before they approach staff' (Student Learning Services, 2006a). This was also consistent with a drive to enhance the student experience and to employ greater numbers of VU students on campus. During 2007, a pilot program will be funded by Teaching and Learning Support to use Student Rovers in the City Flinders St Campus Learning Commons.

Student Rovers will function as:

- first tier of student support for Information Technology, Library and Student Learning;
- mentors for student communities of learning and the Learning Commons culture of learning.

(Student Learning Services, 2006b)

The need for careful selection and recruitment of students was an imperative. Therefore Student Rovers will be:

> ...later year students who have demonstrated their understanding of academic systems and learning demands through their academic results. Their credibility as first tier in support services will rest on their training, while their credibility as mentors will rest on their perception as successful students. (Student Learning Services, 2006b)

Students may initially be drawn from existing VU student leadership programs such as Peer Mentoring, Student Circles, or the Host program.

Three methods for rewarding Rovers were initially explored and evaluated: academic credit; certification, and payment (casual employee or honorarium). It was agreed in consultation with the University's Human Resources staff that the model used be payment because it assists students financially, is transparent and understandable, and is consistent with the University's focus on students' learning in and through work.

The student rovers will work for up to 8 hours per week during the 12 week higher education semester. Rovers will work in pairs in various shift combinations between 11.00 a.m. and 6.00 p.m. weekdays. Although their day-to-day work will be coordinated by a Rover Supervisor from the Library, the rovers' training and ongoing development will be provided by a Teaching and Learning Support staff member.

The student rovers will undergo both initial and ongoing training conducted by staff from Library, Teaching and Learning Support and Information Technology. A training agenda has been developed from existing training programs at VU in peer mentoring and refined to suit the specific circumstances. Student rovers will undertake 2 days of paid training, which will include training in helping students with:

- basic IT related problems;
- referring students to appropriate library resources;
- general questions about academic writing, referencing techniques, basic citation and study skills.

The rovers will use social networking software (ELGG) to communicate with one another through a blog, through detailed shift reports and eventually through a Wiki for FAQs. Rovers will be allocated time towards the end of each shift (in a handover period) to use this facility to reflect on their role, refine their responses to students' problems and queries, share insights with their peers and discuss any issues they are having with their supervisors. Both the Rover Supervisor and the Teaching and Learning Support staff member will have access to ELGG and will be able to use it to monitor how the rovers are working in the space and identify what further support and training they need. In addition, rovers will be required to keep basic statistics on student enquiries and whether they have been able to help the student or whether they have referred the student on to a more experienced staff member.

At this stage funding is provided by a one-off grant from TLS (rather than re-current University funding). Although this is not ideal, it was necessary to launch the program. Evaluation of the Student Rover pilot is a high priority in 2007 in order to make a case for continuing the program and obtaining ongoing funding for student rovers in all VU Learning Commons. The evaluation will take a participatory action research approach with student rovers, Library staff, Teaching and Learning Support staff and the researchers being active participants in the evaluation process. A wealth of formative evaluation data will be generated from ELGG and from the statistics on student enquiries, which will be used to continuously modify and improve how we support and train the student rovers. A key focus of the evaluation will be on exploring the effectiveness of rovers not just as additional staff members, but as mentors for student communities of learning. Qualitative focus groups, interviews and questionnaires will be conducted to evaluate the effectiveness of the rovers pilot from the perspective of key stakeholders who are not direct participants in the pilot but who either use the rover service (students and academic staff) or who share a workplace with the rovers (library, Information Technology Services and other teaching and learning support staff). In addition, roving as a form of peer mentoring will be explored as a way of helping students to develop their core graduate attributes and reinforce study and learning skills. Such research could help to inform other mentoring initiatives at VU designed to support student learning.

Reflections on progress to date and where do we go next?

A great deal has been achieved to date as VU works towards a Learning Commons approach across its many campuses. A shared understanding of a Learning Commons at VU has evolved over time but it was not without challenges. Although there was agreement about the need for new student learning spaces there were differences in how it was seen to work in practice, what personnel would staff the Commons, and indeed what models would best support students' learning. One example was the notion of using student rovers. When this was introduced, concerns were raised by some library staff about students being perceived to take existing library jobs while student learning staff saw this as an opportunity to extend existing mentoring programs in the university.

Through working together closely each party gained a better understanding and opportunities for greater collaboration have emerged. An example is the notion of 'triage', with library, student learning and IT professionals as the second and third tier of support after student rovers. This was a helpful concept in understanding how the different parties could work together and maintain professional identities.

While the development of the physical spaces of the Learning Commons at a number of campuses are well underway, the approach to the management and staffing of these new student spaces is still in the early stages of development. The service model needs to be flexible enough to evolve over time and scaleable to accommodate different campuses and student cohorts. The literature highlights the difficulties of merging previously distinct service cultures and warns of a tough period of transition (Crockett et al., 2002). Most commonly the people involved cite different reporting lines, different work culture and lack of knowledge of each other's areas as challenges. Effective referral systems and cross-training to develop multi-skilled staff are also required.

The success of the Commons has been measured thus far by how busy the facilities are and annual student satisfaction surveys. Bennett notes the lack of evaluation of student learning in 240 library construction and renovation projects between 1992 and 2001. He states, 'We need to understand that the success of the academic library is best measured not by the frequency and ease of library use but by the learning that results from that use' (Bennett, 2005; p. 11). Many of the commonly used evaluation mechanisms do not elicit the type of data that is required. More sophisticated approaches to evaluating the VU Learning Commons are needed, which seek to explore the effectiveness of this space as a site of learning.

During 2007, an evaluation of the Flinders St Campus Learning Commons is planned. This will include collecting evaluation data on students' perception of the facilities, the service model particularly the use of student rovers, and student behaviour and study patterns in this space to determine how best to support students in the Learning Commons. It will also include an evaluation of the staff experience of working in a new service environment. Findings from this evaluation will inform the implementation of the Learning Commons at other campuses.

For the Learning Commons to have a meaningful impact on students' learning, it needs to be integrated with the learning that students undertake in their courses. This is the hardest and most fundamental challenge ahead. It will require a university-wide commitment and culture change to ensure that all teaching at VU is consistent with a learner-centred approach and exploits the learning opportunities inherent in new types of learning spaces. Teachers need continuing support to promote and incorporate the development of independent and collaborative learning in the curriculum and the related role of the Learning Commons. A key determinant to moving forward will be in ensuring that the Learning Commons is flexible and adaptable to ensure that the Commons can best meet the changing needs of the University and its learners.

Notes

1. VU is one of five dual-sector universities in Australia providing both higher education and post-secondary technical and further

education (TAFE). The TAFE sector provides a range of qualifications from Certificate I to Advanced Diplomas in general and preparatory education similar to the Community Colleges in the United States as well as industry and trade specific areas. Although mostly post-secondary, they also offer the final year of an Australian secondary education qualification for adults and or alternatives to the final year.

2. Detailed statistics on higher educations student profiles in Australian universities are available from the Australian Department of Education, Science and Training (DEST). (see *http://www.dest.gov.au/sectors/higher_education/publications_ resources/statistics/publications_higher_education_statistics_ collections.htm#studpubs*).

3. In the higher education sector, students on all courses are required to meet the Core Graduate Attributes one of which is 'can work both autonomously and collaboratively as a professional'. In the TAFE sector each qualification addresses the need for students to develop teamwork skills.

References

Barr, R., and Tagg, J. (1995) 'From teaching to learning', *Change*, Nov/Dec: 13–25.

Beagle, D. (2004) 'From Information Commons to Learning Commons', presented at Information Commons: Learning Space Beyond the Classroom, California, 2004.

Bennett, S. (2005) *Righting the Balance*. Washington, D.C.: Council on Library and Information Resources.

Biggs, J. (2003) *Teaching for Quality Learning at University*, vol. 2. Berkshire, UK: The Society for Research into Higher Education/Open University Press.

Boone, M.D. (2003) 'Monastery to marketplace: a paradigm shift', *Library Hi Tech*, 21(3): 358–66.

Chappell, C. (2003) *Changing Pedagogy: Contemporary Vocational Learning*. Sydney, Australia: The Australian

Centre for Organisational, Vocational and Adult Learning.

Church, J. (2005) 'The evolving Information Commons', *Library Hi Tech*, 23(1): 75–81.

Crockett, C., McDaniel, S. and Remy, M. (2002) 'Integrating services in the Information Commons: toward a holistic library and computing environment', *Library Administration and Management*, 16(4): 181–6.

Equity and Social Justice Branch (2003) *Equity Plan 2004–2006*. Melbourne, Australia: Victoria University.

Keating, S., and Gabb, R. (2005) *Putting Learning into the Learning Commons: A Literature Review*. Melbourne, Australia: Melbourne Postcompulsory Education Centre, Victoria University.

McKinstry, J., and McCracken, P. (2003) 'Combining computing and reference desks in an undergraduate library: a brilliant innovation or a serious mistake?', *Portal: Libraries and the Academy*, 2(3): 391–400.

McLennan, B., and Keating, S. (2005) *Making the Links to Student Learning*. Melbourne, Australia: Victoria University.

Remy, M. (2004) 'Information literacy: the Information Commons connection', presented at USC 2004 Teaching and Learning with Technology Conference: Enhancing the Learning Experience, California, 2004.

Sheehan, P., and Wiseman, J. (2004) *Investing in Melbourne's West: A Region in Transition*. Melbourne, Australia: CSES/ICEPA.

Student Learning Services (2006a) *Role Description: Student Rovers in the Learning Commons*. Melbourne, Australia: Victoria University.

Student Learning Services (2006b) *Student Rovers: Roles and Rewards*. Melbourne, Australia: Victoria University.

Victoria University (2004) *Learning and Teaching Policy.* Melbourne, Australia: Victoria University.

Victoria University (2004) Strategic Plan 2004–2008. Melbourne, Australia: Victoria University.

Weimer, M. (2002) *Learner-Centered Teaching: Five Key Changes to Practice.* San Francisco, CA: Jossey-Bass.

9

Improving student life, learning and support through collaboration, integration and innovation
Crit Stuart

The Georgia Institute of Technology is one of the nation's top research universities. The campus occupies 400 acres in the heart of Atlanta, where 18,000 undergraduate and graduate students receive a technologically-based education, with the preponderance of students engaged in engineering disciplines.

The Institute offers many nationally recognised, top-ranked programs. Undergraduate and graduate degrees are offered in Architecture, Engineering, Sciences, Computing, Management, and Liberal Arts. Georgia Tech consistently ranks among the top 10 public universities in the United States according to *U.S. News and World Report*. In a world that increasingly turns to technology for solutions, Georgia Tech is using innovative teaching and advanced research to define the technological university of the twenty-first century.

Engineering student success through critical partnerships

We believe that a great university requires an outstanding library. This is the story of a library that discovered how to be a compelling destination for students and faculty. Our ambition was driven by an alarming realisation that the Georgia Tech Library was rapidly becoming inconsequential to students and faculty. By 2000, annual library visits had dropped an average of 5 per cent per year for 15 years. Our 220,000 sq. ft library, comprised of West and East towers, was an anachronism in the heart of campus.

Our opportunity to imagine a genuinely customer-sensitive library came in 2001. The newly-arrived library Dean initiated an environmental scan to identify how the library could contribute to the learning and research agendas of the university. Students, faculty and administrators were engaged to give their opinions of library services, resources and the physical facility. For the majority of campus constituents, the library played little-to-no role in their academic and intellectual lives. Graduate students and faculty were more likely than undergraduates to use library books, full text databases and other resources for their research, teaching and classroom deliverables. Constituents frequently failed to be aware of the print and electronic information purchased for their academic endeavours. As they considered the library facility, students and even faculty were unsure how to distinguish the service characteristics of the three general and specialised information desks. Reference desks were infrequently visited while consuming significant effort on the part of the library to staff. And the voluminous print reference collections, especially the general collection covering 50 per cent of one floor, were infrequently used.

Graduate and undergraduate students came to the library for one of two purposes: to find a quiet place for concentrated study, and to use a computer. The computers of choice were those supplied by the Office of Information Technology (OIT). These were assembled in two clusters, one PC-based and the other Mac-flavoured. Both OIT installations offered a variety of production software. These clusters had student assistant gate-keepers who did little more than refill toner cartridges and paper trays in printers, but the OIT workstations were clearly better than the library's gesture. Computers offered by the library were little more than information look-up stations with minimal productivity software and expensive page-per-print output. Library machines were scarcely touched, primarily used during midterms and finals when the OIT clusters were overwhelmed. Over the many years that OIT supported computer clusters in the library, they were viewed by library staff as unwelcome interlopers. Library staff rarely consorted with OIT, and OIT in turn offered computing facilities without regard for our information agenda.

A majority of students and faculty complained that the library was disconnected from the university and inconsequential to their academic success. Library staff in turn tended to ignore the dwindling population of customers in our midst except when providing assistance at service points.

Several themes were evident in the feedback we gathered. All constituents wanted the library to provide digital resources over print whenever possible for access from the desktop. They wanted our services to be easier to identify, comprehend and use. Students especially made note of the drearily uninspiring spaces the library set aside for study. Interiors were drab and scarcely improved over several decades, and a high percentage of original user space was consumed by collections. Students were outspoken in their desire for better workstations and productivity tools to facilitate their work.

The implications of the Dean's environmental scan were obvious: either change or become obsolete. Our response was threefold: accelerate the transition from print collections of journal and conference titles to comprehensive digital subscriptions, consolidate service points, and focus on the productivity and learning needs of students.

When we surveyed academic libraries for inspiring learning spaces, we were struck by how little attention this seemingly logical initiative received. Even in new structures and renovations, we noted that libraries frequently failed to comprehend and address the life cycle of students with their need for study and productivity accommodations. We were convinced that the academic library was the logical agent to fill this gap, and so the Georgia Tech Library embarked on a series of transformations to spaces that reveal compelling data about student study habits and learning requirements. The work is centred in an evolving Learning Commons, created in two phases across the span of 4 years.

Georgia Tech finds that Learning Commons, if thoughtfully conceived and nurtured, are epicentres of student academic life and suggest next steps in needed library transformations and partnerships. The lessons we have learned appear to have universal application and appeal. In this report you will learn how Georgia Tech Library came to be essential to the university's core mission to educate the leaders of tomorrow.

Planning the library's West Commons

Upon completion of the environmental scan, and in the midst of consolidating public services into fewer and more apparent service destinations for students and faculty, the library Dean asked us to collaborate with OIT to create an Information Commons (the West Commons) just inside the doors of the library. The Dean had recently completed a tour of some of the country's best academic libraries in the company of university administrators and OIT personnel. The tourists were struck by Information or Learning Commons that relied on both library and IT staff to create improved facilities for student productivity. This collaborative model of a library Commons appealed to both Georgia Tech Library and OIT administrators.

The West Commons greets students as soon as they enter the library. The two-storey space had devolved over the years into a drab, individual-study, cubicle maze planted next to the Circulation desk. OIT administrators aspired to create a next-generation computer cluster in a dynamic setting. Library administrators felt the partnership would benefit us by putting support for the technology infrastructure into OIT's practiced hands, thereby freeing us to focus on our information agenda. From this renovated location, reference staff would work from a consolidated information service desk on the margins of the West Commons. The Circulation desk was moved to a different location. Building hours were expanded, with permanent library staff continuously on hand from Sunday noon to early evening Friday, and all day Saturday.

Fifty-five staff from the library and OIT engaged to create the West Commons. Most library participants came from the Information Services department. OIT's participants came, for the most part, from units that provided classroom and computer cluster support, or from their student computer support team. The work of this very large group was facilitated by a lead team of six individuals from the two organisations, lead by the library's Associate Director for Public Services. The West Commons was programmed and designed for construction bid in 4 short months.

During this initial programming phase and the ensuing months we were required to address training issues for both library and OIT staff, market the enterprise to the university, and sustain its performance once it was built. The staffing model was difficult to discern. We wanted to build a team of library and OIT staff to handle both information and technical requests. Library staff at the Information Services desk could be expected to assist students with login authentication, printing problems and perhaps even help with basic software applications. And we imagined that OIT staff and student assistants might also provide basic assistance with information requests. Not knowing exactly how life would be in the West Commons, we imagined a combined enterprise where a student might look to any employee for help. For staff who had only worked in one subject, discipline or technical domain, these broadened expectations were not always welcome.

An overriding concern was that individuals were wary of working with counterparts from the opposing organisation. We had no prior history of working together. For years the library had ignored OIT staff and student assistants who worked in the two IT computer clusters. As we attempted to organise individuals into teams, mistrust and doubt were palpable. Within a few weeks, our work had ground to a halt. In our rush to detail the technical, physical, service and organisational aspects of the West Commons, library and OIT leaders had not addressed staff fears associated with organisational change and the complexities of collaboration. Some individuals were on board from the start, but others were unable to move forward without first addressing personal concerns about this new service structure. And strain was coming from other quarters. Simultaneous with this work, the library's Public Services division was consolidating service points so that staff would be freed up for other tasks, and to stretch existing staff over expanded hours of service. Some specialised reference staff regretted that both the government information and microforms reference desks would be consolidated into a single service point offering comprehensive information assistance. Our customers had told us that one comprehensive service point would suffice. But this was not our historic model of reference and information service. Some reference staff imagined that customers would suffer from the consolidation and be left behind in the rush to create a new model of library service. Staff in OIT were similarly concerned that their commitment to the West Commons would undermine other duties.

In order to get the process back on track, the lead team addressed these staff concerns by giving time to each individual to explore fears, and to indicate the specific assurances they needed to move forward. 'Will I lose my job if I can't learn the new technical or information skills expected of me?' 'Will students and faculty no longer use the library's specialised information services if we create a facility that focuses on student productivity?' 'If the preponderance of print reference materials are returned to the general stacks, will our ability to provide great reference assistance suffer?'. The lead team came to the realisation that our combined staff would work best if they were given broad choices for contributing to the evolution of the West Commons, and for imagining changes to their work responsibilities. We could see opportunities in the emerging service structure for some individuals to carry on as before, while others would take on additional challenges and new skills. Each person was assured that his or her job would be secure, and over time and with careful consideration, changes would be implemented to meet the requirements of the new setting. We allotted time for staff from both organisations to talk about their current jobs, expertise, and value to their respective organisations. We came to appreciate what each person had to offer, and to understand

and respect the work of each organisation to foster student success at the university. With this new appreciation for each individual in the large group, our work was accelerated and even exciting. The big lesson we learned about creating a genuine collaboration is that time must be given to engendering trust, self-confidence and mutual consideration for individuals in the 'other organisation'. From this point forward our work was focused, rapid and collegial.

Life in the West Commons: a general productivity centre for individual learners coupled with a multimedia studio[1]

The West Commons (Figure 9.1) opened in autumn 2002 and is composed of two elements, a general productivity centre and a multimedia studio. It is designed for individual workers rather than for groups.

General productivity centre in the West Commons

Funding for the West Commons renovation (~$1,000,000) came from undesignated library endowments, a technology fee committee grant, OIT, and the provost's office. This facility hosts approximately 90 computers on a mix of long tables laid out in rows and horseshoe configurations (Figure 9.2a,b). Each machine has a minimum of 4 ft of lateral space, though we believe now that a minimum of 6 ft of lateral workspace is better suited for a single individual. There is no segregation or walling-in of stations, opting instead for an 'open landscape' so that each station has an unobstructed

Figure 9.1 West Commons floor plan – general productivity multimedia studio

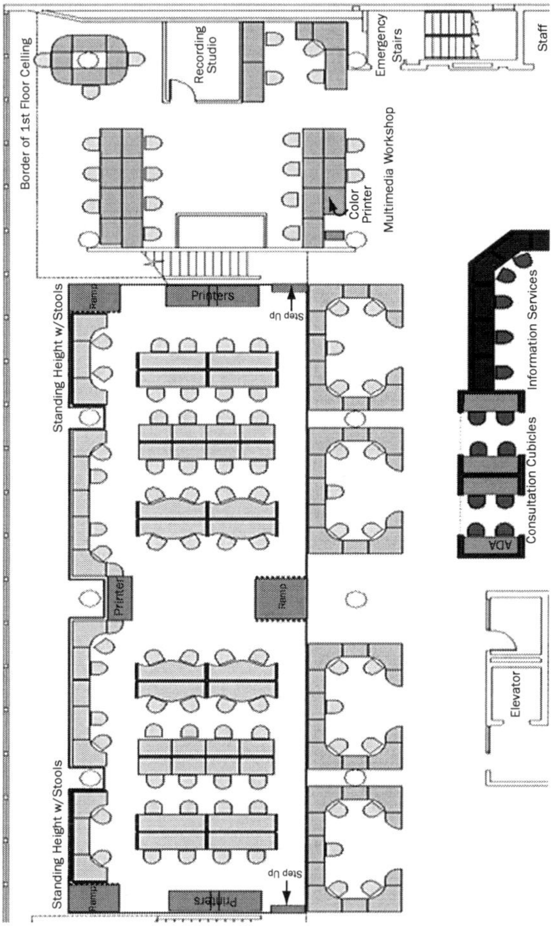

Figure 9.2 General productivity center in the West Commons

(a)

(b)

view of the two-storey, north-facing glass wall. A clearly designated entry point in the middle of the room forms a natural queuing spot for customers. Login authentication restricts use to currently enrolled students, and current employees of the university. A rich offering of approximately 70 software applications is available from the desktop and updated by OIT each semester. Headphones with microphones are attached to each machine. High capacity printers, both colour and black-and-white, are placed at the periphery of the general productivity centre, providing customers 100 free pages the first week of the semester, and with an addition of 50 pages each successive week (no more than 100 pages accrue to an individual's account at any time). A dozen scanners are concentrated in one aspect of the Commons, and these also link to the nearby printers.

A help desk in the centre of the general productivity installation is staffed with OIT student assistants from 8 a.m. to midnight most days. These assistants are trained to rove about the floor looking for students who might have issues with desktop performance and, more frequently, to manage printer performance (re-supplying paper, toner, fixing jams, and monitoring overall performance of the in-house print management system).

From the week it opened, the general productivity centre has been overwhelmingly popular. It has become a place to see and be seen, and hosts a continually changing mix of focused work and light social engagement. Extra chairs are provided for groups of friends who gather around single stations, offering a gesture toward group accommodation. In a year, 800,000 print jobs are generated on the machines, which are each logged in an average of 3,200 hours. A queue typically forms by 10 a.m. each day, and persists until late into the evening.

The Information Services desk sits along the margin of the West Commons. A mix of librarians and library assistants are on duty every hour the library is open providing information assistance to walk-up clients and those at a distance. Several paraprofessional staff are upgraded to

Figure 9.3 Student tutor at reserved workstation

'information associate', a new position necessitated by the demands of the West Commons. Information associates are grounded in both information and technical skills, and principally work the second and third shifts.

At one end of the Information Services counter are four workstations reserved for student tutors providing evening and weekend assistance with MATLab and other complex software (Figure 9.3). This request came from faculty in engineering who wanted a more central and student-popular location for providing this assistance after typical tutoring hours. It is a big hit with students seeking just-in-time and repeated help with homework assignments.

As we considered the production cycles of students, we noticed there were no logical spaces on campus for them to practice group presentations. Students were creating presentations in the West Commons, then departing for locations in abandoned classrooms, dormitories and other

Figure 9.4   Presentation rehearsal studio

'found spaces' to rehearse prior to appearance in class. In early 2004 we created a presentation rehearsal studio that could be booked online for 2-hour reservations. We remodeled a little-used office adjacent to the West Commons, supplying it with a technology podium, 50" plasma screen, and custom furniture to accommodate a group of up to 14 individuals. A digital camera can be deployed to record the rehearsal, with the option to save the recorded session to a storage medium or to a streaming server for 30-day access. Today the space is heavily used for the exclusive purpose of presentation practice. An average of 800 reservations are placed each year, for any time of day in a 24-hour cycle. The space has inspired the creation of two additional rehearsal spaces in writing centres across campus (Figure 9.4).

Multimedia studio of the West Commons

This second aspect of the West Commons is a startling success. Prior to the creation of the West Commons, a few high-end multimedia workstations were installed in a little-used space in OIT's principal building. Hours were limited, with the facility advertised exclusively to faculty. Students seldom discovered the space. Once set up and greatly expanded in the West Commons, the Multimedia Studio was an immediate hit with students. Today it houses 24 high-end PC and Mac stations with approximately 35 software applications covering movie editing, web page design, 3D rendering and other graphics tools, and with peripheral equipment for scanning, audio and video editing, and other conversion activities. Each station provides 6 lateral ft of desktop workspace. One permanent OIT staff person runs the studio with help from two full time employees (FTEs) in the form of student assistants. The area is staffed from 8 a.m. to midnight most days. Together the Multimedia staff carry expertise across all applications offered in the facility. Staff training is intensive and on going.

After the first year of operation we realised that short courses in specialised multimedia software would benefit student customers and conserve staff time. There is an unending demand for every level of technical assistance, and faculty frequently direct entire classes to our facility for in-depth training in one or more applications. The OIT manager anticipates demand for specific software by meeting at the beginning of the academic term with faculty who are known to refer to the facility. Special training units for the multimedia assignments in these classes are offered at critical moments in the semester to capitalise on students' motivation to learn. The ambiance of the Studio contributes to creative output (Figure 9.5a–d). The surrounding walls are typically decorated with images of student work created in the Studio. At other times it is jazzed up in a hot theme, with the current look for this semester (spring 2007) inspired by the videogame Super Mario World. The student photography and feature-length movie-making clubs hold

Figure 9.5 Life in the Multimedia Studio

(a)

(b)

weekly meetings in the space, and these students help to popularise the area as a student-centric, student-friendly zone. Today the student demand for multimedia workstations

Figure 9.5 (*Cont'd*)

(c)

(d)

outstrips what we can supply. We imagine a future expansion of the Studio supplying triple the current number of workstations. In our view, today's multimedia software will be tomorrow's standard work tools as students and faculty discover the power of graphic expression.

Impact of the West Commons

This first Learning Commons for Georgia Tech Library was a sensation for both library customers, the library and OIT. Library attendance leapt 65 per cent in the first week of operation and was sustained. Student acclaim for the West Commons resulted in their designating it the most important improvement at Georgia Tech after its first year of operation, this in a year when the university built or renovated approximately $250,000,000 in campus structures. In the same year, students voted it the best place to study on campus. It became the place to see and be seen in the act of study, a convening ground for individual productivity that at times pulses with energy and studious commotion.

Information Services staff quickly adjusted to living on the margin of the West Commons. The department's strategic plan was broadened to include innovative marketing of library services. These staff joined OIT colleagues to create annual welcome back events that feature gaming in the Commons, performances by singing and comedy groups, movies and board games. Library staff also initiated a monthly faculty speaker series, Tuesday Talks, aimed to 'bring research to the rest of us'. In these talks, outstanding research faculty present their work to students in an informal setting where inquiry and frank discourse are encouraged. Information Services staff, joined by colleagues from other library units, significantly increased their participation in Georgia Tech's freshman seminar course, and now comprise the largest group of faculty volunteer teachers outside the course's home department. This exposure to freshmen also gives our reference staff a better sense of how to influence information skills in other classroom venues.

The East Commons: an experiment in refreshment of mind and body[2]

The West Commons focused on the productivity needs of single individuals. It continues to do this very well. But we wanted to expand our Commons facility to address group work. The need for this expansion was reinforced through the findings of two library-conducted studies, the first of which looked at the most popular study destinations on campus.

For the first survey in autumn 2003, the library worked with Steelcase Corporation's research division to do, in Steelcase's research parlance, a 'deep dive' into student study and productivity dynamics. Pairs of library and OIT staff traveled to the six most popular study locations on campus to photograph hundreds of groups of students engaged in homework assignments. We interviewed each group for a sense of what attracted students to these preferred locales. Students identified these spaces as having good aesthetics, relatively good food and drink from vending machines or cafes, comfortable furniture, and the likelihood that one might run into friends or helpful individuals during the course of one's stay. They studied together because they were working on a similar assignment, or if the work were dissimilar, because they were reinforced and sustained by their study cohorts. At the end of each interview, we asked students why they were not studying in the library, and what would attract them to our facility. The majority of respondents said the library was a logical entity to host their individual and group work 'if' we effectively addressed several issues: improve aesthetics, provide terrific refreshment, provide group work accommodations including spacious computer workstations, and attract their friends to our setting. With this data in hand, the Steelcase researchers proposed a renovation of a floor of the library to deliver these qualities. The library and OIT began to work out the details for the renovation, but university funding was not forthcoming due to budgetary constraints. In spite of the temporary setback, we were emboldened by the findings.

In autumn 2004, several student leaders approached library administration to commend the direction we had taken with the West Commons, and to offer to help us in some way. We had recently read Scott Bennett's influential study, *Libraries Designed For Learning*.[3] Bennett suggests that academic libraries should consider how to construct productive relationships with students, perhaps utilising a student ombudsman to facilitate communication and awareness. For our purposes, we decided to create a student advisory council that, with us and our partner OIT, might address policy issues and the postponed renovation for group study. The student leaders liked the idea and agreed to serve on our first Library and Partners Student Advisory Council.[4]

University finances had improved in the ensuing year. The library and campus administrators felt the time was right to renovate the first floor of the East tower as a Learning Commons catering to groups. With assistance from Student Advisory Council members, we conducted a second study of group learning behaviours. An affinity focus group technique was employed for gathering programming data.[5] (This process is composed of four exercises: idea generation/brainstorming, sorting of ideas into 'affinity groups', and then labeling the groupings of ideas with both literal and metaphoric titles.) We convened four focus groups comprised of students, and one each of academic faculty and library/OIT staff. The 1-hour sessions revealed amazingly consistent themes for programming the East Commons.[6] The data also reinforced the findings of the previous year's deep dive into campus study spaces.

The overarching theme for the East Commons is 'refreshment for mind and body'. For students to stay in the library for long stretches of time, they require refreshment and amenities to sustain them. A café and good vending machines were frequently mentioned. They imagined great lighting, student-created art, exhibits celebrating the best-and-brightest student and faculty research at Georgia Tech, and an energising aesthetic. Students desired a mix of easy-to-configure furniture that accommodated group work while also allowing for moments of relaxation and chilling out. And they wanted group computer workstations to facilitate collaboration, with whiteboards and flipcharts to track brainstorming sessions and homework reviews.

We now had indisputable programming content for the East Commons. The university eventually pledged several hundred thousand dollars to the project because we had gained their trust and commitment via the successful West Commons. And members of our Student Advisory Council provided complementary support in a successful campaign to acquire both technology fee funds and a handsome pledge from a 50th year alumni class fundraiser.

The East Commons (Figure 9.6) covers approximately 8,000 sq. ft of the first floor East tower, immediately down the hallway from the West Commons. It opened in autumn 2006 with the following elements:

- a refurbished Circulation department and service desk;
- two group computer zones with 30 workstations, in addition to six walk-up computers for short-term use and four visitor workstations that also can be used by students;

Figure 9.6 East Commons floor plan

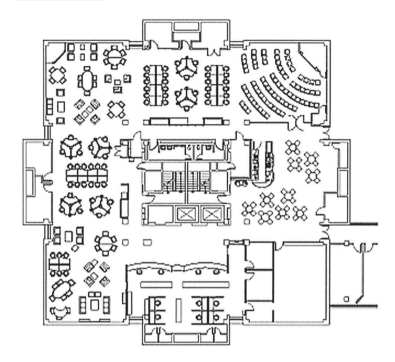

- three study zones set up with a mix of portable tables and chairs, over-stuffed chairs and sofas, flipcharts and ceiling-mounted power cords;

- a study zone that transforms into a presentation space seating 85 guests, with 80" rear-projection screen, speakers and microphones, and a digital camera mounted in the ceiling to capture performances and presentations;

- a Jazzman's Café open from early morning to late evening, and 24 hours a day as finals approach.

We wanted an infrastructure solution for the East Commons to facilitate on-the-fly additions and modifications to the spaces. We selected a new product from Herman Miller, Convia®, a ceiling-based lighting management system with the capacity to push power and data drops to any location throughout the zones. The East Commons carries the flexibility of a theater stage as we extemporise adjustments to lighting schemes, introduce equipment like camcorders and wireless projectors, and install micro-exhibits with custom lighting and data ports at any location under the ceiling grid (Figure 9.7a–f). Fabric walls by Herman Miller articulate to almost any shape and divide the East Commons into variously-flavoured study zones. Along the periphery, walls can be washed in standard light or 'painted' from a palette of colour options.

The East Commons is coordinated by two new library positions, re-engineered from existing Circulation staff positions. These coordinators (think 'concierges'!) manage the art, exhibits and programming in the presentation space as well as attend to the technology, lighting and additions of new hardware throughout the floor. At the Circulation desk, new laptops, digital cameras, camcorders, webcams and other technology devices are checked out to students for multimedia work and extemporised videoconferencing with fellow students.

A high percentage of students in the East Commons are regular inhabitants who are drawn to a remarkable new home in the East Commons. Its heterogeneous mix of learning environments has something to offer to any student or group looking for an inspiring, superbly equipped facility. At the end of a 24-hour cycle, students have rearranged furniture to suit their immediate group study needs, worked through tablets of flipchart paper, crashed on couches and comfortable chairs, and produced hundreds of documents to print out on a new array of printers. In the first semester of operation, 17 programs were presented in the presentation

Figure 9.7 East Commons – refreshment for mind and body

(a)

(b)

space (when it wasn't functioning as a study venue). Student art enlivens the peripheral walls, and clever micro-exhibits colour the interior spaces. For the library's autumn 'welcome back' event, 800 students, mostly freshmen,

Figure 9.7 (*Cont'd*)

(c)

(d)

jammed the East Commons, West Commons and adjacent spaces to enjoy board games, improvisational comedy, speed dating, Ninja tag, student-produced short films and free food and drink (Figure 9.8a–c). An honors program class

Figure 9.7 *(Cont'd)*

(e)

(f)

studying ideal 'dwelling spaces' selected the East Commons for the final class project that produced a 20-minute documentary of the setting. By the end of the first semester of existence of the East Commons, library attendance had shot up another 25 per cent to historic highs.

Figure 9.8 Programming for academic and social aspects of student life

(a)

(b)

Figure 9.8 *(Cont'd)*

(c)

Collaboration, oversight and assessment in the Commons

The collaboration between the library and OIT is structured through a memorandum of understanding.[7] It outlines the governance, service, staffing, technology and financial responsibilities of each party to sustain the two Commons and the Resource Center. An advisory council meets monthly to provide oversight of the operations, and is comprised of two library administrators and three OIT administrators and staff. More immediate and detailed guidance is attained through an oversight council comprised of several line staff in both of our operations, facilitated by a pair of individuals from the advisory council. Issues that cannot be resolved by the oversight council are bounced up to the advisory council.

In general, OIT absorbs technology costs associated with the Commons: printers and printing costs including paper and toner, servers, two full-time staff with student assistants for both aspects of the West Commons, and productivity software and the applications images pushed to the various workstations. The library staffs the Information Services desk and maintains the physical environment. Together the two units petition the university or the technology fee committee for funds to refresh the technology suffusing the Commons enterprises. And together we interview both full-time and student assistant applicants who work in the Commons, and provide a limited degree of cross-training to the other's staff as appropriate. The primary concern for both the advisory and oversight councils is to maintain excellent communication between the two entities.

Assessment of the Commons is a collaborative effort. Upon completion of the West Commons, a detailed report characterised the relative success of the installation, and of the collaboration.[8] Together we also compiled an exhaustive report card at the end of the first year of operation.[9] After 4 years of intimate collaboration, we have the sense that we are succeeding at our work. The same can be said of student reactions to the Commons spaces.

OIT maintains detailed statistics of software usage, and in a generalised way, of the types of students using our installations. These data help us to know what software applications to drop, and which to sustain. We also entertain requests from students for new software, software training aids, and peripheral equipment, which are reviewed on a semester basis.

Student opinion is sampled in a variety of ways. We are able to push questionnaires and surveys to the Commons workstations for students to voluntarily respond, though this seems to irritate students so we do it sparingly. Printed questionnaires are scattered about the Commons spaces addressing discrete topics related to amenities, technology, ambiance and programming (the first survey created for the East Commons is available from *http://librarycommons.gatech.edu/about/docs/LEC_questions_feedback.pdf*). The return rate is approximately 20 per cent, and this gives us ample data to react to. A 'send us your comments' button on the library home page generates feedback from students, but use is fairly low. The Multimedia Studio also provides a suggestion box to solicit feedback. And we periodically put up a flipchart in the East Commons seeking student reaction to a topic, and for random comments. Focus groups are sporadically gathered for focused conversations, and the Library and Partners Student Advisory Council frequently offer theirs and their friends' reactions to library services. The library has participated in LibQUAL three times in the past 5 years so that we are able to benchmark and track student and faculty reaction to the physical building and services within. We have seen an extraordinary improvement in students' impressions of the physical library and amenities, centred around accolades for the Commons spaces. Taken together these techniques for sampling customer opinion and suggestions help us to sustain environments and services to benefit student learning and productivity outcomes.

A rush of new collaborations

The transformed library appears to be on everyone's radar. In the past year, several campus departments focusing on student and faculty success approached us for space in our dynamic settings. The library and OIT decided to create a destination space, the Resource Center, for several of these entities (Figure 9.9a,b). The library provided 3,500 sq. ft of space for OIT to renovate at its expense. We then offered the new quarters to several of the most attractive campus enterprises. A new undergraduate academic advisement office has opened a satellite service for academic counseling. OIT has moved its computer assistance walk-in service into the library, with hours expanded into nights and weekends. The campus's most outstanding tutoring program offers expanded evening hours in another corner of the Resource Center. And a second presentation rehearsal studio handles the extreme demand for group practice space during midterms and finals.

The university has been rather slow to endorse a writing/communications centre in the library. The literature department, along with other campus agents, are committed to the initiative, but concern arises from department-based writing centres on campus who want to see it done well. We hope to win over these skeptics in time.

Elsewhere in the library, we host a myriad of student and faculty functions. The Center for the Enhancement of Teaching and Learning holds its monthly faculty training seminars in library space, along with its annual poster session of campus experiments in pedagogy and student learning. The Counseling Center moved its monthly student seminars into the library and impressively increased student attendance. In the library entrance rotunda, and in Jazzman's Café in the East Commons, musicians occasionally serenade fellow students with violin and guitar performances, and we are testing poetry and literature readings in the Café. Campus a cappella groups offer spontaneous, brief performances on a balcony overlooking the West Commons. Both undergraduate student

Figure 9.9 The Resource Center – a collaboration of student support services

(a)

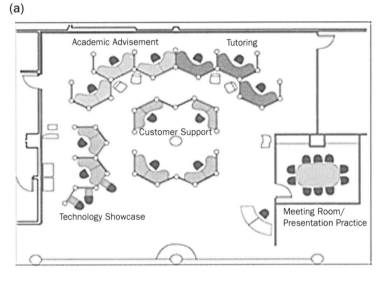

(b)

government and the residence hall association offer free food and drink in the library rotunda leading up to and during exam week. Space and support is provided to Campus MovieFest® @ GT for its annual short movie competition, and this in turn helps to popularise the Multimedia Studio. A handsome seventh-floor meeting venue in the East tower is freshly renovated for the use of academic departments, campus development officers, and student honor societies to hold special ceremonies, programs and receptions. The Library and Partners Student Advisory Council has initiated a freshman book program that touches 50 per cent of all new students, as well as launching a book club whose added purpose is to spawn other book clubs on special topics. For years tours of campus avoided the library. Daily tours now showcase the West and East Commons to prospective students and to faculty recruits. Wherever one turns in our new spaces, there is evidence of student ownership and identity.

A *re-engineered library*

Georgia Tech Library is profoundly transformed in 4 years. Much of our success in creating great learning spaces is due to the sustained contribution from our now invaluable partner, OIT. Together we have discovered that in order to create compelling learning spaces, we have to be in ongoing dialogue with students, faculty and others who care passionately about learning outcomes. As our partnership with OIT and other campus agencies flourishes, we recognise the importance of just-in-time tutoring, instruction and intervention, and of providing highly skilled assistance with emerging technologies and software applications loosely referred to as multimedia. Our students, when asked to comment on their learning needs, consistently mention secure and inspiring spaces that qualify as neutral ground, imbued to refresh mind and body, with active and quiet zones, and with robust technology and assistance. They want to see-and-be-seen in the act of learning. For our students, the library is the logical destination for their productive output, academic socialising, critical commentary and presentation rehearsal.

The work we are engaged in represents an experiment in transformation, and of looking beyond the library's borders to engage the perfect mix of practical partners in our enterprise. The grand outcome we strive for is to positively affect student retention.

Today, the Georgia Tech Library is the premiere learning space on campus, the 'third place' that joins living/sleeping quarters and classrooms/labs in the holy trinity of student destinations. Our students wouldn't have it any other way!

Notes

1. Georgia Tech Library and Information Center (2007) *The Commons at Georgia Tech Library: West Commons*. Available at *http://librarycommons.gatech.edu/lwc/index.php* (accessed 23 March 2007).
2. Georgia Tech Library and Information Center (2007) *The Commons at Georgia Tech Library: East Commons*. Available at *http://librarycommons.gatech.edu/lec/index.php* (accessed 23 March 2007).
3. Bennett, S. (2003) *Libraries Designed for Learning*. Washington, D.C.: Council on Library Resources.
4. Georgia Tech Library and Information Center (2007) *The Commons at Georgia Tech Library: Library Student Advisory Council Mission & Charge*. Available at *http://librarycommons. gatech.edu/about/docs/lsa_mission_charge.pdf* (accessed 23 March 2007).
5. Georgia Tech Library and Information Center (2007) *The Commons at Georgia Tech Library: Affinity Focus Group Exercise*. Available at *http://librarycommons.gatech.edu/ about/docs/affinity_exercise.pdf* (accessed 23 March 2007).
6. Georgia Tech Library and Information Center (2007) *The Commons at Georgia Tech Library: East Commons Focus*

Group Findings – March 2005. Available at *http://library commons.gatech.edu/about/docs/focus_group_findings.pdf* (accessed 23 March 2007).

7. Georgia Tech Library and Information Center (2007) *The Commons at Georgia Tech Library: Library Commons Memo of Understanding.* Available at *http://librarycommons. gatech.edu/about/docs/memo_of_understanding.pdf* (accessed 23 March 2007).

8. Georgia Tech Library and Information Center (2007) *The Commons at Georgia Tech Library: West Commons Project Closeout Report.* Available at *http://librarycommons.gatech. edu/about/docs/LWC_project_closeout_report.pdf* (accessed 23 March 2007).

9. Georgia Tech Library and Information Center (2007) *The Commons at Georgia Tech Library: West Commons 1st Year Report Card.* Available at *http://librarycommons.gatech. edu/about/docs/LWC_report_card.pdf* (accessed 23 March 2007).

10

The Information Commons at the University of Auckland; improving student life, learning and support through co-location, collaboration, integration and innovation

Hester Mountifield

This chapter presents a case study of the Information Commons Group at The University of Auckland, focusing on the purpose-built Kate Edger Information Commons. It outlines the strategic and operational planning undertaken to create the large student-centred learning facility that provides proactive integrated learning support in a collaborative, interdisciplinary physical and virtual learning environment. It also discusses the reengineering of the original service model to accommodate changes in learning, technology and student needs.

Introduction

The aim to be 'student-centred' has been a strong focus at The University of Auckland over a number of years. The Student

Life Commission and the Curriculum Commission of 2002 were two major initiatives to enhance student learning and life on all campuses. Another was the establishment of the highly successful Kate Edger Information Commons that provides a student-centred infrastructure for integrated learning support and information services. It is the largest of the Information Commons Group of services managed by the University Library in partnership with the University's Information Technology Services (ITS).

The University of Auckland is the largest university in New Zealand and was established in 1883. It is New Zealand's top-ranked tertiary institution based on research quality. Its mission is to be an internationally recognised, research-led university, known for the excellence of its teaching, research, and service to its local, national and international communities. The University is a member of two international university collaborations – Universitas 21 and the Association of Pacific Rim Universities. Teaching and research is conducted in eight faculties – Arts, Business and Economics, National Institute of Creative Arts and Industries (music, sound recording and design, dance, fine and visual arts, architecture, planning and urban design), Education, Engineering, Law, Medical and Health Sciences and Science. There is also a School of Theology, 37 research centres and nine research institutes.

The University has five campuses:

- The City Campus, the largest covering an area of 16 hectares or 39.5 acres, is located in the Auckland central business district. Most faculties and the School of Theology are located on this campus, as well as University Management and central service divisions such as the Centre for Academic Development (CAD), Facilities Management, Finance, ITS, Human Resources and Student Administration. The large General Library, focusing on Arts, Science, Business and Economics, and five subject libraries are based on the City Campus in close proximity to the associated faculties. The Kate Edger Information Commons is located across the street from the General Library.

- The Grafton Campus for Medical and Health Sciences is near the major Auckland City Hospital. The Philson Library and Grafton Information Commons are located in the centre of this campus and linked via an internal stairwell.

- The Epsom Campus was added after the 2004 amalgamation of The University of Auckland and the former Auckland College of Education. The Epsom Information Commons is located within the Sylvia Ashton-Warner Library.

- The Tai Tokerau Campus for Education and its small subject library is located north of Auckland in Whangarei.

- The Tamaki Campus has a strong focus on population and community health, inter-faculty research and research collaboration with government and industry. The Tamaki Campus Library supports the information needs of the campus.

The University of Auckland has a diverse student body in terms of ethnicity, English language capability and levels of academic preparation. The University experienced a significant growth in student numbers from 14,213 in 1990 to 37,924 in 2005. Most of the students fall into the 17–21 age group and have grown up with technology.

The University Library (*http://www.library.auckland.ac.nz/*) is the largest in New Zealand and ranks with the top five Australian university libraries in terms of expenditure and size. The University Library system comprises decentralised client services delivered in 12 subject libraries, three Information Commons and centralised units such as Information Commons and Learning Services, Corporate Services, IT Services, Document Delivery, Acquisitions, Serials and Cataloguing, all with system-wide roles and responsibilities.

The University of Auckland operates a federated system for the governance and delivery of IT services. ITS is responsible for implementing the University IT strategic plan, enterprise system operation, IT architecture planning, network services management, lecture theatre management, telephony services, IT procurement coordination, information security strategy and end user support for staff. The Information Commons Group provides student user support. Faculty IT Services provides input into central services and are responsible for local application development and support, as well as end user support.

The Information Commons Group

The Information Commons Group (*http://www.information-commons.auckland.ac.nz/*) consists of the Kate Edger, Grafton and Epsom Information Commons. All three facilities operate within the same IT and service infrastructure (Table 10.1).

The Kate Edger Information Commons

The Kate Edger Information Commons is an integrated learning and social environment located in a purpose-built facility. An assortment of services, environments and

Table 10.1 The Information Commons Group

	Kate Edger	Grafton	Epsom
Established	April 2003	April 2004	1999 as the @Ace Rooms, reviewed and integrated into IC Group – January 2006
Location	Purpose-built facility on the City Campus	Close proximity to Philson Library on the Grafton Campus	Inside Sylvia Ashton-Warner Library (SAW) on the Epsom Campus
Size and layout	6,647 square metres 73,700 sq. ft Five levels: Level 0: collaborative study and computers space Level 1: Short Loan and ELSAC Level 2: IC Helpdesk and collaborative computer space Level 3: quiet computer space Level 4: quiet study space	490 square metres 5,274 sq. ft One level	235 square metres 2,529 sq. ft Three rooms
Client group	Approximately 28,835 students from Arts, Business and Economics, Creative Arts, Music, Architecture, Law Engineering and Science	Approximately 3,670 Medical and Health Sciences students	Approximately 6,250 Education students

Table 10.1	The Information Commons Group *(Cont'd)*		
	Kate Edger	Grafton	Epsom
Computers	443	88	51
Laptops	38	–	13
Group seats		28	None in the
(around tables)	236		Epsom IC but
		–	42 in the SAW
Formal			Library
individual seats	185	12	None in the
			Epsom IC but
Casual seats	266	18 with	160 in the SAW
		computers	Library
Teaching room	171 (including	146	None in the
seats	66 computers)		Epsom IC but
Total study			43 in the SAW
spaces	1,339		Library
			10 with
			computers
			74
Printers	13	3	2
Photocopiers	17	1	1
Scanners	10	5	1
Software	**Operating** **system** Windows XP **UoA enterprise** **systems** Cecil Portal nDeva Printing Systems **Productivity** Endnote Microsoft Access 2003 Microsoft Excel 2003 Microsoft Word 2003 Microsoft PowerPoint 2003	Same as Kate Edger plus: Scope and Chart Image Pro Brain Storm Pharma-CAL-ogy suite	Same as Kate Edger plus: BibleWorks Fonts Geometers' Sketchpad Fathom Tinkerplots Google SketchUp

Table 10.1 The Information Commons Group *(Cont'd)*

	Kate Edger	Grafton	Epsom
	Microsoft Publisher 2003 Macromedia Studio 8 Adobe 7 Pro **Statistics** R SPSS **Multimedia software** QuickTime Player Real One Player Windows Media Player Windows Movie Maker Power DVD **Accessories** Calculator Notepad Adobe Acrobat Reader Winzip **Web page creation** Microsoft FrontPage 2002 **Web browser** Mozilla Firefox 1.5 Microsoft Internet Explorer **Library database reader** Ebrary Cduser **Software development**		

| **Table 10.1** | The Information Commons Group *(Cont'd)* |

	Kate Edger	Grafton	Epsom
	Visual Studio net Framework **GIS, spatial data and maps** ESRI Arcview 8 **Built in players (Explorer)** Macromedia Authorware Macromedia Flash Macromedia Shockwave **Imaging software** Microsoft Imaging for Windows Gimp **Features** Swap mouse buttons **Virus Tools** Symantec Antivirus **Remote console** PuTTY **Terminal connections** Xwin 32 VNC Windows Terminal Server client Citrix ICA client **Keyboard inputs** Maori keyboard Dvorak keyboard **Language inputs**		

Table 10.1 The Information Commons Group *(Cont'd)*

	Kate Edger	Grafton	Epsom
	English (NZ) Japanese Chinese (PRC) Chinese (Taiwan) German (Germany) Russian Italian Spanish (International) Thai Vietnamese Korean French Arabic		
Teaching rooms	2 seminar rooms 1 small group room 4 computer training rooms	1 computer training room, open to students outside teaching times	1 computer training room, open to students outside teaching times
Staff	IC Helpdesk: Weekdays: 6 between 7 a.m. and 7 p.m.; 3 between 7 p.m. and midnight Weekends: 3 between 8 a.m. and 10 p.m. Short Loan: Weekdays: 6 between 8 a.m. and 5 p.m.; 1 between 5 p.m. and 10 p.m. Weekends: 1 between 8 a.m. and 10 p.m.	Weekdays: 1 Weekends: 1	Weekdays: 1 Weekends: 1

Table 10.1 The Information Commons Group *(Cont'd)*

	Kate Edger	Grafton	Epsom
	ELSAC: 3 between 9 a.m. and 5 p.m. weekdays Learning Services: 5 between 8 a.m. and 5 p.m. weekdays		
Opening hours	Weekdays 7 a.m. to midnight Weekends 8 a.m. to 10 p.m. Extended weekend hours during examination periods	Monday – Thursday 7.30 a.m. to 10 p.m. Friday 7.30 a.m. to 6 p.m. Saturday 10 a.m. to 6 p.m. Sunday 12 midday to 8 p.m.	Monday – Thursday 7.30 a.m. to 10 p.m. Friday 7.30 a.m. to 6 p.m. Saturday – Sunday 10 a.m. to 4 p.m.

functions interact to create an attractive and popular student-centred hub at the physical centre of the City Campus. The Information Commons building was named after Kate Edger, the first female graduate of the University of New Zealand and the British Empire, who graduated with a BA in 1877 and a MA in 1882.

Physical facility and associated environments

The Kate Edger Information Commons (Figure 10.1) occupies one side of a major building that was constructed between October 2001 and June 2003. Warren and Mahoney were the principal architects for the project. The five-storey building opened in April 2003 and the substantial

Figure 10.1 The Kate Edger Building – the two sides of the building are linked with a glass atruim and walkways

size of the facility (11,442 m²/123,161 sq. ft) allowed for the co-location of related learning support and student services, as well as a range of retail and food suppliers. The other side of the building, the Student Commons, houses Health and Counselling, Student Association offices, Student Accommodation Centre, Postgraduate Lounge, International Student Centre and retailers such as a bank, pharmacy, bookshop, hairdresser, travel agent, IT store, and cafes. The 2002 Student Life Commission pointed out that there was much room for improving the nature, variety and quality of retail and food services on campus. A project team, consisting of staff and students, worked with a retail consultancy service to determine students' preferred retail outlets, design concepts and hours of opening for retail outlets and service agencies in the building.

The Kate Edger Information Commons offers over 1,300 study spaces in flexible configurations matching different learning styles and preferences. Collaborative learning is encouraged on the lower floors with group spaces and a greater tolerance of noise and activity. Provision is made for quiet study on the two top floors with individual study spaces (Figure 10.2a–e).

Level 0 floor plan – group study and computer space

Level 1 floor plan – High demand collection and ELSAC

Level 2 floor plan – IC Helpdesk, computer space and computer training room

Level 3 floor plan – Student Learning Centre and computer space

Level 4 floor plan – silent study space and teaching rooms

Figure 10.2 The Kate Edger Building

(a)

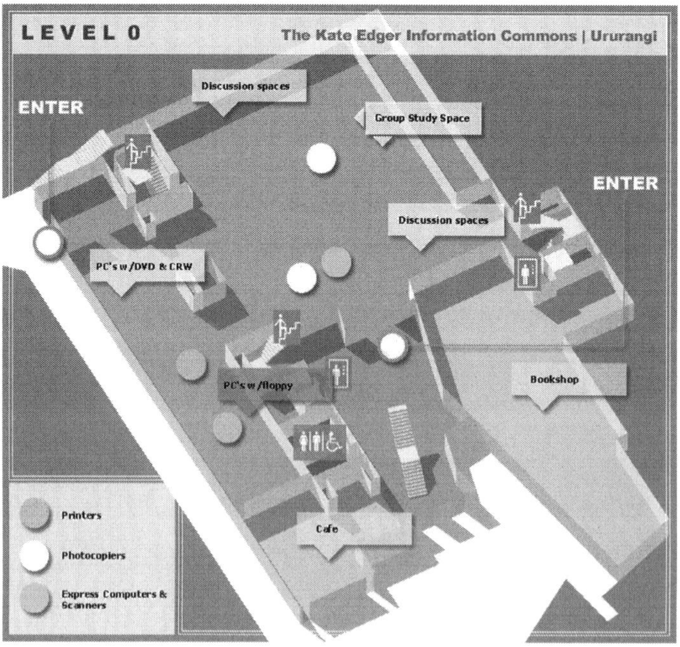

Figure 10.2 *(Cont'd)*

(b)
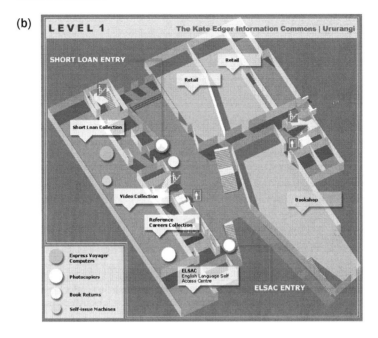

(c)
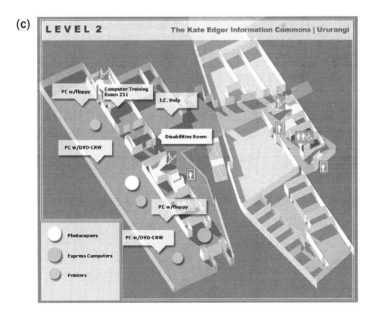

Figure 10.2 *(Cont'd)*

(d)
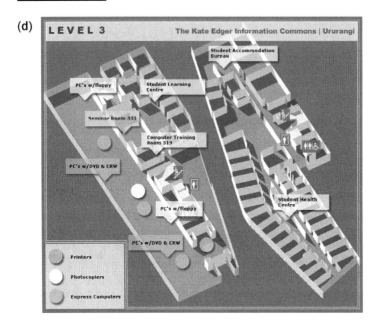

(e)
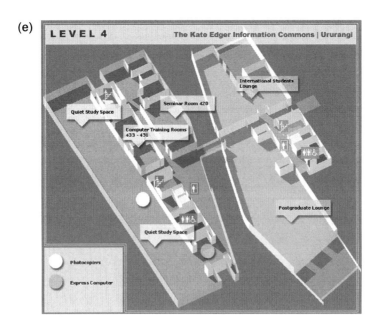

The building is at the physical and social centre of the campus effectively connecting the wider campus and creating a vibrant hub where the university community loves to gather. It is a leading-edge building that demonstrates the university's commitment to learning and technology. The virtual learning environment is visible through the glass exterior (Figure 10.3) and mesh screens and looks particularly vibrant after dark through the clever positioning of computers, coloured lighting and artwork.

The information technology infrastructure was designed to provide maximum flexibility to adapt to ongoing changes in teaching and learning technology requirements and

Figure 10.3 The Kate Edger Building exterior – attractive use of glass, colour and light

services. The design is based on conventional wired networking architectures with provision for wireless technology through several wireless access points on all levels. Students have access to over 500 computer workstations (Figure 10.4a,b) for group and individual work as well as 38 wireless laptops available for borrowing via the Voyager library management system. The IT environment provides printing, scanning, photocopying and file storage capabilities.

Student electronic services are managed through the proprietary NetAccount authentication and authorisation system. All students receive a Net login and password when they enrol. NetAccount provides access to the Internet, printing and photocopying on campus and access to enterprise systems such as the Cecil learning management system, the nDeva student enrolment system, Library electronic resources, student email and file storage on and off campus. User charges for Internet, photocopying and printing are levied by direct debit to students' NetAccount. All students receive an annual allocation for Internet access and some departments allocate print credits to their students for printing course-related work and additional credits for Internet access. The Library subsidises staff and student access to electronic resources, including web-based licensed databases, electronic course readings, e-journals and e-books, and some selected Internet resources. Students deposit funds in their NetAccounts in the Information Commons and other points of sale on the different campuses.

When the Information Commons opened in 2003, it offered a new enterprise software environment for all students regardless of which faculty they belonged to. Students have access to standard productivity software, enterprise systems and University and Library web pages

Figure 10.4 High demand computer areas (a) and group study areas with NetGen appeal (b)

(a)

(b)

and electronic resources. The new student desktop environment was a strategic development at the University of Auckland. It became a driver for change in departmental computer laboratories and for the implementation of a single sign-on authentication system. Single sign-on to all enterprise systems via NetAccount was introduced in mid-2005. Prior to its implementation students had a separate login for the nDeva student enrolment system and used NetAccount for all other systems. Needless to say it caused confusion and frustration amid students and support staff. With single sign-on, and once logged on, students automatically have seamless access to the Cecil learning management system, the nDeva student enrolment system, WebMail, AFS file storage and Library electronic resources and electronic course material readings on and off campus.

Another significant improvement was made in the area of student file storage. AFS file storage was initially only available in the Information Commons and students were also able to access their faculty or departmental file storage from any computer in the Information Commons. Students soon started to demand an enterprise approach to file storage and now have access to AFS from all libraries and most departmental computer labs and from off campus via web-services.

Planning

There were several key drivers contributing to the development of the facility. These included goals articulated in The University of Auckland strategic documents and many practical issues facing student services. The University of Auckland Academic Plan (2001) articulated the University's commitment to providing 'its students an intellectually stimulating education, which focuses on enquiry, critical thinking, experiential learning, open discussion, and which fosters a lifelong love and enjoyment of ideas, discovery and learning'. The plan also stated that the University is committed to:

- Developing an information literacy policy and support systems that enable students to locate, evaluate and use information effectively

- Identifying a level of computer skill that all students must acquire and the support systems needed to achieve these levels.

The University of Auckland Graduate Profile (2003; p. 1) points out that graduates should have:

- An ability to recognise when information is needed and a capacity to locate, evaluate and use this information effectively.

- An ability to make appropriate use of advanced information and communication technologies.

Study space was at a premium with the libraries constantly overcrowded. Learning support services for students were located in different buildings on campus. The Student Learning Centre, providing academic learning and performance skills development and some computer skills training, had inadequate teaching facilities and staff offices. ELSAC, the English Language Self-Access Centre, was located approximately 1.5 km from the centre of the City Campus. The Student Union facilities were in an urgent need of upgrading as these were built when student numbers were significantly lower. Student expectations were changing fast. Incoming students are typical of the Net Generation. They are digital natives who are comfortable in a world characterised by fast changing technologies (Prensky, 2001; 1). Oblinger and Oblinger (2005; sections 2.5–2.7) described them as always connected, digitally literate, able to multitask, comfortable in a visual-rich environment, favouring teamwork and experimental learning, able to move seamlessly between the physical and virtual environments, and expecting excellent and adaptable services. Students arrived at university expecting access to learning facilities, including computers, which provided an integrated suite of tools, resources and services (Figure 10.5a–c).

The University Library presented University Management with a discussion document that outlined its vision for enhanced services based on the development of an Information Commons. The proposed concept was complementary to a long-standing university strategy to improve student facilities on the City Campus and as a result

Figure 10.5 Seating and study areas

(a)

378

Figure 10.5 *(Cont'd)*

(b)

(c)

the Student Commons and Information Commons Project was given priority status early in 2001. A project team, consisting of the University Library, ITS, Student Administration and student representatives, developed a design brief for the Information Commons and Student Commons. The project team was later divided into the Information Commons and the Student Commons groups for the detailed planning of the different areas. Both had very specific but different goals and requirements. For the purpose of this chapter, the discussion will concentrate on the Information Commons. There was, however, ongoing consultation and collaboration between the groups to ensure a strategic fit.

The Information Commons was a collaborative project between the University Library and ITS. It was an innovative new service that crossed departmental boundaries. An IC Steering Group was established in 2002 to facilitate planning for the new IT and customer services. Staff members from the University Library and ITS worked on projects such as: networking, layout and furniture, disability requirements, hardware and software environment, student support services, student access and billing, desktop implementation and support, and IT security. Detailed project plans were developed by the teams and gradually implemented after approval by the IC Steering Group. The position of Library Manager – Learning Services was established to manage the facility and develop the associated customer services. This position also acted as the senior Library project manager and was a key member of all project planning groups. It was critical to the success of the development that one person had detailed knowledge of all aspects of planning in order to provide continuity between projects. The position title later changed to Assistant

University Librarian (Information Commons and Learning Services).

For the purpose of the strategic and tactical planning of the integrated learning support service, information on various distributed support services in the Libraries, Student Computer Laboratories and other Enquiry and Resources Centres on campus was gathered and analysed. Several official student surveys undertaken by the University in preceding years provided useful information. Negative comments about specific services and support were carefully considered in the planning process.

The initial broad vision for the Information Commons was that it would be a modern student-centred facility that provided a variety of easily identified and conveniently located spaces, computer workstations and access to information resources, technologies and expert staff that supported different learning needs in one physical location. It was refined during the planning process and the documented vision for the Kate Edger Information Commons is to:

> Provide a highly visible, modern and unique facility which will inspire students to acquire new skills so that they can participate more actively in the learning process. *http://www.information-commons.auckland.ac. nz/?page=vision*

Four desired outcomes, based on the vision, underpin the service design and delivery; skills development, effective information access, access to quality facilities and improved support. Developing students' information literacy and IT skills is the pedagogical intent common to the outcomes (Mountifield, 2006; p. 178).

Desired outcome one – skills development

Assist students to acquire skills to locate, retrieve, evaluate and use information effectively through:

- Courses in computer, information and learning skills presented in flexible teaching spaces that include state of the art equipment.
- Individualised instruction provided in consultation spaces throughout the building and during user transactions.
- Several layers of instruction, catering for different needs and preferences, in a wide-ranging collection of guides and self-paced tutorials in both print and electronic format.

Desired outcome two – effective information access

Students are able to access information to facilitate learning through:

- Searching and use of all databases to which the University Library has established access.
- Searching for and use of information available on the Internet and the University's website.
- Availability of the University Library's high demand print and audiovisual collection.
- Expert staff providing support.

Desired outcome three – access to quality facilities

IT and a mixture of spaces in the Information Commons facilitate student learning through access to:

- Flexible computer workstation and study areas designed for both group and individual work.

- Group study spaces that are fully wired and equipped.

- Spaces for laptop users and laptops for loan.

- Printing, downloading, file transfer and storage, scanning, and photocopying capabilities.

- Audiovisual equipment in a well-designed space.

- Specialist technologies and space adequate to the needs of students with disabilities.

Desired outcome four – improved support

Expert support structures are in place to facilitate learning through:

- Providing expert support to facilitate learning through an integrated service delivered by multi-skilled staff.

- Assistance in the location, retrieval, evaluation and use of information.

- Assistance in the capture, manipulation, storage, articulation and transfer of information.

- Providing specialist support to students in English language skills development.

- Collaboration between other University IT service points and facilities to identify resources and expertise that will complement the activities of the Information Commons.

- Clear and effective system of referral and escalation of queries and problems.

(See *http://www.information-commons.auckland.ac.nz/?page =vision* for more information.)

The outcomes are based on a planning document from The University of Calgary Library (Ritchie, 1999).

The outcomes and service model were developed after comprehensive research of other Information Commons facilities. The research included studying journal articles, websites and email communication with Information Commons planners and managers who were generous with their time and provided very valuable advice.

It was determined that in early 2000 many Information Commons facilities in North America had separate reference and computing services desks staffed by experts. Crockett, McDaniel and Remy at the Leavey Library of the University of Southern California found that students were frustrated by having to differentiate between computer-based or research-based questions. Restructuring of their service resulted in an integrated service with appropriate staff training as an important component (Crockett et al., 2002; 183–4).

The decision to adopt an integrated learning support model was based on student needs and feedback, advice from colleagues at other Information Commons and on research findings recorded in the literature. Bailey and Tierney (2002; 284) identified the Information Commons model that focuses on integrating research, teaching, and learning activities within the digital and physical environments as the most successful. This model takes into consideration the needs and characteristics of the student as well as changes in higher education. It is a collaborative environment that provides a holistic approach to student learning. This can be achieved by integrating the facilities, tools, resources and expertise of learning support providers such as IT professionals, librarians, learning advisors, instructional technologists, multi-media producers, language advisors, writing advisors and others (Mountifield, 2006; p. 174).

The planning process for the service philosophy and model consisted of several steps, always with the Information Commons vision, desired outcomes and customer needs as the guiding elements. Existing roles within the University Library and ITS were examined, identifying each team's strengths and weaknesses. A new service model, based on collaboration between the University Library and ITS, was developed in draft format and submitted to key stakeholders and managers for comment. The draft proposal described the components of the service, proposed management and staffing structure, new procedures, standards, training requirements and the budget. The strategic advantages that the new service model would bring to the University of Auckland student body were highlighted. Several months of detailed operational planning took place after the model was approved and the associated budget assigned. The planning included developing position descriptions, training and recruitment plans; procedural manuals including reporting methods; access and security measures; and a marketing and communication campaign.

Guidelines for the use of the Information Commons (*http://www.information-commons.auckland.ac.nz/?page= guidelines*) and associated food and drink guidelines (*http://www.information-commons.auckland.ac.nz/?page= fooddrink*) were developed to encourage acceptable use of the facility, equipment and services and to manage student behaviour.

Establishing a successful Information Commons facility requires strategic thinking and positioning as well as tactical or short-term planning. Strategic thinking and planning will ensure that the facility and associated services are strongly aligned with the institutional mission, strategy and values and with student requirements. It is also critical in obtaining the required budget for the implementation and ongoing operation.

Service model

The University Library, ITS, the Student Learning Centre and the English Language Self-Access Centre collaborate to provide a proactive integrated learning support environment for students. The development of computer and information literacy, academic and English language skills are key focus areas of the Information Commons. Opportunities for training are integrated into all aspects of the service. The new building and associated services facilitated the blending of some services and the rethinking of traditional organisational boundaries that are often not student-centred. Facilities, resources, services and student support were co-located and integrated to varying degrees. The two main learning support providers in the Information Commons are the University Library's Information Commons and Learning Services department and the Student Learning Centre, a unit within the University's Centre for Academic Development.

The Information Commons and Learning Services department consists of four teams: the IC Helpdesk, Short Loan, ELSAC and Learning Services. Staff collaborate on many levels and often have roles and responsibilities across teams. All staff are appointed to the Information Commons and Learning Services department and may be required to work in any team or location that is part of the department. A statement to this effect is included in all job descriptions and training programmes ensure staff are multi-skilled.

Courses and workshops in information literacy, IT literacy, language and learning skills are presented in flexible teaching spaces. Individualised instruction is provided in consultation spaces throughout the building. IT literacy workshops are provided by the Student Learning Centre while IC Helpdesk Consultants provide point-of-need roaming support throughout the building. Support material, catering for different needs and preferences, are available in a wide-ranging collection of print and online guides and self-paced tutorials. Frequently asked questions are available from the Information Commons web pages. Students who are unable to attend library courses can download the course handout from the online bookings website.

IC Helpdesk service

The IC Helpdesk service was a new model founded on the amalgamation of existing services and the establishment of new positions. The ITS Electronic Campus Helpdesk service merged with the University Library's Learning Services to form the IC Helpdesk Service. The service operated in a cross-functional multi-skilled team environment and consisted of two components, walk-in and roaming support. The IC Helpdesk area provides walk-in support to students, NetAccount sales and open consultation space, which could be used by staff members from the different student support departments. Roaming support (Figure 10.6) is provided on all levels. The staffing consisted of a full-time Help Desk Manager, six part-time After-hours Supervisors and a large number of Information Commons Consultants who were students employed on a casual basis. The Grafton Information Commons and Epsom Information Commons are managed as extensions of the Kate Edger Information Commons. Staff work in any location that is part of the Information Commons Group.

The role of the Information Commons Consultants was to serve as student support staff in the Information Commons. They provided a roving consultation service by assisting students using the computers in the Information Commons, work shifts on the IC Help desk, and assist with special

Figure 10.6 IC Helpdesk roving support

projects on a point of need basis. A detailed training
programme ensured IC Consultants were able to support the
use of electronic resources, enterprise systems and Library
databases. They were familiar with Microsoft Office
software, provided general PC skills support (e.g. accessing
files from drives) and supported the printing, scanning and
photocopying systems. Appropriate cross-training to
develop skills in many areas was vital to the delivery of the
service. Ongoing training and refreshers were provided at
regular intervals. Senior students, preferably postgraduate,
were employed to work in the Information Commons. They
were expected to be available to work a minimum of 9 hours
and no more than 20 hours per week. Shifts were usually
between 3 and 6 hours long. A relatively large number of
students, approximately 30–35, were employed to cover all
shifts during opening hours. The Information Commons

soon became a sought after place for employment on campus. Although the model worked well and suited student employees with its flexibility, it was also not without its challenges in terms of continuity of service, communication and staff administrative processes. The service was reviewed at the end of 2006 and changes were implemented – see 'Transformation and Repositioning'.

An Automatic Call Diversion (ACD) system was implemented in 2005 in order to make telephone assistance from the various Information Commons locations more efficient as well as to collect operational statistics. The ACD system distributes incoming calls evenly to the members of a number of answering groups, ensuring all calls are answered in a timely fashion.

The IC Helpdesk service is jointly managed by the University Library and ITS. The University Library is responsible for the day-to-day management of the service in the Information Commons. ITS takes responsibility for the IT infrastructure, associated hardware and software and the NetAccount support and development. All IT related problems and service requests are logged through the online enterprise SolveIT system.

The English Language Self Access Centre (ELSAC)

The ELSAC (Figure 10.7; *http://www.elsac.auckland.ac.nz/*) provides learning support to the growing number of 'English as another language' students at The University of Auckland. Students can improve their English language skills through guided self-study and through consultations with language advisors. The electronic learning environment, a software application that was developed in-house, gives students access to learning resources, monitors

Figure 10.7 ELSAC Language Advisor assisting a student

their learning and aids in the development of successful self-study skills. The ELSAC was transferred to the University Library's Information Commons and Learning Services department and relocated to the Information Commons in 2003. ELSAC also provides podcasts and iPod-compatable language learning exercises to students.

Learning services

The University Library offers a multifaceted information literacy programme (Figure 10.8) with specialised subject-based and generic components to students and staff. The Learning Services team, based in the Information Commons, provides leadership in designing, developing, delivering and evaluating the programme and its associated teaching activities, initiatives and resources. The team collaborate

Figure 10.8 ELSAC Students attending an information literacy course

with subject librarians across the Library system, learning designers from the Centre for Academic Development (CAD) and faculty to integrate information literacy into academic courses. The team offers a comprehensive range of activity-based library courses in the Information Commons. Students and staff use an online bookings database (*http://www.library.auckland.ac.nz/bookings*) to enrol in courses and to evaluate courses afterwards. The Learning Services team, in partnership with CAD, developed an interactive online tutorial for the Voyager catalogue. It is in the style of a graphic novel and teaches students how to use the Voyager catalogue through simulations. It follows three fictional students as they conduct research for an assignment and gain valuable information literacy skills along the way (*http://www.library.auckland.ac.nz/voyagertutorial/*).

Short loan

The high demand print and video collection for Arts, Science and Business and Economics students are housed in the Short Loan area. The collection consists of over 14,000 prescribed and recommended texts and is selected by teaching staff. The service provides controlled access to material in high demand through 1 hour, 2 hours, 3 hours, 3 days, and 7 days loan periods. Students use 3M RFID SelfCheck equipment for borrowing and returning short loan material. The Short Loan department manages the University Library's electronic course material service. Journal articles and book chapters are digitised or linked to electronic holdings and made available through the Voyager library catalogue and the Cecil learning management system. There are over 5,000 items in the electronic course material collection (*http://www.library.auckland.ac.nz/slc/slchome.htm*).

The Student Learning Centre

The Student Learning Centre is part of the Centre for Academic Development and assists students with the development of learning and performance skills. The Centre provides support for undergraduates and postgraduates through workshops and individual consultations (*http://cad.auckland.ac.nz/index.php?p=slc*).

ITS Desktop Services

ITS Desktop Services are responsible for the hardware and software environment and support in all Information Commons locations. Three staff members are located in the Kate Edger Information Commons. The main responsibility of these staff members is technical support for the Information Commons Group but they also provide services to other university departments.

Collaboration

A student-centred learning environment that improved student life and learning was achieved through strategic partnerships and collaboration between learning support providers. The Information Commons student support service model is underpinned by a commitment to service innovation, excellence and collaboration.

The partnership between the University Library and ITS is governed by a service level agreement that outlines the roles and responsibilities of each. It is revised annually. Strategic and operational priorities are discussed at monthly meetings. Requests for new software by staff and students are evaluated against a set of predefined criteria and an updated software image is installed prior to the beginning of each semester.

One of the strategic goals during the planning process of the Information Commons was to encourage a more coherent and integrated approach to IT literacy, information literacy, language and learning skills development. The University Library, Student Learning Centre and ELSAC, collaboratively and individually, contribute to the development of information literacy, IT literacy, language and learning competencies through a multifaceted programme that comprise discipline-specific and generic components. They work with academic staff to integrate these competencies into course curricula. Collaboration between learning support providers has evolved and strengthened over the past 3 years. They promoted an institutional and strategic approach to learning support at every opportunity. An institutional information literacy policy was approved by Senate in March 2006 and together with The University of Auckland strategic plan, academic plan and graduate profiles highlights the institutional focus on information literacy and IT literacy programmes, activities and support (Beatty and Mountifield, 2006; 239).

A new collaborative initiative between the University Library, Centre for Academic Development, Student Learning Centre, Postgraduate Careers and Academic Departments is the development of a Doctoral Skills Programme (*http://www.auckland.ac.nz/doctoralskills*). The programme, which started in March 2007, is governed by representatives from these units and administrative and marketing support is provided by the Graduate Centre. The programme offers a variety of courses and individual consultations to support and assist doctoral students in two ways:

- to help students further develop their academic and professional skills so that they can complete their doctorates successfully and in a timely manner;

- to help students with career planning and professional development, in order that they may better achieve their goals following completion of the doctorate.

One of the ways that IT literacy is addressed in the Information Commons is through the use of MELL (Microsoft E-Learning). Information Commons and Student Learning Centre staff work together to promote the resource library and support students using the package. The MELL software is available on all computers in the Kate Edger, Grafton and Epsom Information Commons.

Outcomes

The Information Commons is a rich learning environment for the Net Generation student. It encourages collaborative and socio-cultural learning by offering, in one location, a modern IT infrastructure, flexible learning spaces and tailored learning support. It promotes social and learning communities by providing convenient, central and comfortable spaces for learning and socialising. It is ideal for collaboration, group work (Figure 10.9), discussions and peer coaching.

The Information Commons is consistently given the highest satisfaction rating of any University of Auckland service or facility evaluated in undergraduate and

Figure 10.9 Small group collaboration

postgraduate student surveys. It is clear from occupancy as measured by automatic door counts and manual head counts as well as network logins that the Information Commons is the preferred learning and social space on campus. Students are encouraged to provide feedback to the Information Commons management via focus group meetings and via the electronic suggestions box. Students seem to appreciate the opportunity to contribute based on the number of suggestions received and their willingness to participate in focus groups.

There was also a substantial increase in the use of various learning support services after co-location in the Kate Edger Information Commons. Membership of the ELSAC increased from 200 in 2002 to 1,200 in 2006. The Student Learning Centre reported an increase in attendance of workshops and individual consultations. Daily issues of short loan material have been increasing steadily each year since the opening of the Information Commons.

The majority of all information literacy courses are offered in the teaching rooms located in the Information Commons. There has been a significant increase in student and faculty participation in the information literacy programme since the opening of the Information Commons. In 2003 there was a 36 per cent increase in student attendance at all library courses, followed by 21 per cent increase in 2004 and 30 per cent increase in 2005. An unexpected but pleasing outcome was that attendance of optional generic courses grew by 109 per cent in 2003 and by 22 per cent in 2004. It indicates that students value opportunities to develop their information literacy and are increasingly aware that it enhances their learning. The high visibility of the programme, targeted marketing, increased tailoring of content and the excellent teaching facilities in the Information Commons are major contributors to its ongoing success.

Table 10.2 Information literacy statistics

	2002	2003	2004	2005
Presentations to groups	898	1,527	1,838	2056
Participants in group presentations	13,409	17,924	21,606	27,797

Source: CONZUL statistics (*http://www.aut.ac.nz/CONZUL/statistics.htm*).

The University Library's information literacy statistics show a considerable upwards trend since the opening of the Kate Edger Information Commons in 2003 (Table 10.2).

The learning support providers in the Kate Edger Information Commons have found that working collaboratively offers benefits such as the sharing of resources and expertise, a cross-functional multi-skilled team environment, more student-centred programmes and the development of new standards and best practice models.

Beagle (2006; p. 35), Mountifield (2006; pp. 174–5) and White et al. (2005; p. 6) encapsulate the benefits and outcomes of the integrated Information Commons as:

- Convenience; a one-stop shop for IT, information, language and learning needs.

- Expert support; collaboration between librarians, IT professionals, writing consultants, media specialists, language and learning advisors.

- Continuum of service; supporting the access, use, evaluation, management, integration, and creation of information.

- Integrated technology-enabled learning environment; latest hardware, software, multimedia, networks and file storage.

- Flexibility to adapt the physical, virtual and service environments to accommodate changes in technology and in the expectations and needs of students.

- Catering for collaborative and individual learning styles and social needs.
- Promoting IT and information literacy development.
- Service excellence; self service, satisfaction, seamlessness.
- Comfort and collaboration.
- Formal and informal learning groups and communities of scholarship.

Transformation and repositioning

A key objective of the Information Commons Management is to ensure that the service model continues to meet the changing needs of learners. Student and staff feedback provided useful information for the periodic appraisal of services, activities and operations. Several refinements have been made to customer services, the IT environment and staff management processes since the opening of each facility. Conducting research into current and emerging trends in higher education, information and communication technology and e-learning ensures that the strategic role of the Information Commons continues and strengthens.

It became clear after 3 years of operating the service that the original Information Commons Helpdesk service model was no longer meeting the diversifying student requirements in an efficient and effective manner. Several factors contributed to the decision to review the service in mid-2006. Changes in university enterprise systems such improved identity management resulting in single sign-on and the development of self-service financial services had a significant impact on the service. The Information Commons also moved towards a fully cashless environment at the start of 2006 by discontinuing all cash-based functions and making cash-taking autoloaders available. The deployment of self service NetAccount ePOS (electronic point of sale) units in all the IC Group locations had a considerable impact on desk-based activities. The ePOS system allows students to add credit to their NetAccount via a self service Eft-POS terminal and touch screen. Since the implementation of ePOS in August 2006 the number of Helpdesk transactions at Kate Edger and Grafton Helpdesks has decreased noticeably to just over half what they were the previous year during the same period.

The service model was one that employed a large number of casual student staff, all working various hours. A lack of continuity in the delivery of services and effective communication became problematic. The ongoing recruitment, training and scheduling of casual staff and the associated administrative processes consumed an undue amount of managerial time. As the range of self-service options grew, staff were able to devote more time on increasingly complex individual queries and support. It became evident that employing part-time students was no longer suitable for the type of role that was emerging.

The Assistant University Librarian (Information Commons and Learning Services) and the IC Helpdesk Manager undertook a review of the service and staffing model during September and October 2006. The purpose of review was to examine, evaluate and make recommendations on the services and staffing structure of the IC Helpdesk.

The following questions were asked to inform the review:

1. What are student needs and expectations?

2. What are the main components of the service?

3. What are the desirable components of the service?

4. What are basic services and what are advanced services?

5. How many staff should be on duty during various periods in the Kate Edger?

6. How many staff members are required at specific periods for optimal service delivery?

7. How many staff members are required after 7 p.m. and over weekend for security and safety purposes?

8. What are the best hours for the summer vacation – should they match General Library's hours?

9. How can we work with Campus Security to ensure a safe environment?

10. What IC Supervisors work patterns are optimum for service excellence?

11. Which IC Supervisors portfolios are critical?

12. What are the housekeeping tasks that are performed every day; at what intervals?

13. What is the impact of the self service options?

14. What university-wide deployment of ePOS systems is planned?

15. What further service integration is required in the Information Commons?

   – relationship between IC Helpdesk and Learning Service.

   – relationship between IC Helpdesk and Short Loan.

16. What is the current level of collaboration with the Student Learning Centre?

17. What level of collaboration with the Philson Library on the Grafton Campus is possible and desirable?

18. What level of collaboration with Sylvia Ashton-Warner Library on the Epsom Campus is possible and desirable?

Statistical data for all locations was obtained to determine usage patterns. Hourly head counts, people counter statistics and computer logins were analysed for the period shown in Table 10.3.

Table 10.3 Analysis period

Weekdays	Weekends
7–8 a.m.	8–9 a.m.
8–9 a.m.	9–10 a.m.
5–6 p.m.	10–11 a.m.
6–7 p.m.	11 a.m.–noon
7–8 p.m.	Noon–5 p.m.
8–9 p.m.	5–7 p.m.
10–midnight	7–10 p.m.

The enquiry statistics, NetAccount POS transactions (at the desk with staff helping) and NetAccount ePOS transactions (self service) provided useful trends.

A new service and staffing model was developed with 03 January 2007 as implementation date. IC Management articulated a service focus for 2007 to be that of providing more advanced support for IT consultations and drop in sessions in collaboration with the Student Learning Centre, as well as increasing the range of IT and information literacy courses and support materials in collaboration with Learning Services. Staff meetings were held in November to introduce and explain the new model.

The new staffing model of the Information Commons Helpdesk service is based on an increase in permanent staff with fewer casual staff. The new model called for the establishment of three full-time permanent positions (each 37.5 hours per week) and one full-time fixed-term contract position (37.5 hours per week, from March to November). These positions have daily work patterns of 7.5 hours between 7 a.m. and 7 p.m. The six permanent part-time staff (20 hours per week) remained and continue to work after hours and over weekends. Twelve casual positions working after hours and over weekends remained.

New permanent positions were advertised at the end of 2006 and in January 2007. A number of existing casual and part-time staff accepted permanent full-time positions and new staff have also been appointed. The review and the reallocation of the existing budget created the opportunity to create a new full-time position in the Learning Services team. Responsibilities have also changed within this team as it has been agreed that the team will take greater responsibility for the professional development and training of library staff in close collaboration with the Library Staff Development Advisory Group, the Library Human Resources Manager and the Library Management Team.

Future challenges

The ongoing operational challenge is to ensure that the service model continues to evolve to ensure excellent frontline services as well as the further blending of learning support services to match student needs. To achieve continuous growth requires a flexible design that can adapt in response to changes in technology, pedagogy and learning needs. Collaborators' ability to integrate their services, capabilities and potential into the learning process and campus-wide learning initiatives, and to involve faculty in the process, will ensure that the Information Commons continues to provide a strategic advantage for The University of Auckland.

Conclusion

The Information Commons at the University of Auckland provides much more than access to computers. It is a general learning environment that is considerably different from any other on campus. It encourages social leaning, group collaboration, social activities, and is likely to be closer to the working environments that students will experience in their future careers. It accommodates different styles of learning and the open and flexible nature provides students with greater choice of where, when and how they learn.

Note

All floor plans in this chapter are reproduced courtesy of Warren and Mahoney Architects, Auckland, New Zealand.

References

Bailey, R. and Tierney, B. (2002) 'Information Commons redux: concept, evolution, and transcending the tragedy of the Commons', *The Journal of Academic Librarianship*, 28(5): 277–86.

Beagle, D.R. (2006) *The Information Commons Handbook*. New York: Neal-Schuman Publishers.

Beatty, S. and Mountifield, H. (2006) 'Collaboration in an Information Commons: key elements for successful support of eliteracy', *ITALICS*, 5(4): 229–45.

Crockett, C., McDaniel, S. and Remy, M. (2002) 'Integrating services in the Information Commons', *Library Administration & Management*, 16(4): 181–6.

Mountifield, H. (2006) 'The Information Commons: a student-centred environment for IT and information literacy development', in Martin, A. and Madigan, D. (eds) *Digital Literacies for Learning*. London: Facet Publishing; pp. 172–81.

Oblinger, D. and Oblinger, J. (2005) 'Is it age or IT: first steps toward understanding the Net Generation', in Oblinger, D. and Oblinger, J. (eds) *Educating the Net Generation*. Washington, D.C.: EDUCAUSE; sections 2.1–2.20.

Prensky, M. (2001) 'Digital natives, digital immigrants', *On the Horizon*, 9(5): 1–6.

Ritchie, L., Clarke, H., Esche, H., Morrall, M., Neary, S., Thrasher, R., Warren, D., White, P. and Wilson, M. (1999) *Information Hub Planning Document*. Calgary, Canada: University of Calgary. Available at *http://www .ucalgary.ca/IR/infocommons/conceptdoc.htm* (accessed 30 June 2007).

University of Auckland (2001) *The University of Auckland Academic Plan 2001–2003*. Auckland, New Zealand: University of Auckland.

University of Auckland (2001) *The University of Auckland Graduate Profile*. Auckland, New Zealand: University of Auckland. Available at *http://www.auckland.ac.nz/uoa/fms/ default/uoa/about/teaching/objectivesplans/docs/graduate _profile.pdf* (accessed 30 June 2007).

White, P., Beatty, S. and Warren, D. (2005) 'Information Commons', in *Encyclopedia of Library and Information Science*, vol. 1.1. New York: Dekker.

11

Beyond Facebook: thinking of the Learning Commons as a social network

Jill McKinstry

There was a time when celebrating the social network of an academic library would have been considered heresy. Good libraries were quiet and orderly – sanctuaries for solitary research and scholarly preparation. Enormous resources and space were dedicated to the storage and preservation of the collective history in anticipation of future use. Today that picture has changed. There is serious competition. Space for humans is being considered as important as space for collections in libraries. Furthermore, space and resources that foster social interaction in the physical and virtual academic environment is transforming the more traditional warehouse of knowledge. If we agree with the views of John Seely Brown about the importance of the social process on the way to gaining knowledge, the core of the learning and intellectual Commons is the interaction.

> Learning is a remarkably social process. In truth, it occurs not as a response to teaching, but rather as a result of a social framework that fosters learning.[1]

The library offers a venue where academic work can be carried out in a social context – a context that is supported physically, intellectually, and remotely. While the undergraduate library may have always had group study rooms and a dedicated mission to helping undergraduates become academically comfortable at large research universities, it has been the willingness to experiment with collaborative spaces and technology that has set the undergraduate library apart and made it a leader in advocating and promoting the Learning Commons within libraries. As Scott Bennett has noted in *Libraries Designed for Learning*, the library design should not be dominated by information resources and their delivery, but should 'incorporate a deeper understanding of the independent, active learning behaviour of students and the teaching strategies of faculty meant to support those behaviours'.[2] The independent and active behaviour of students is an important concept in understanding the Learning Commons as distinguished from the Information Commons.

> The core activity of a Learning Commons would not be the manipulation and mastery of information, as in an Information Commons, but the collaborative learning by which students turn information into knowledge and sometimes into wisdom. A Learning Commons would be built around the social dimensions of learning and knowledge and would be managed by students themselves for learning purposes that vary greatly and change frequently.[3]

Or as an architect once advised, 'Try to think of the library as an environment rather than a facility—a place of interaction, learning, and experiencing rather than a place for storage and equipment'.[4]

Library as Human

With the ubiquitous integration of technology into our lives, libraries no longer have a hold on access to academic resources, as Michael Stephens points out, 'Conversations are taking place online, with or without you'.[5] Understanding this phenomenon and how students are working and communicating, while being attentive to the opportunities that come our way to insinuate ourselves into this process is crucial for libraries of the twenty-first century.

> 'One of the principles of web 2.0 and the corresponding library 2.0 meme is that 'the library is human' because it makes the library a social and emotionally engaging center for learning and experience. Librarian 2.0, then, is the strategy guide for helping users find information, gather knowledge and create content'.[6]

What we have learned from Barnes and Noble and from watching the gate count in our different libraries is that students will seek out the most comfortable, most accommodating, and most wired space that they can find (Figures 11.1 and 11.2). The noise in an undergraduate library and the preference of students to study together was a characteristic that most undergraduate librarians would just as soon not have advertised or even admitted in earlier decades, but now, 'studying together' or 'being noisy' is not necessarily bad nor automatically equated with the non-academic or less scholarly activities. As students try on different disciplines, they need space to wrestle with the issues, and it may not be quiet. 'Mark Maves, a senior vice president at the SmithGroup, an architecture and planning firm, says that he is 'fascinated' to see some librarians

Figure 11.1 Students are creating their own Learning Commons with ubiquitous wireless connectivity in the library

Figure 11.2 The openness of the Odegaard undergraduate library stairways provides a welcoming visual index to the building

describe their building 'not so much as a library but as the academic counterpart to the student center'.[7]

I would like to have been able to say that our journey into imagining this new role for the Odegaard Undergraduate Library at the University of Washington was an intentional plan to revolutionise our spaces based on what we knew about how students learn and how the libraries could create environments to foster that learning. It turned out to be more evolutionary than revolutionary, taking small steps along the way, making great use of the 'pilot project', and most importantly, being open to new opportunities even when we had no idea how it would turn out.

History

Stepping back just for a moment to set the context, the University of Washington (UW), in Seattle, Washington, USA, founded in 1861, is one of the foremost public institutions of higher education in the nation, richly combining its research, instructional and public service missions. Its internationally acclaimed faculty includes five Nobel Laureates and the winner of the 1990 National Book Award for Fiction. The UW student body on the Seattle campus totals about 40,000. The UW also has campuses in Bothell and Tacoma. Total enrollment at these campuses is about 4,000.

Among the largest academic research libraries in North America, the University of Washington Libraries has a collection of more than six million catalogueed volumes, an equal number in microform format, more than 50,000 serial titles, and several million items in other formats. It is a system of over 20 libraries and a staff of over 400 with an equal number of student employees.

The idea of a Learning Commons at the University of Washington began in 1994 when the University Libraries was approached by a colleague from the Office of Undergraduate Education 'to do something with this new technology'. This request had been prompted by an inquiry from the then-provost Wayne Clough, currently the President of Georgia Institute of Technology, who knew that some very interesting things were going on in academia with technology and he wanted to be a part of it. With the impetus and interest of the provost, a collaborative effort between the Office of Undergraduate Education, the University Libraries, and Computing & Communications was launched. That first joint initiative was called, 'UWired'.[8] In that first year of 1994, a plug n' play classroom was built for instruction and training, called the 'UWired Collaboratory'. Ninety students were given a laptop and a full year of training in information and technology literacy by three full time instructors, the 'UWired Librarians'. While it was a successful program for the 90 students that first year, it did not scale well for a large undergraduate population. The second year, instead of three year-long classes with 30 students each, the program was expanded to include 10 one-quarter, one-credit classes of 30 each, built on the Freshman Interest Group (FIG) and taught by 10 librarians. That was also performed for only 1 year, followed by the creation of what would become the beginning of the computing Commons, which included a general access lab of 60 computers in the library, a drop-in facility for faculty, and the development of a curriculum of information literacy and technology workshops. We continually evolved and asked questions as the computing and academic landscape changed each year. What began as an initiative to get the latest computing technology into the hands of students and to guide that usage to enhance academic work, evolved into an effort to facilitate, (and in some ways to get out of the way) in order to allow students to make their own connections. While the introduction and use of technology was the initial focus of UWired and the OUGL Computing Commons, access to a high speed network on state of the art computing stations became an expected backdrop for students and the focus changed to provide more innovative and collaborative spaces and tools for the students to use. We have found over the past 13 years that the good ideas have withstood the test of time. No amount of promoting or pushing the use of technology or innovations prevailed, unless it was found to be authentically useful and to make a difference in the ease and effectiveness of learning for students and faculty. To promote 'technology in the *service* of learning' has been the goal for many of UWired's initiatives. The challenge, of course, is that we often don't know until after a technology has been introduced whether it has been an enhancement or a hindrance in the learning process.

The UWired pilot of 13 years ago is now a 24-hour wireless library with two computer classrooms, 14 group study rooms, a 356-seat computer lab or 'Learning Commons' as it is now called, 50+ computers scattered throughout the building, a multimedia centre, a drop-in centre for faculty, and enhanced technology spaces that include facilities to digitally edit audio and video, to capture and create streaming presentations, and to participate in video conferencing (Figure 11.3). Most importantly, consulting and training services are available along with drop-in workshops for students.[9] Reference and technology help is available at a combined desk in the centre of the Commons,[10] along with a research and writing centre, staffed by students and teaching assistants from the College of Arts and Sciences. As mentioned earlier, the approach at the Odegaard

Figure 11.3 Twenty-four hours a day, students access the 400 computers in the Odegaard undergraduate library Learning Commons

Undergraduate Library has been evolutionary rather than revolutionary. We did not have the opportunity to design or build a new facility. But, rather, what success we may have achieved may be linked to a willingness to partner with others, to be open to change, to observe students and to ask them about their use of technology in their academic work,[11] and to question our traditional dedication of library space and staff to book storage and solitary study.

Undergraduate libraries are often the perfect partners for innovation in services and space in that it is easier to dedicate the entire building, rather than just a room, to integrated spaces supported by other academic partners. There is a convergence in an undergraduate library of many disciplines and services. Libraries in general are integrated broader and deeper across campus than any other entity and have relationships with both the academic and support side of the house.

As mentioned earlier, our planning process for creating a Learning Commons was often a vision of no more than 2 years ahead. But, as the renowned management consultant Peter Drucker, advises, 'Unexpected success is often the first sign of an opportunity'.[12]

Another crucial component to success of a program is a renewable source of funding for the continued improvement and maintenance of a learning space. At the University of Washington, in addition to the initial dedication of funds from the respective partners to renovate spaces, purchase equipment, and assign staff for support and oversight, the most important source of funding for innovation and renewal has been the Student Technology Fee (STF). The students and administration supported a successful legislative effort to enable the establishment of a fee in 1996 that would be used 'exclusively for technology resources for general student use'. Washington State statute (RCW 28B.15.051)[13] allowed the University to establish the fee (currently around $120 per year) upon the agreement of the student government. Unlike tuition increases, the Student Technology Fee, as directed by statute, is to be spent only on technology for students. State law directs that the annual expenditure plans for the fee be approved by students rather than by the administration or the Board of Regents. The Student Technology Fee Committee, run solely by students, reviews proposals from campus departments and decides which proposals are funded with the goal of improving the environment for computing and accessibility to computer resources at the UW. This quarterly student-assessed fee generates over $ 4.5 million dollars per year. At the Odegaard Undergraduate Library, the Catalyst (formerly UWired) team has done an excellent job in creating excitement and enthusiasm for proposed enhancements to the computer labs and technology suites that resonate with students. (Last year, the library submitted a proposal for self-check machines, thinking that the self-sufficient, automated option would appeal to students who use ATMs, movie kiosks for tickets, and self-check at the grocery store. Not so. We heard back from many that they enjoyed the exchange at the service desk and that while machines might make 'our jobs easier', it was not necessarily an enhancement to theirs. The students on the STF committee have a strong commitment to the students that they represent and have set a high bar to demonstrate the usefulness of technologies for students.

Another crucial element in a successful collaborative venture is to put together the right team. At the University of Washington, we have found that our best partners thrive on innovation – innovation in technology, teaching, and service. These may not seem extraordinary or unusual, but it is amazing how many roadblocks can be created if one partner feels that every new idea needs to be studied at length or that each problem requires extensive evaluation before moving on. Moving on is the key characteristic and the rate at which this happens may also turn out to be a crucial factor in the collaboration.

The validation for the Learning Commons has come from our students. Voting with their feet, close to 10,000 students per day come into the Odegaard Undergraduate Library during the academic week. This is the highest gate count of any library on campus. The high numbers are due in part to the large number of workstations, the high speed wireless network, the enhanced spaces for collaboration, the ready access to technical, research, and writing help and the long hours (24/5). But, there is also a feeling of 'ownership' by the students. They are comfortable there and while we are chagrined at times to see how comfortable they are, we are loath to set up more rules and regulations to try to inhibit the interaction and active learning that is going on

Figure 11.4 Students seek comfort, even when viewing media in a converted study carrel

(Figure 11.4). As Duane Webster, the executive director of the Association of Research Libraries recently pointed out, 'There really is a new breed of librarian out there. There's this notion that as these facilities are in such prominent places on campus, they would be better devoted to people than collections'.[14]

To the extent that we are creating inviting, comfortable spaces with integrated services that are relevant, that are valued and are perceived to make real contributions to enhancing the full educational experiences of students – they are used.

Another important aspect in planning and creating a Learning Commons is to look at the characteristics of students today. It is absolutely essential that we understand how libraries can best serve this generation and make explicit choices to make changes that 'privilege the Millennials', our emerging generation of scholars. That has always been our role, but the transition may be harder for us as a profession now because it takes the attention away from us and our resources and focuses on our users. The importance of 'user-centred services' has been celebrated in libraries for a long time, but I would propose that we thought more about those services from our perspective, the information specialists, than from the student or user. Times have changed and we have competition on all fronts and must strategically place ourselves to be in the arena of learning and not assume that libraries will be the next generation's choice for information resources.

John Beck, President of the North Star Leadership Group and Senior Research Fellow at the University of Southern California's Annenberg Center for the Digital Future is convinced that the gamer 'generation, born after 1970 and raised on video games is about 4 to 5 years away from dominating society'.[15] He says that the experience of games has molded a generation with these characteristics:

> **Motivated**: Gamers are competitive and love a challenge. Winning is very important to them...They believe that anything is possible...however, they do not have an appreciation for doing things 'just because'.

> **Resilient**: Failure isn't the end of the world; gamers have each failed thousands of times on their way to success...persistence pays off in the end.

> **Confident**: Gamers think of themselves as experts and want to tackle problems head on. They are used to being the hero and have a more positive outlook on life than nongamers. They are more flexible about change.

> **Sociable**: As a lot is done with friends and over the Internet, gamers value other people and have a greater need for human relationships than other groups. They

are great team players and loyal to the teams and organisations of which they are a part.

Analytical: Gamers learn from the games they play. By sampling so many different realities through games, they become very good at seeking problems in a deeper, strategic perspective and at handling risk and uncertainty'.[16]

Beck is convinced that game playing is a generation-shaping activity that over time 'will reshape behaviour patterns, beliefs, art, business, institutions – the entire culture'.[17]

Marc Prensky, in his work, *Digital Game-Based Learning*, echoes this view:

Today's average college grads have spent less than 5,000 hours of their lives reading, but over 10,000 hours playing video games. Today's students think and process information fundamentally differently from their predecessors.[18]

'Zone in on your users' is the advice given to satisfy the gamers and the boomers. Create blended spaces and create zones. As the boomers prefer quiet, the gamers 'thrive on all the commotion'.[19] Gamers need social space and boomers need a 'third place'.

'Gamers are technologically savvy and take in multiple streams of information while they socialise. They multitask! They need a space with all kinds of simultaneous activities – music, television, video streaming, computers'. This shift away from print has been seen in many libraries with declining circulation rates of printed materials and the expansion of DVDs, audiobooks, e-books, podcasting, CDs, streaming and, in some libraries, the once ignored genre of games.

'Given that this generation of college students has grown up with computers and video games, the students have become accustomed to multimedia environments: figuring things out for themselves without consulting manuals; working in groups; and multitasking. These qualities differ from those found in traditional library environments, which, by and large, are text-based, require learning the system from experts (librarians), were constructed for individual use, and assume that work progresses in a logical, linear fashion'.[20]

In the 90s the focus was on getting technology into libraries. Now that technology is in the libraries, there is focused attention on 'learning spaces', a concept that might have brought to mind the 'classroom' in earlier decades rather than the library, which might have been referred to as 'study space' or 'research space'. More learning is taking place outside of the classroom than ever before in virtual and real spaces.

We may teach and learn in virtual spaces, but, as physical beings, we can't escape real space. We can, however, improve upon it.[21]'

That is the premise for 'Designing Spaces for Effective Learning: A Guide to 21st Century Learning Space Design', an inspiring publication from the Joint Information Systems Committee in the UK. Using case studies and architects' floor plans, the publication explores 'the relationship between learning technologies and innovative examples of physical space design...the design of our learning spaces should become a physical representation of the institution's vision and strategy for learning – responsive, inclusive, and supportive of attainment by all' (Figure 11.5).[22]

Figure 11.5 Considerations of light, openness, and comfortable seating are important components in "Designing Spaces for Effective Learning" (reproduced courtesy of the Joint Information Systems Committee)

From a design perspective, some of the best changes in new libraries across the country have embraced some fundamental principles. They are inviting to all – males and females. They are an open network, facilitating communication in a spatial, social, and intellectual relationship. They are light and open, accomplishing what I heard one public librarian say is their motto in their space: 'To satisfy and delight'. It's hard to imagine an academic library stating that as a goal, but that is exactly what we hope happens – that our students will choose our library as their home and be delighted. Many of the delightful new libraries are bold, flexible, and embody what has been termed 'future-proof'. There is an energy and creative spirit that inspires users' collaborative work style.

Libraries as Learning Commons

Making the library strategically indispensable on the university campus is absolutely crucial. One of the best ways to do that is to provide integrated services that no other unit or entity on campus can or is willing to provide. The popularity of the one-stop or 'no-stop' on site or virtual services have made libraries the perfect Learning Commons for students today. Libraries are the best organisation on campus to provide this because:

- libraries have space;
- libraries are interdisciplinary and committed to serve everyone;
- libraries are integrated broader and deeper across campus than any other entity;
- libraries see collaboration as their job;
- libraries have time, expertise, and are dedicated to staying relevant in serving their users.

Libraries with support, both financial and philosophical, from the top administration have the greatest chance of success in collaboration. There also must be openness to sharing information, trusting your partners, and being willing to give up some control on facilities and staffing. It is often the case that a particular program or initiative is mutually beneficial for both partners – it is solving a mutual problem with a strong motivation to make it work. Partners will often have the same goals, but a different vision of how to get there. Continually scanning the campus for potential opportunities in new partnerships and services is vital in keeping the library in the mainstream of learning.

In 2004, after 10 years of collaborating with our technology partners to provide enhanced technology and support spaces in Odegaard, we noticed that we had repeated requests from students for help with their writing. While there are other writing centres on campus, they are often departmental facilities with limited hours and a disciplinary focus. One exception to this is the writing centre in the CLUE (Center for Learning and Undergraduate Enrichment)[23] that provides writing assistance to all students up until midnight. But, students were often looking for some help while they were working in the library and didn't want to go to another building. So, in 2004, OUGL partnered with the College of Arts and Sciences to create the Odegaard Research and Writing Center. As the introduction page for the service states, the library is a wonderful place for a writing centre:

> Isn't the best location for a writing center a place where one does a lot of writing? And what could be better than having both writing tutors and librarians on call to help you through all phases of the writing and research process?[24]

As we work to provide a convergence of services in the library, we're often caught in the middle, holding on to the icons of the past while forging ahead with the latest in new technologies and conveniences. As Joan Lippincott has remarked, the book has been the icon for the library. When the physical book is not there, how can you find the library?[25]

Perhaps it will be what one British newspaper called, an 'Idea Store'. In a BBC news article covering a renovation of the Bow Library in east London, the headline reads: 'The word library is set to fade from our vocabulary – but not because we've fallen out of love with books. Today's libraries are being made over as 'idea stores', complete with cafes, crèches, and multimedia offerings.[26]

Learning Commons as 'idea store'

If ideas generate ideas, how do you promote that exchange in a library? As libraries are a crossroads of ideas, the more we can bring these ideas to life, the more exciting intellectual environment is created. It is also a place to promote a convergence of differing perspectives. At the University of Washington, the Odegaard Undergraduate Library has partnered with the office of Undergraduate Research to sponsor a lunchtime series of faculty lectures in the library to talk about their research. This series, 'Research Exposed' has become a popular one credit lunchtime class to introduce undergraduates to research in the different disciplines and plant the idea that they could become involved in research.

Celebrating the research projects of undergraduates is also another initiative that was started in the Odegaard Undergraduate Library with the 'Library Research Award for Undergraduates'. This program, now in its fourth year, has become one of the favourite initiatives of the libraries, as faculty work with librarians in evaluating the best research projects for the year and award monetary prizes for the most exemplary. Not only are the faculty and students thrilled with the prize, but we have learned a lot about how undergraduates conduct their research and how we might better help in that area. We also display the photos and the project titles for the winning submissions in the Learning Commons hoping to encourage students to participate the following year. As one student said, 'Library research has been one of the most comprehensive learning experiences of my academic career. It has been a very valuable part of my education. It is one thing to read about the facts in a class; it's another to try and discover them yourself'.

Exhibits and displays are another way that libraries can provide a stimulating environment for students. We have an ambitious program of exhibits and displays in Odegaard, which brings life to the surroundings and stimulates curiosity. As students take a break from studying or working at the computer, a stroll around the library can be a welcome relief from the task at hand. The new book display tables at the front of the library are another way to bring the collection to life. The books, still wearing their colourful publisher jackets, invite browsing, much like the bookstore model. Joan Frye Williams suggests that libraries create environments in which 'students trip over ideas – they can't avoid it' (Figure 11.6).[27] One great way to promote synergy between formats is to provide mixed space, mixed use, and mixed access to multiple formats of information whether it is print, electronic, or digital. With so many access points for information, it is still important to provide a physical space

Figure 11.6 Books on display in the Odegaard undergraduate Library invite browsing and stimulate reading for pleasure and research

to mingle, a mixing chamber of sorts, that can be a powerful component of learning. As Dr Moeser, the President of University of North Carolina, Chapel Hill recently noted, 'Philosophical connections sometimes happen when you make physical connections'.[28]

Conclusion

Tom Klein reminds us that the new learning is collaborative and socially constructed. It is interconnected and contextual and happens in and outside of classrooms.[29] Facebook may be the virtual social network community – but I would propose that the library as Learning Commons is the perfect social and intellectual network (Figure 11.7). As a trusted,

Figure 11.7 "Walk up, Join In, and Work Together" is what collaboration is all about – Tidebreak TeamSpot technology helps make that happen in the Odegaard Collaboration Studio

neutral entity of learning on campus, the library bridges the gap between the more formalised classrooms and the informal domain of personal learning. 'Learning is joining a community. Joining a community is entering a figured world of knowledge'[30] a place where libraries have always been.

Notes

1. Brown, J.S. and Duguid, P. (2000) *The Social Life of Information*. Cambridge, MA: Harvard Business School Press.
2. Bennett, S. (2003) 'Libraries designed for learning', *CLIR*, Nov: 39.
3. Ibid; 38.
4. Boone, M.D. (2002) 'Library design – the architect's view: a discussion with Tom Findley', *Library Hi Tech*, 20(3): 392.
5. Stephens, M. (2006) 'Ten top technologies for librarians 2006'. Online Programming for All Libraries (OPAL), available at *http://www.opal-online.org/Stephens200604_files/frame.htm* (accessed 28 June 2007).
6. Stephens, M. (2006) 'Into a new world of librarianship: sharpen these skills for Librarian 2.0', *NextSpace*, 2: 8.
7. Carlson, S. (2006) 'Thoughtful design keeps new libraries relevant: not everything students want and need is online', *The Chronicle of Higher Education*, 52(6): B1.
8. Zald, A., Sreebny, O., Mudrock, T., Laden, B. and Bartelstein, A. (1998) 'UWired: a collaborative model for integrating technology and information skills across the curriculum', in LaGuardia, C. and Mitchell, B.A. (eds) *Finding Common Ground: Creating the Library of the Future Without Diminishing the Library of the Past*. New York: Neal-Schuman Publishers.
9. Seeley, S., Collins, K., Holmes, J. and Davis, A. (2006) 'Learning @ Odegaard', University of Washington Libraries, available at *http://www.lib.washington.edu/ougl/walkins/* (accessed 28 June 2007).

10. McKinstry, J.M. and McCracken, P. (2002) 'Combining computing and reference desks in an undergraduate library: a brilliant innovation or a serious mistake?', *Portal: Libraries and the Academy*, 2(3).

11. Lane, C. and Yamashiro, G. 'Educational technology at the University of Washington: report on the 2005 Instructor and Student Survey'. Available at *http://catalyst.washington.edu/ projects/edtech_2005report.pdf* (accessed 28 June 2007).

12. Drucker, P.F. and Senge, P.M. (2001) *Leading in a Time of Change*. Video recording by The Drucker Foundation. San Francisco: Jossey-Bass.

13. Revised Code of Washington (RCW). Available at *http://apps. leg.wa.gov/RCW/default.aspx?cite=28b.15.051* (accessed 28 June 2007).

14. Vaznis, J. (2006) 'Coffee's on, dusty books are out at UMass Library: extras aimed at drawing students', *Boston Globe*, 25 Nov. Available at *http://tinyurl.com/ygbxtf* (accessed 28 June 2007).

15. Storey, T. (2005) 'The big bang', *OCLC Newsletter*, Jan/Feb/ Mar: 7-8.

16. Ibid, 8.

17. Ibid, 9.

18. Ibid.

19. Ibid, 11.

20. Lippincott, J. (2005) 'Net Generation students and libraries', in Oblinger, D.G. and Oblinger, J. (eds) *Educating the Net Generation*. Boulder, CO: EDUCAUSE.

21. 'Designing spaces for effective learning: a guide to 21st century learning space design', report by Joint Information Systems Committee (JISC), a strategic advisory committee working on behalf of the funding bodies for further and higher education in England, Scotland, Wales and Northern Ireland; p. 4. Available at *http://www.jisc.ac.uk/uploaded_ documents/JISClearningspaces.pdf* (accessed 28 June 2007).

22. Ibid.

23. Center for Learning and Undergraduate Enrichment at the University of Washington. Available at *http://depts.washington. edu/clue/writingcenter.html* (accessed 28 June 2007).

24. Odegaard Research and Writing Center at the University of Washington. Available at *http://depts.washington.edu/owrc/* (accessed 28 June 2007).

25. Lippincott, J. (2006) Personal communication.

26. Lane, M. (2003) 'Is this the library of the future?', *BBC News Online*, 18 March 2003; available at *http://news.bbc.co.uk/1/hi/uk/2859845.stm*.

27. Williams, J.F. (2004) 'Innovation and risk-taking'. Strategic Planning Seminar, University of Washington Libraries, 8 June, Seattle, Washington.

28. 'Transforming the culture: undergraduate education and the multiple functions of the research university'. The Reinvention Center Conference, Washington, D.C., 9–10 November. Available at *http://www.stonybrook.edu/reinventioncenter* (accessed 28 June 2007).

29. Klein, T. (2002) 'The Search for a college Commons', *About Campus*, 7(3): 9–16.

30. O'Connor, R. (2005) 'Planning for learning: creating 'knowledge islands' in the information ocean', presented at Building the Future: Designing Academic Libraries as Learning Spaces, CIC Center for Library Initiatives Conference 2–3 May, Gleacher Center, Chicago, IL. Available at *http://www.cic.uiuc.edu/programs/CenterForLibraryInitiatives/Archive/ConferencePresentation/LibrarySpacesConference2005/CIC Richard O'Connor library talk final.ppt*.

Index